THE MIDNIGHT WAR

The American Intervention in Russia, 1918–1920

THE MIDNIGHT WAR

The American Intervention in Russia, 1918–1920

by

RICHARD GOLDHURST

McGraw-Hill Book Company
New York · St. Louis · San Francisco
Toronto · Düsseldorf · Mexico

DWG, who bore with grace and fortitude

Book design by Milton Jackson.
Copyright © 1978 by Richard Goldhurst. All rights reserved. Printed
in the United States of America. No part of this publication may be
reproduced, stored in a retrieval system, or transmitted, in any form or
by any means, electronic, mechanical, photocopying, recording, or otherwise, without the prior written permission of the publisher.

1 2 3 4 5 6 7 8 9 0 D O D O 7 8 3 2 1 0 9 8

Library of Congress Cataloging in Publication Data

Goldhurst, Richard.
The midnight war.
Bibliography: p.
Includes index.
1. Russia—History—Allied intervention, 1918–
1920.   I. Title.
DK265.42.U5G64   940.4'147   78–9762
ISBN 0–07–023663–1

Now Nestor yelled at the Argive soldiers: "My friends,
Danaan heroes and comrades of Ares, let no man
Drop behind greedy to pounce on the spoils
And go to the ships with the heaviest of the loot!
But keep killing men."

> —*The Iliad of Homer*
> Lattimore Translation

Military action is admissible in Russia, as the Government
of the United States sees the circumstances, only to help the
Czecho-Slovaks consolidate their forces and get into successful cooperation with their Slavic kinsmen and to steady any
efforts at self-government or self-defense in which the Russians themselves may be willing to accept assistance.

> —Woodrow Wilson
> *Aide-Mémoire,* July 17, 1918

The day will come when it will be recognized without a doubt
throughout the civilized world that the strangling of Bolshevism at birth would have been an untold blessing to the
human race.

> —Winston Churchill
> to the House of Commons, May 11, 1953

ACKNOWLEDGMENTS

My colleague at Fairfield University, Professor Jiri Nadela, translated the Czechoslovak for me. When I introduced myself to him and explained my purpose in describing the action of the Czech Legion in Russia, he stared hard for several seconds before throwing wide his arms and shouting, "My father was a legionnaire!" Edward Allen McCormick of the City University of New York helped me with the German and read the manuscript with sympathy. Henri Peyre located the Bergson for me at the Sterling Library at Yale. Mr. Ronald Bulatoff of the Hoover Institution mailed me a complete catalogue of its Siberian Collection and proved unfailingly courteous and helpful while I was there. Mr. Timothy Nenninger of the National Archives got me what I wanted at the moment I wanted it. Mrs. Marie T. Capps of the United States Military Academy Library made sure I overlooked nothing and corresponded regularly to inform me of new acquisitions I might find useful.

CONTENTS

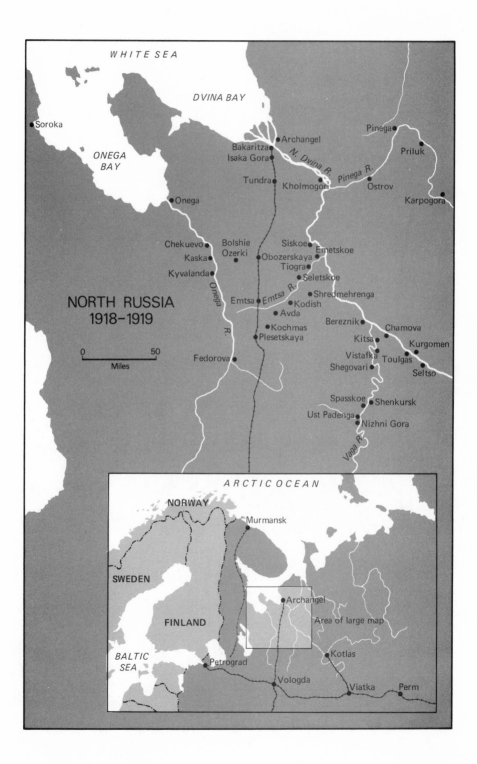

WHITE SEA

DVINA BAY

ONEGA BAY

Soroka

Pinega

Bakaritza • Archangel
Isaka Gora

Priluk

N. Dvina R.

Tundra

Kholmogori

Pinega R.

Ostrov

Onega

Karpogora

Chekuevo

Bolshie Ozerki

Siskoe

Emetskoe

Kaska

Obozerskaya

Kyvalanda

Tiogra

Seletskoe

NORTH RUSSIA
1918-1919

Onega R.

Emtsa

Emtsa R.

Shredmehrenga

Kodish

Bereznik

Chamova

Avda

0   50
Miles

Kochmas
Plesetskaya

Kitsa

Kurgomen

Fedorova

Vistafka

Toulgas

Shegovari

Seltso

Spasskoe

Shenkursk

Ust Padenga

Nizhni Gora

Vaga R.

ARCTIC OCEAN

NORWAY

Murmansk

SWEDEN

FINLAND

Archangel

Area of large map

BALTIC SEA

Petrograd

Kotlas

Vologda

Viatka

Perm

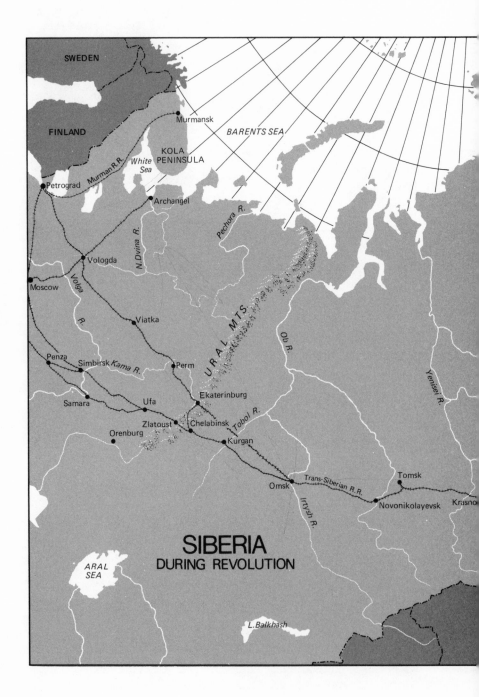

SIBERIA
DURING REVOLUTION

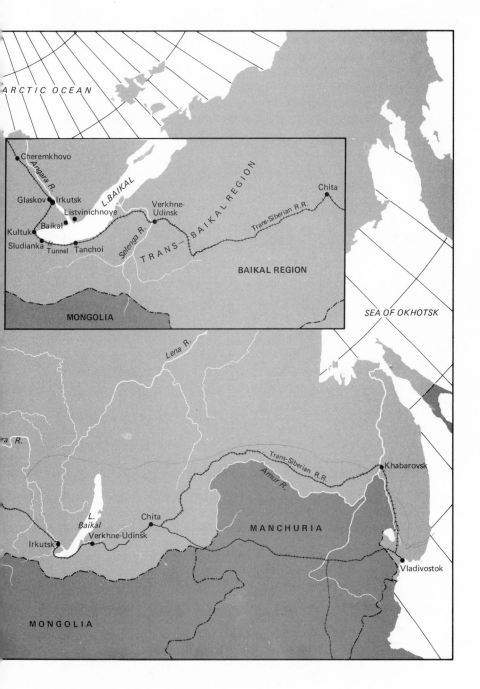

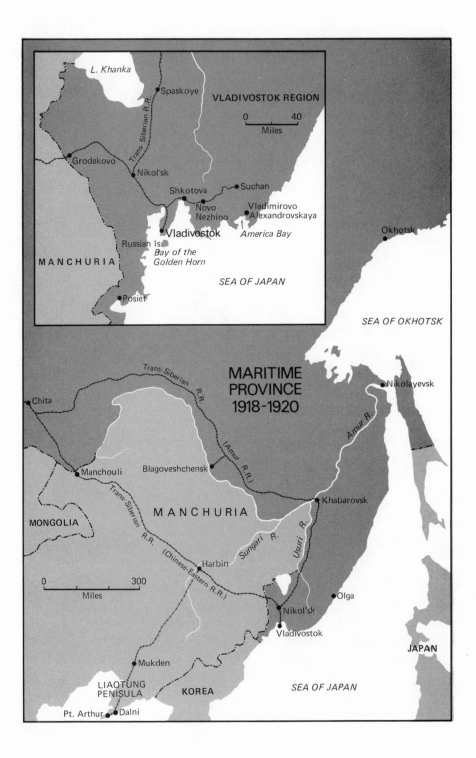

INTRODUCTION

Two months before World War I ended with an armistice on the Western Front, President Woodrow Wilson sent five thousand American soldiers to the north Russian port of Archangel on the White Sea. He sent another eight thousand troops to Vladivostok on the Bay of the Golden Horn at the eastern tip of Siberia, and long after their buddies in France had gone home, these soldiers continued to fight a desperate, forgotten war.

There were many reasons why these doughboys came to Russia, but there was only one reason why they stayed: to intervene in a civil war to see who would govern the new Russia—the largest country in the world.

The intervention in Russia was not the first time Woodrow Wilson had embroiled himself in the internal affairs of another country. He intervened in the Mexican Revolution in April 1914 by occupying the port of Vera Cruz. He intervened in Haiti in 1915 when he ordered the resident United States naval commander to dissolve the Haitian congress and write a new constitution (an action, incidentally, that lasted nineteen years). He intervened again in the Mexican Revolution by ordering the Pershing Punitive Expedition into Chihuahua to run Pancho Villa to earth.

Such interventions were not solely the province of Woodrow

Wilson. President William McKinley had intervened in the Cuban insurgency in 1898; and Theodore Roosevelt, after he became President, intervened in the Boxer Rebellion in China in 1900. Each of these interventions had been attended by grave political, military, and moral risks. Yet each had the approval of the voting public. And each was successful to a degree in that the intervention accomplished what it set out to do. But the Russian intervention failed—completely and ignobly. It failed for a variety of reasons, the most important of which was that the Bolsheviks fought to bring about its collapse. It also failed because it was conceived in panic.

Failed because of the nature in which it was conceived

The Allies won the war against Germany and the Central Powers in November 1918, but they were perilously close to defeat in March of the same year. Statesmen and generals thought the way to avert defeat in the spring of 1918 was to counter the ever-stronger German army on the Western Front by sending an Allied expedition to reopen the Eastern Front in Russia. But to believe that a few thousand soldiers could make a difference in a country where vast distances are the one profound reality was a lunatic plan. Siberia alone is large enough to contain the whole of the continental United States. And European Russia itself could contain the United States from Maine to Mississippi. However, the spring of 1918 was a lunatic time and lunatic things kept happening.

Another reason for the failure of the intervention was because it was undertaken with grievous political misconceptions. One of these was that because the Bolsheviks were wicked and ruthless, therefore they were weak. Moreover, Woodrow Wilson and many of his countrymen wanted the two Russian revolutions in 1917 to conform in all particulars to the American Revolution of 1776. It was not to be.

After the armistice of 1918, America and its European and Asiatic allies maintained expeditionary forces in Russia in the hopes of instilling in Russians a desire to rid the world of Bolshevism. The Allies had won a war against Germany, but they had devastated their manhood and virtually bankrupted their treasuries. They saw their victory being menaced by Bolshevism, which kept Russia—one sixth of the world's surface—and Eastern

Europe in tumult. America and the Allies interpreted their victory over Germany as the triumph of democracy over autocracy. However, the Bolsheviks declared a new war: between capitalism and socialism.

Thus, the American intervention in Russia was the first intervention in which the United States could not even pretend it had accomplished what it set out to do. Hundreds of young Americans died on foreign soil for a hopeless cause. It is even more tragic to realize that the lessons which could have been learned from the Russian intervention were not learned. In the years that followed, American politicians, newspapers and historians suppressed or ignored the bitter facts of the failure. Had these facts been revealed openly, interventions similarly doomed to failure might have been avoided in the future.

CHAPTER 1

THE WESTERN FRONT:

MARCH 1918

On March 3, 1918, the political leaders of the Allied world and the generals in their field headquarters knew the worst had come to pass. A Bolshevik delegation, headed by Leon Trotsky, had left Brest-Litovsk, a rail center in Byelorussia, with a treaty that would end the war on the Eastern Front. Russia had negotiated a separate peace with Germany.

Since seizing power five months before, the Bolsheviks had wreaked havoc on the Allied cause. They had published the secret treaties concluded between Russia, Britain, France, Italy, and Japan in 1915, which disappointed millions who imagined the war had been fought for more altruistic ends. Then the Bolsheviks canceled the war debts of Imperial Russia, which totaled billions in pounds sterling, francs and dollars. But the separate peace with Germany was the arch-betrayal. It enabled Germany to exploit the resources of the Ukraine—minerals, wheat, oil—and thus lessen the strangling effects of the British blockade. More importantly, it enabled General Erich Ludendorff of the German High Command to transfer some forty divisions from the Eastern Front in Russia to the west, where, for the first time, the Germans possessed numerical superiority in the trenches.

The Allies had contained the Germans in the west for three and a half years of bloody war largely because of the prolonged sacrifice of Russia. Six million Russian soldiers had been killed. Their deaths kept two million Germans occupied on the Eastern Front. This slaughter had wracked Russia, destroying its economy and the morale of its people. A revolution had erupted in February 1917, fomented by workingmen in St. Petersburg, whose city-wide demonstration persuaded elite Czarist troops not to fire upon them. The February Revolution forced the abdication of the Czar and the inauguration of a Provisional Government that promised the people a constitution and representative government. It also promised the Allies that Russia would fight on.

Among the many factions contributing to the February Revolution was the militant wing of the Socialist Workers Party who called themselves "Bolsheviks." Their goal was to reorganize Russia, to free her people from the bondage of the Czarist elite and from the agony of a never-ending war. But the February Revolution failed to achieve either goal, and the Germans, seeing how the situation might be turned to their advantage, seized the political initiative. Thus the Germans transported through their lines one Nikolai Lenin, who had been exiled in Switzerland, and they freed him at Finland Station. Once he was reunited with his Bolshevik comrades, Lenin redefined the purposes of the revolution, promising the war-weary Russian masses "Peace, Land, and Bread," as inspiring a messianic program as any ever offered in history. And within a short time, a small cohort of Bolsheviks seized power in Russia by storming the Winter Palace in St. Petersburg, where they dismissed the ministers of the Provisional Government at gunpoint.

Despite the Bolshevik promises, the peasants never got the land, and famine soon followed the revolution. But "Peace" was achieved by Lenin and Leon Trotsky when they asked Germany for an armistice to conclude an end to the war.

Germany had whelped Red terror. In return, Germany was able to separate the Ukraine from Greater Russia, which not only gave her food and raw materials for her beleaguered people but access to a fair-sized industrial plant as well. Germany was also able to send a division, under Graf von der Goltz, to Helsinki to help Baron Carl Gustave Mannerheim win Finland's independence

Submarine base at Murmansk

from the Soviet Government. Once Mannerheim was successful, Germany could move across the Finnish border to seize the northern Russian ports of Murmansk and Archangel for submarine bases. But above all, Germany now had the reserves with which to beat France and Britain in the west.

At that truce in March 1918, Allied strength in the trenches was 173 divisions, a little more than two million men. German strength was 177 divisions, with another forty divisions moving over from Russia. Thus the German forces would number more than three million men—crushing superiority. With this powerful reserve on the way, Ludendorff did not hesitate. On March 21, he launched the first of five hammer-stroke offensives on the Western Front. Six thousand guns and more than 100 divisions drove the British Fifth Army back thirty miles, inflicting 120,000 casualties. The Allies knew this was Germany's opening gambit, that other equally murderous blows would fall elsewhere on the front and fall soon. In this desperate situation it is not surprising that desperate initiatives were born. One of these was a plan that the Allies should intervene in Russia to rally pro-Allied Russians and lead them back to their trenches on the now deserted Eastern Front.

The formal plans for this campaign came out of the deliberations of the Permanent Military Representatives, the military adjunct of the Allied Supreme War Council, which had been set up in late 1917 to coordinate the winning of the war by the four great powers, Britain, France, Italy, and the United States. It was composed of the Prime Ministers and Foreign Secretaries of each, though by virtue of geography Woodrow Wilson and Secretary of State Robert Lansing could not convene with the others. From the time of its inception until the Armistice, the Supreme War Council met only eight times. Its deliberations were *pro forma*, its decisions cut and dried because it was advised by auxiliary committees: the Allied Naval Council, Allied Food Council, Allied Council on Purchases and Finance, groups that thoroughly discussed and thrashed out the recommendations they forwarded. The most important of these groups was the Permanent Military Representatives, which was charged with determining grand strategy. From

Planning of operation

January 1918 until the Armistice, they met fifty-one times. It was they who worked out such complicated programs as a unified Allied command, the creation of a general reserve, the disposition of the American Army, and the shipping priorities necessary in the wake of a U-boat war.

The men designated as Permanent Military Representatives were distinguished Allied generals who served outside the regular and staff commands of their respective armies. They were, in effect, ambassadors whose duty it was to coordinate the military efforts of their respective countries into one cohesive campaign. These generals assembled twice a week in the gilded ballroom of the Trianon Hotel in Versailles, where, over a burnished table that perfectly reflected their tunic ribbons and decorations and surrounded by maps on three-legged stands, they argued about how best to salvage the current situation and then go on and win the war. It was in these deliberations that the concept of a Russian intervention became a formal and diplomatic reality.

Presiding over the Permanent Military Representatives was France's Maxime Weygand, dapper, trim, of royal parentage. He was a lifelong student of war and confidant of Ferdinand Foch, destined to become the Allied commander-in-chief. (Two generations later, Weygand would succeed Maurice Gamelin as commanding general of the French Army and, in June 1940, report to his government that the war against Nazi Germany was beyond repair.)

General Henry Hugh Wilson sat for Britain. As the British ambassador to the French General Staff, Henry Wilson was also a firm believer in the brilliance of Foch. He was also an ebullient Irishman with a natural gift for politicking and destined to succeed Sir William Robertson as Chief of the Imperial Staff. (Later, Wilson would serve in Parliament, where he was assassinated by Irish terrorists in 1922.)

The resplendent but mournful Luigi Conte Cadorna was Italy's representative. He was a forceful, imaginative, and vigorous soldier, but his military insights were dimmed by the burden of defeat. He had commanded the Italian Army when it suffered disastrous defeat at Caporetto in October 1917. As a consequence, Italy had little to contribute to these sessions.

Lieutenant General Tasker H. Bliss was Woodrow Wilson's representative. A big man—he was called the "big Bliss" by his West Point classmates of 1875—Bliss was a *rara avis,* an intellectual military man, fluent in several languages, well informed on politics and economics, a geologist of repute, and a proficient tactician and strategist. He had been jumped from major to brigadier general in the Spanish-American War and in 1917, as Chief-of-Staff, had worked out the plans for the mobilization of the American Army. Bliss took his seat among the Permanent Military Representatives in January. He was the only one of the representatives to serve throughout the war. This tenure, added to his own considerable accomplishments, made him a prestigious figure. One reason for the unanimity of the Permanent Military Representatives was Bliss's skill as a mediator.

National policies, often at cross-purposes, divided these men. France wanted a unity of command on the Western Front, a command vested in a French general who would fight to the death to save Paris and concentrate every available resource on its defense. Britain feared that the French, in defense of Paris, would abandon the vital cross-Channel ports and strand British Tommies on the Continent. There were also high-ranking British soldiers and statesmen, among them General Henry Wilson and Prime Minister David Lloyd George, who believed the war could be won elsewhere than on the Western Front. Britain already had sent an expedition to Gallipoli in the Dardanelles, had committed fifty thousand men to a front in Salonica, and waged successful and romantic campaigns in the Middle East in pursuit of this strategy.

The one point on which the British, French, and Italians agreed was how to deploy the growing American Army. They wanted Yanks integrated into depleted British, French, and Italian divisions. However, John J. Pershing, commander of the American Expeditionary Force, unalterably opposed this plan. He wanted an American Army in France commanded wholly by American officers, fighting in an American sector of the line. In the beginning, Bliss had agreed with the British, French, and Italians. Pershing unceremoniously told him to change his mind, and Bliss knew an order when he heard one.

Meanwhile, the subject of intervention in Russia came before the Permanent Military Representatives as soon as it became apparent what might be the terrifying prospects of a separate Russo-German peace. Weygand, seconded by Sir Henry, suggested an immediate Allied occupation of the Trans-Siberian Railway from Vladivostok on the Pacific to Harbin in Manchuria, a distance of 300 miles. Such an occupation would deny Germany the use of military stores piled up in Vladivostok, as well as access to the Pacific for U-boats. To do the occupying, Weygand said a Japanese force supervised by an Allied commission would be quick and sure.

Japan had been at war with the Central Powers since August 1914, although her only contribution to the fighting had been to seize the German colony on the Shantung Peninsula and to occupy other German possessions in the Pacific. A Russian collapse, Weygand thought, could easily transform Germany into a Far Eastern power. Weygand's plan, such as it was, went on to specify that if the United States and Japan, as Pacific powers, took military possession of the whole of the Trans-Siberian Railway, the Allies could ship supplies to the Rumanian Army, which could serve as a nucleus for anti-Bolshevik forces who wished to continue fighting against Germany.

Bliss had immediate reservations, the least of which was that the Trans-Siberian Railway was 6,000 miles long. Bringing Japan into Siberia, Bliss wired Newton D. Baker, Secretary of War, was dangerous. This move would give Moscow every reason to suspect that the Japanese were doing to Russia in the east what the Germans were doing to it in the west.

"The intervention," wrote Bliss, "over a large part of Siberia, of a large Japanese army, raises the question of when and how they can be made to get out. I have often thought that this war, instead of being the last one, may be only the breeder of still more."[1] The purely military advantages the Allies wanted, Bliss concluded, could be secured by the simple occupation of Vladivostok.

Nevertheless, the Permanent Military Representatives sent Weygand's recommendation on to the Supreme War Council, whose ministers asked for Woodrow Wilson's approval. Wilson replied that a Japanese intervention would antagonize the Russians, that any occupation of Siberia should be a joint Allied venture, and that the United States did not regard favorably a unilateral move by Japan into Siberia. But that was hardly the end of it.

Of all the Allies, the British were the most insistent on intervention in Russia. The British had a gem to guard—India—and they would guard it with the same ferocity as they guarded the home islands. They knew that what happened in Moscow affected Bokhara and what affected Bokhara affected Bombay. The British wanted to depose the Bolsheviks, who were calling for a worldwide proletarian revolution, and in late 1917 the British began supplying money and arms in unending quantity to Cossacks in Transcaucasia and to anti-Bolsheviks mobilizing armies along the Don in southern Russia. They had given limited support to Captain Grigori Semenov, a Cossack who had established himself at the head of 750 men in eastern Siberia. And they had, without a by-your-leave from their allies, landed 160 British Marines at Murmansk on March 6, 1918. Murmansk was the northernmost port in European Russia, just below the Arctic Circle, and tacticians knew that any intervention in European Russia would have to start from there. The British Imperial Staff explained the move by saying the marines were in Murmansk only to guard military supplies.

The British, in short, were ready to go to Russia at the drop of a hat. But they lacked the manpower to assemble a strong intervening force. They would have to coax or persuade or hoodwink Woodrow Wilson into supplying them with troops. To achieve this, the British had an ace to play.

There was, in the spring of 1918, a small Allied military force still in Russia. It was a legion composed of Czechoslovaks who had fought for Russia against Germany. The legion comprised 40,000 excellent soldiers and was, in fact, the only force to fight bravely and well for the Provisional Government. Under the conditions of the Treaty of Brest-Litovsk, the Bolsheviks had ordered all Allied military units from Russia. Thus, a Czech Legion was making its way eastward from the Ukraine toward Vladivostok, from where it would cross the Pacific and the continental United States and proceed to France. There it would come under the command of the French General Staff and go into the trenches. At the moment, some of the legionnaires had begun the trek across Siberia. But many more of them were still in European Russia.

Sir Henry Wilson explained to the Permanent Military Representatives that it would be easier to bring the Czech Legion to the Western Front by having those legionnaires still in European Russia make a ninety-degree turn and march directly north to the ports of Murmansk and Archangel. It was an appreciably shorter trek from Omsk to Murmansk than it was from Omsk to Vladivostok, but it was still 1,600 miles, about the distance from Jacksonville to New York. Sir Henry also argued that if the Czechs went to Murmansk and Archangel, they could be used to guard these cities if the Germans in Finland pushed into North Russia.

Tasker Bliss saw the merit of bringing the Czechs northward as soon as possible in order to get them into the trenches in France. Therefore, he endorsed Sir Henry's proposal, which went up to the Supreme War Council on April 27 as Joint Note 25.

The British needed nothing more than this endorsement. Straightaway, the Imperial General Staff reinforced the marines at Murmansk with a military mission of 560 officers. Ostensibly this mission was to train and equip the Czechs when they arrived. Along with the mission came three companies: one machine gun, one engineering, and one infantry, who were to guard the ports while the training went on. Because Britain had now sent more than one thousand men to Russia, Sir Henry next asked the Permanent Military Representatives to recommend that their respective governments detail troops to this force.

Bliss concurred in detailing to Murmansk one battalion of American soldiers, which would serve with units from France, Italy, and Britain. The overall force had grown to four to six battalions, all under British command, their purpose being to supply and train the Czech Legion. Bliss's concurrence was dependent on Pershing's and Woodrow Wilson's approval, and he further stated that if an American battalion went to Russia, it went at the expense of the American commitment to the Western Front.

Though initially John J. Pershing was opposed to the idea, he, too, said he would concur, provided General Foch, who had by now been appointed generalissimo, had no objections. Indeed, Foch did not. In fact, Foch called on Woodrow Wilson to detail not just a battalion to North Russia but a regiment, an escalation that outraged Bliss. Meeting at Abbeville on May 2, the Allied Supreme War Council approved the recommendation and passed it on to Washington, where, on June 1, Woodrow Wilson authorized the diversion of troops from France to Murmansk.

Wilson sends the boys

Having won half a loaf, the British with the French and the Italians conspired to win the whole. They had Allied troops in the North; now they wanted Allied troops in the east. The foreign ministers—Arthur Balfour of Britain, Stephane Pichon of France, and Sydney Sonnino of Italy—once more importuned the Japanese to go to Siberia. They asked of Japan only that she "respect the territorial integrity of Russia, taking no sides in its internal politics, advancing as far as possible for the purpose of encountering Germans."[2]

Japan informed the foreign ministers that if she intervened she would go no further than Irkutsk, which was almost one-third of the way across Siberia. She would intervene only to halt the spread of German anarchy and end German intrigue. Nor would she intervene with America uncommitted. The Japanese did not want to risk an exhausting struggle in Siberia while the United States stood aside conserving its own Pacific forces. Japan had no intention of establishing trade centers in and around Vladivostok only to have the Allies order them closed after the war.

Arthur Balfour took it upon himself to convince Woodrow Wilson of the essential decency of the Japanese demands. "Since Russia cannot help herself," wrote Balfour to the American President, "she must be helped by friends. It is therefore to Japan that in the opinion of the Council appeal should be made to aid Russia in her present helpless condition."[3] The British Foreign Minister also passed along to Washington the report of the British Imperial General Staff which concluded that "unless Allied intervention is undertaken in Siberia forthwith, we have no chance of being ultimately victorious and shall incur serious risk of defeat in the meantime."[4]

Amazingly enough, this evaluation was still valid. The war on the Western Front continued to go badly and the fears that animated these men were real fears. By June, Ludendorff had thrown three hammer strokes at the Allied lines—the first on the Somme in late March, the second on the Lys in early April, and the third on the Aisne in late May. These attacks had driven ever deeper into France. Now Paris itself was under artillery bombardment. More frightening still was the knowledge that Ludendorff was readying even more powerful assaults.

Ferdinand Foch addressed a personal letter to Woodrow Wilson dated June 27:

> . . . in the interests of military success in Europe, I consider the expedition to Siberia as a very important factor for victory, provided action be immediate, on account of the season being already advanced, I take the liberty of insisting on this last point.[5]

Foch sent off his letter as a covering explanation to the plans for a Siberian intervention as proposed by the Permanent Military Representatives. Even so there were those who saw the expeditions to Russia as less than salvation. Tasker Bliss was one. He cabled a specific warning to the War Department:

> It seems to me our Allies want the United States to commit ourselves to various places where, after the war, they alone will have special interests.[6]

NOTES

1. Quoted by Peyton C. March, *The Nation at War.* New York: Doubleday, Doran, 1932, p. 100.
2. George F. Kennan, *Soviet-American Relations:* Vol. 2: *The Decision to Intervene.* New York: Atheneum, 1967, p. 384.

3. Frederick Palmer, *Bliss, Peacemaker: The Life and Letters of General Tasker Howard Bliss.* New York: Dodd, Mead, 1934, p. 303.
4. Richard H. Ullman, *Anglo-Soviet Relations, 1917–1921:* Vol. 1: *Intervention and the War.* Princeton: Princeton University Press, 1961, p. 5.
5. Ray Stannard Baker, *Woodrow Wilson: Life and Letters,* Vol. 8: *Armistice.* New York: Doubleday, Doran, 1939, p. 232.
6. Palmer, *op. cit.,* p. 293.

CHAPTER 2

WASHINGTON, D.C.:

JUNE 1–JULY 6, 1918

From the moment the Allies first broached the idea, President Wilson felt that an intervention in Russia was a perilous undertaking. But Britain and France were insistent on the necessity for it. He saw the Allied proposals as two separate endeavors. Intervention in the north of Russia would put troops just south of the Arctic Ocean; intervention in Siberia, a third of the world away, would put troops just west of the Japanese islands. Wilson did not think either endeavor endangered Russian hegemony. Therefore, he instructed Tasker Bliss to tell the Permanent Military Representatives that

> . . . Russia's misfortunes impose upon us at this time the obligation of unswerving fidelity to the principle of Russian territorial integrity and political independence. Intervention via Vladivostok is considered impracticable and the idea of compensating Japan by territory in Asiatic Russia inadmissable. *But* the President is heartily in sympathy with any practical military effort which can be made at and from Murmansk or Archangel, but such efforts should proceed if at all upon the sure sympathy of the Russian people and should not have as their ultimate object any restoration of the ancient regime or any other interference with the political liberty of the Russian people.[1]

[handwritten margin note: U.S. not meant to add too Japanese influence in Pacific]

On June 1, Wilson authorized diverting troops from France to Murmansk. He also detached for duty in North Russian waters the USS *Olympia,* Dewey's flagship at Manila Bay, which had been serving as a training ship at Annapolis.

When Secretary of War Newton D. Baker argued that the diversion was unwise, Wilson said he "felt obliged to do it anyhow because the British and French were pressing it on his attention so hard and he had refused so many of their requests that they were beginning to feel he was not a good associate much less a good ally."[2]

There is no question that Woodrow Wilson had received several warnings, including particularly judicious ones from his military advisers, to stay out of Russia. And when he first learned of the Weygand Plan calling for a Japanese occupation of Vladivostok, the President saw that this move might sacrifice some large American interests in Siberia. Among others, International Harvester, the Singer Sewing Machine Company, J. M. Coates (who supplied 60 percent of all the thread used in Russia), and the Westinghouse Company had made large investments there. So he continued to say no to a Siberian expedition.

Though Wilson had made a serious policy determination regarding his country's best interests, still pressures continued to build to make him change his mind. The British Military Mission to the United States General Staff pointed out to the White House that Japan and China had concluded a military agreement which allowed Japanese troops to enter Manchuria unopposed. Japanese troops were coming onto the Asian continent and taking up positions along the Siberian border. The subtle French sent over Henri Bergson, the Academie Française's preeminent philosopher whose books on the *élan vital* and creative evolution had made him hailed as a new Plato. Instructed by Clemenceau to put before Wilson the need to reconstitute an Eastern Front, Bergson had four *tête-à-têtes* with the President in June. The President remained obdurate. Woodrow Wilson had had long experience in dealing with preeminent philosophy professors when he was president of Princeton University.[3]

Just as the Allies kept pressuring for a Siberian intervention, so did domestic politicians. Ex-President William Howard Taft wrote a widely reprinted editorial for the *Philadelphia Public Ledger* calling for immediate action in Russia. Republican Senator James Wadsworth and ex-President Theodore Roosevelt publicly asked for forceful and positive action in dealing with the Bolsheviks. Senator James E. King introduced a resolution on the floor directing the President to send an expedition to Russia to repel German invaders. An astute politician, Wilson saw that inaction would give the Republicans an advantage in the coming fall elections.

If Wilson needed to renew his resolve, the man to do it was at hand. He was Thomas G. Masaryk, and he had arrived in the United States in June to rally support for Czechoslovakian independence. Masaryk's arrival was attended by widespread publicity and clamor. More Czechs lived in Chicago than any city outside of Prague, and almost as many Slovaks lived in Pittsburgh.

Thomas Garrigue Masaryk was a sixty-four-year-old philosophy professor at the University of Prague and a member of the Austrian *Reichsrat* when the war broke out in 1914. Long champions of Czechoslovakian independence from the Austro-Hungarian Empire, Masaryk, Eduard Beneš, and Milan Stefanik made their way from Prague to Paris, where they set up a Czech government-in-exile known as the National Council of Czechoslovakian Countries. Its purpose was to secure independence for Czechoslovakia by mustering men and money for the Allied Army to defeat Germany and Austro-Hungary.

Czech communities in the United States raised millions of dollars to finance legions which fought in France, Italy, and Russia. Of these, the most important was the Czech Legion in Russia, the very legion the British had asked to proceed to Murmansk and Archangel from Omsk. This legion was Masaryk's own creation. After the February Revolution of 1917 that established the Provisional Government in Russia, Masaryk made his way to St. Petersburg, where he persuaded Alexander Kerensky, the Prime Minister, to recruit the 250,000 Czech prisoners of war into an army corps to fight against Germany. Virtually all of these Czechs had deserted from the Austro-Hungarian Army. The 1st Prague Regiment, in fact, had not only abandoned their positions *en masse* but had marched into Russian captivity preceded by its military band. In captivity, these Czechs had formed shadow military commands in the hope that they could fight for Russia. When Kerensky authorized the formation of the legion, Masaryk quickly mustered 40,000 men in two divisions. They were in the line within a month, an incredible accomplishment in a country whose transport, communications, and administration were chaotic. The Czech Legion acquitted itself brilliantly at the battle of Zborov, Russia's last offensive against Germany. When the offensive failed, the Czechs were the only disciplined corps in the Ukraine, the Russian Army having melted away.

When the Bolsheviks signed the Treaty of Brest-Litovsk, Masaryk supervised the evacuation of the legion. He warned its officers to maintain strict neutrality in regard to Russian party dissensions. Assured by the Bolsheviks of the legion's safe passage across Siberia, Masaryk embarked at Vladivostok for the United States. Masaryk had made heroism glow again for the Czechs, a heroism extinguished when the Hapsburgs overwhelmed Bohemia centuries before.

More importantly for Woodrow Wilson, Masaryk was the one European statesman with a thorough and firsthand experience of Bolshevik strength and determination.

As Masaryk made his pilgrimage to the White House in June the Czech Legion had suddenly exploded against the Bolsheviks. Badgered and harassed by local soviets, the legion had disobeyed Masaryk's orders for strict neutrality and had resolved to fight its way across Siberia. Though news of its derring-do was sketchy, its bold action enthralled Americans. Masaryk was less sanguine. He urgently desired an audience with the American President not only to plead for the recognition of Czech rights but also to warn him that the Bolsheviks were going to govern Russia.

The two leaders met on June 19. "My first impression of Wilson," Masaryk said many years later, "was of such perfect neatness. I said to myself it's obvious he has a wife who loves him."

He offered Wilson direct and succinct advice: stay out of Russia. He advised *de facto* recognition of the Bolshevik regime, which had more staying power than any suspected. He was unenthusiastic about intervention for which neither clear plans nor goals had been formulated. A Japanese intervention, Masaryk told Wilson, would alienate the Russian people and it would be difficult to pay off the Japanese. When Wilson replied that America would finance the Japanese intervention, Masaryk cautioned that it was too little, that the Japanese would want Russian territory. Masaryk ventured that it would take one million men to wage a successful intervention, a military commitment Japan was hardly ready to undertake. Masaryk told Wilson that the Czechs wanted independence and that they wanted the Czech Legion out of Russia as soon as possible.[4]

When Wilson reported the gist of this conversation to Newton D. Baker, the Secretary of War agreed with the Czechs. "I would like to take everyone out of Russia except the Russians, including diplomatic representatives, political agents, propagandists and casual visitors and let the Russians settle down and settle their own business."

Wilson offered no demurrers. Nevertheless, he was still of two minds about intervention. He wrote his trusted adviser Colonel Edward M. House, "I have been sweating blood over the question what is right and feasible (*possible*) to do in Russia. It goes to pieces like quicksilver under my touch."

Indeed the American President had been sweating blood over Russia for the past eighteen months because he saw that Russia's position in Europe was the key to peace. He had been as preoccupied in keeping Russia in the camp of the West as he had been with any other problem connected with winning the war. Wilson saw to it that the United States was the first Western nation to recognize the Provisional Government which had emerged from the February Revolution of 1917. When Wilson asked Congress for a declaration of war against Germany, he cited this revolution to make clear that the war was fought to make the world safe for democracy. In ringing declamation, Wilson noted that the Russian people had thrown off the autocracy and in their naïve majesty and might joined the forces fighting for freedom in the world, for peace, for justice. "Here," he concluded, "is a fit partner for a league of honor."

He had also dispatched a good-will mission to the Provisional Government. The mission was headed by the Mr. Republican of his day, Senator Elihu Root, who had served in Theodore Roosevelt's two cabinets. Root's main purpose, as he understood it, was to bring the United States and the Provisional Government together in closer prosecution of the war. It was an impossible mission. The Provisional Government was wracked by dissension, lacked money, and its army was beaten. Root and members of his mission simply got in the way of harassed ministers who dared not reveal to anyone the imminence of the Provisional Government's collapse. Thus Root was as surprised as anyone to learn a few weeks after he had returned to the United States that the Bolsheviks had toppled the Provisional Government. This second revolution in Russia nevertheless motivated one of Wilson's Fourteen Points, the sixth:

> The evacuation of all Russian territory and such a settlement of all questions affecting Russia as will secure the best and freest co-operation of the other nations of the world in obtaining for her an unhampered and unembarrassed opportunity for the independent determination of her own political development and national policy. . . . The treatment accorded Russia by her sister nations in the months to come will be the acid test of their good will.[5]

This sixth point was a proffered bribe. Wilson was promising that Russia could go her own way with Allied help and American loans if the Bolsheviks would keep Russia in the war. Hundreds of thousands of mimeographed copies of this speech were distributed by American consular services in Russia.

Despite blandishments, threats of economic reprisals, and the rhetoric of moral outrage, the Bolsheviks were impervious to Allied demands. Intervention might change this. And Wilson again turned toward it in late June. What helped him change his mind about going to Siberia was the progress of the Czech Legion,

which was fighting its way out of Russia. The legion was smiting
the Bolsheviks hip and thigh. The British and the French pointed
out to Wilson that the Czech Legion virtually constituted an Allied
army in Siberia. Now Wilson listened. He wrote Secretary of State
Robert M. Lansing that there seemed to emerge from the Czech
Legion the "shadow of a plan" by which the United States might
work an intervention with Japan.

Wilson wanted intervention as a lever to manipulate the
Allies at the peace table. In the fourteen months the United States
had been at war, he had built up considerable friction between
America and the three major warring powers—Italy, France, and
Britain. Wilson had refused to bind himself to the ends the Allies
wanted to realize in victory, he had refused to integrate the Yanks
in decimated Allied divisions, and there was every chance he
would offer magnanimous terms to the defeated. Wilson wanted
to cool the friction in order to have his way at the peace table; he
wanted the peace treaty to incorporate a covenant of a League of
Nations which would regulate a congeries of liberal-capitalist states
in which American interests would best flourish. A Siberian intervention became a *quid pro quo*. If he sanctioned a Siberian intervention, the Allied statesmen could hardly deny him later.

Wilson fired off a presidential memorandum to Peyton C.
March, Chief of the United States General Staff, asking him to
draw up plans for a proposed Siberian intervention by a force of
10,000 to 15,000 men comprising American, British, French, and
Italian units who would subsist by living off the country.

A brilliantly incisive West Pointer, March was probably the
only American general who never looked like a general. A tall,
lanky man with a graying Van Dyke beard, he was always uncom-
fortable in uniforms that seemed too short. He had been Chief of
Artillery when Baker recalled him from France to take over the
faltering and bewildered General Staff in the first winter of the war.

March offered serious opposition to Wilson's proposed intervention. He argued cogently that the solution of the Russian question by intervention meant giving Japan a portion of Siberia.
There was, the general went on, no way to reconstitute Russia into
a military machine. He spoke from experience: He had been an

observer in the Russo-Japanese War twelve years before. If the United States simply concentrated on winning the war on the Western Front, it could dictate a solution to Russia's internal troubles come what may at the peace table. As for living off the country

> . . . it is to be noted that while the supply of grain and cattle in Siberia was properly used in the Russo-Japanese War for feeding the people, it is now proposed without regard for the inhabitants of Siberia to subsist an army of invasion on the food supplies which naturally go to feeding the inhabitants themselves. This to my mind is practically out of the question.[6]

The President ignored March's objections. Bliss, Baker, Pershing, and now March had seriously questioned the advisability of a military intervention. Wilson, who in the past had listened to the advice of his military planners, in this instance did not. There was in Woodrow Wilson a streak of the stubborn know-it-all. This was the moment he chose to display it to his general as he had displayed it to the Princeton faculty some years before which cost him the presidency of the university. The same stubbornness with Republican Senators some years hence cost him the League of Nations.

On July 2, the Supreme War Council appealed to the President to reconsider an urgent intervention in Siberia because the Czechs were in danger of being cut off and the Allies must save them. Wilson decided yes. Aboard the presidential yacht *Mayflower* on a torpid July 3, Wilson and Lansing found the key with which to turn the lock. "The Czech Legion," wrote Lansing in a shipboard memo, "has materially changed the situation by introducing a sentimental element into the question of our duty." Three days later, Wilson authorized a State Department announcement that the United States regarded the Czech forces in Russia as an "inspiring element of the military forces now engaged against the Central Powers, deserving of support and approval of all governments engaged in the war."

On July 6, the President summoned Lansing, Baker, Secre-

tary of the Navy Josephus Daniels, Admiral W. S. Benson, Chief
of Naval Operations, and General March to a late-evening meeting in one of the upper rooms of the White House. They had
seated themselves in order of rank when Wilson entered with a
yellow pad and, standing in the manner of a schoolteacher, as
March put it, read off the proposal that the United States would
share with Japan the expense of providing small arms, ammunition, and machine guns to the Czechs along with supplemental
supplies; and that with the Japanese the United States would land
a military force at Vladivostok to guard the Czech line of communication to Irkutsk. For this purpose the United States and
Japan would send detachments numbering no more than 7,000
troops—7,000 because that was the table of organization for the
two Philippine regiments, the only troops the General Staff said
the American Army could spare from France.

Wilson took a voice vote. March kept shaking his head vigorously.

> [The President] said with some asperity, "Why are you
> shaking your head, General?" and instantly went on, "You
> are opposed to this because you do not think Japan will
> limit herself to 7,000 men and that the decision will further
> her schemes for territorial aggrandizement." I have never
> been a "yes-man" so I said in reply, "Just that, and for
> other military reasons which I have already told you."[7]

Newton D. Baker also disagreed with the decision, the only
real disagreement he ever had with his chief. "The expedition was
nonsense from the beginning," he wrote years later, "and always
seemed to me one of those sideshows born of desperation and
organized for the purpose of keeping up home morale rather than
because of any clear view of the military situation."

When the meeting broke up at midnight, Baker wired Admiral Austin M. Knight on the USS *Brooklyn,* which was off
Vladivostok in easternmost Siberia in Golden Horn Bay protecting the American consulates and gathering intelligence, to keep
Vladivostok available as a base for the escape of the Czechs. At
the same time, the President forwarded credits in the amount of

$7,000,000 to the Czech Legion from monies the Congress had appropriated for his discretionary use.

In the days that followed, Woodrow Wilson devoted himself to composing on his portable typewriter an *aide-mémoire* in which he gave his reasons for sending the United States into Russia. That *aide-mémoire,* which was circulated secretly among the Allies— for the American public didn't know about either of the Russian expeditions until August—is the only statement ever offered by the twenty-eighth President for the intervention.

Wilson began by killing his own arguments. Military intervention, he said, would add to the present sad confusion in Russia rather than cure it, injure her rather than help her, and would be of no advantage in the prosecution of the Allies' main design, to win the war against Germany. But then he picked up the argument:

> Military action is admissable in Russia, as the Government of the United States sees the circumstances, only to help the Czecho-Slovaks consolidate their forces and get into successful cooperation with their Slavic kinsmen and to steady any efforts at self-government or self-defense in which the Russians themselves may be willing to accept assistance. Whether from Vladivostok or from Murmansk and Archangel, the only legitimate object for which American or Allied troops can be employed, it submits, is to guard military stores which may subsequently be needed by Russian forces and to render such aid as may be acceptable to the Russians in the organization of their own self-defense . . . the United States is glad to contribute the small force at its disposal for that purpose. It yields, also, to the judgment of the Supreme Command in the matter of establishing a small force at Murmansk, to guard the military stores at Kola, and to make it safe for the Russian forces to come together in organized bodies in the north. . . .
>
> It is the hope and purpose of the Government of the United States to take advantage of the earliest opportunity to send to Siberia a commission of merchants, agricultural experts, labor advisers, Red Cross representatives and agents of the Young Men's Christian Association accus-

tomed to organizing the best methods of spreading useful information and rendering educational help of a modest sort, in order in some systematic manner to relieve the immediate economic necessities of the people there in every way for which opportunity may open. The execution of this plan will follow and will not be permitted to embarrass the military assistance rendered in the rear of the westward-moving forces of the Czecho-Slovaks.[8]

A curious statement. On the one hand the note insists the United States cannot countenance a Russian intervention, then on the other details how such an intervention will not disturb Russian internal disputes. It dismisses the possibility of reconstituting the Eastern Front—the express purpose of the Allies—in favor of guarding military stores which may be needed by the Russians. But the note does not say for what purpose the Russians may need them. On the one hand, the note says the United States is going to Russia to rescue the Czechs but on the other does not explore the obvious question of what is to become of the rescuing force once the Czechs are secure.

Wilson was obviously hoping the intervention would accomplish something else. What he hoped for, suggests George F. Kennan, was that the arrival of the Japanese and American forces "would elicit so powerful and friendly a reaction among the population that a pro-Allied authority would be initiated throughout Siberia and in North Russia by spontaneous democratic action."[9]

There is a key word in the *aide-mémoire* which appears in the document's last sentence—"the *westward*-moving forces of the Czecho-Slovaks." Nobody picked up this confusion at the time. If the Czechs wanted rescue, they could only move *east* to find it. To move west meant the Czechs were moving against the centers of Bolshevik power, that they were attacking toward Moscow. Indeed this is what had happened. The Czechs were no longer fighting their way toward Vladivostok but toward the Volga. Wilson said "westward-moving forces" because he probably knew the British and the French had persuaded the legion to war against the Bolsheviks, promising Czechoslovakia independence in return. Indeed, French recognition of Czech rights came on July 8 and British recognition of Czechoslovakia as an Allied nation on August 9.*

There was steady pressure on Wilson both from the Allies and from politicians at home to intervene. Intervention finally turned on the Czech Legion, which had an influence out of all proportion to its size. It was as though a small star, no more than a pinprick of light in a telescope, had suddenly exploded, irradiating the heavens with its intense light. That explosion had been building up for more than a year. To understand the forces which ignited the star and compelled Woodrow Wilson's attention, we must go back to the star itself.

NOTES

1. Baker, *op. cit.,* p. 175.
2. *Ibid.,* p. 147.
3. Henri Bergson, *Ecrits et Paroles.* "Ma Missions, 1917–1918." Paris: Presses Universitaires de France, 1959.
4. Victor S. Matamey, *The United States and East Central Europe, 1914–1918.* Princeton: Princeton University Press, 1957, pp. 280–86.
5. Stanley S. Jados, *Documents on Russian-American Relations.* Washington, D.C.: Catholic University of America, 1965, p. 43.
6. March, *op. cit.,* pp. 116–20.
7. *Ibid.,* p. 126.
8. Jados, *op. cit.,* pp. 51–52.
9. Kennan, *op. cit.,* p. 404.

* The United States recognized a state of war between Czechoslovakia and Germany on September 3.

CHAPTER 3

SIBERIA:

MARCH 3–JULY 7, 1918

Czech legionnaires wore visored caps with red and white ribbons for emblems, belted Russian blouses for tunics, and khaki pants tucked into high boots. They slung their pack on one shoulder and on the other carried a variety of arms which made ammunition supply difficult. Their shoulder patches portrayed the Hussite chalice and the Bohemian lion, which led Russians to nickname them *rjumotshky* and *sobatshky*—"wineglasses" and "puppy dogs." Their flag consisted of equal fields of red and white emblazoned with the crests of the lands which composed their embryonic republic—Bohemia, Moravia, and Slovakia. The legion was commanded by Milo K. Dietrichs, formerly a general of the Imperial Russian Army.

In the late winter of 1917, the Allied Supreme War Council recognized an autonomous Czechoslovak Army made up of the French, Italian, and Russian legions. This recognition heartened the Czech Legion in Russia, which by February 1918 was virtually alone in the face of a German push through the Ukraine. The Treaty of Brest-Litovsk bought them a little time.

Apprised by the Bolsheviks that they would have to withdraw their military missions from Russia, the Supreme War Council decided to evacuate the legion by the 6,000-mile transit across Siberia where the British would provide the tonnage for its transport to France. In at least one respect this was a chimerical goal: There was no available tonnage for the Czechs once they reached Vladivostok. Vladivostok was a dead end.

Masaryk assented to the proposed transfer and secured the agreement of Kotsubinsky, the military secretary of the Ukrainian Soviet, and Murayev, the Soviet's commander-in-chief, to recognize and respect the armed neutrality of the legion and keep it supplied until it moved onto Bolshevik soil. The Bolsheviks at this time stipulated only that the legion would continue to maintain order wherever it was garrisoned. Masaryk put Jiri Klecenda and Prokop Maxa in charge of this evacuation. Klecenda was a young administrator who did exactly as he was told. Maxa, a schoolteacher, had survived three years in Turkestan POW camps. The legionnaires said Maxa was a cunning man but one who had an excessive regard for his own life. Klecenda and Maxa maintained headquarters in Moscow to deal with the Bolsheviks as the evacuation proceeded.

Carefully the Czechs began to withdraw from their positions near Kiev, entraining for the rail terminal of Penza on the west bank of the Volga. But as soon as the Treaty of Brest-Litovsk was ratified, German troops began to occupy the Ukraine. The German High Command had no intention of permitting the easy withdrawal of 40,000 disciplined soldiers for the Western Front. Two Panzer divisions raced for Bachmach, the capture of which would trap the legion. The Czechs barely beat the Germans to it. The Czechs were lucky: In the yards at Bachmach they found twenty-seven locomotives and 750 boxcars, enough to evacuate the entire corps. While most of the 1st and 2nd Czech divisions embarked on these trains, a determined rear guard moved west to delay the Germans. They encountered the 224th German Infantry and halted the advance. The German commander reported the legionnaires showed

> ... class, offensive enthusiasm, good discipline and marksmanship. Germans should neither underestimate their numbers nor their combat value. They fought with great bravery and operated so cleverly that they reached their goal of an orderly withdrawal.[1]

The Czechs left eighty dead sprawled across the railway ties. So close was their escape that German advance units opened fire on the last of the fleeing echelons. As the legion drew out of the Germans' range, the Bolshevik Government in Moscow approved their passage across Soviet territory. On March 18, Commissar of Foreign Nationalities, Josef Stalin, agreed to the evacuation of the Czechs on three conditions: that they leave at once, that non-Communist Russian officers with the exception of General Dietrichs resign from the legion, and that the legionnaires proceed "not as fighting units but as free citizens taking with them a certain quantity of arms for self-defense against counter-revolutionists."[2]

The legionnaires had armed themselves by capturing German weapons, by retrieving Russian arms from the battlefield, and by improvisation. Nevertheless at Kursk the Czechs grudgingly began to turn these over to the local soviet, which then allowed them to proceed. Aboard each train there was only one company of armed men with 168 rifles, 300 rounds per man, one machine gun with 1,200 rounds, a single trench mortar, and a small number of hand grenades.

The Czechs were far from naïve. They began secreting their arms in the small stoves which heated their vans, under the floorboards, below their bunks, and in the bags of provisions. When the Czechs reached Penza, 400 miles east of Kursk, their boxcars were as explosive as the interior of an anarchist's suitcase. Here, the legion began its protracted exodus from European Russia across the steppes to the Great Ocean.*

The legion proceeded on this journey echelon by echelon, spaced a day and sometimes a week apart. An echelon consisted of twenty boxcars or vans which the Czechs called *teplushkas*. Twenty was not an arbitrary number; it was the maximum load a wood- or coal-burning Russian locomotive could haul. In each *teplushka* there were forty men. Eight hundred men to an echelon did not constitute a battalion, a dispersal the Czechs thought seriously endangered their movement. A soldier in 1918 believed the

---

* Geographically, Russia's eastern shores lie along the Sea of Japan, the Strait of Tartary, the Sea of Okhtosk, the Bering Sea, and the Bering Strait. Russians have always called these waters the Great Ocean.

only way to prevail against an enemy armed with machine guns was by heavy artillery bombardment and an attack in the mass, and now the legion had neither. Vast though it was, the Czechs knew Siberia was a plain on which dissident armies were maneuvering for a civil war, where hordes of Cossacks preyed on the weak and where mythical German prisoners of war, armed and organized, marched to seize military vantage points.

Under optimum conditions the best speed an echelon could make was 600 miles a day, which meant a ten-day journey across Siberia. Having started in late March, the first echelons did not begin to reach Vladivostok until late April. Locomotives broke down, Czechs had to stop and forage for provisions, and keeping echelons in communication with one another was time-consuming. By the beginning of May, however, 14,000 Czechs under Dietrichs had crossed Siberia, while 4,000 were still in Penza waiting to entrain. It was as though 14,000 Czechs had reached New York while 4,000 remained in Honolulu with another 22,000 spread across the Pacific and in small towns in the United States. These 22,000 between these two points contended daily against the most serious obstacle to their passage: the unwillingness of the Bolsheviks to let them go on.

When an echelon drew into Samara on the east bank of the Volga, the local soviet demanded it surrender even more of its weapons than it had handed over at Kursk. To the protest of the Czechs who produced Stalin's visa, the commissars replied that Comrade Stalin's authority did not extend to Samara, that the local Bolsheviks needed weapons even more than the Czechs, that the weapons were Russian property, and that unless the departing legionnaires turned over thirty rifles the railway personnel would neither provide a locomotive nor switch the echelon onto the main track. The Czech officers complained to Maxa, the National Councilman in Moscow, who promptly advised that the legion must maintain friendly relations with the Bolsheviks at all costs. So in dozens of towns along the way the local soviets indulged in blackmail of one sort or another, delaying the echelon until its officers persuaded the men they had no option.

At Balasov, an echelon found itself in the middle of a fierce fight between Bolsheviks and Socialist Revolutionaries. The Socialists held the station, the Bolsheviks the town. The Socialists begged the Czech commander, Lieutenant Cehovsky, for help, which he refused. Aware that the Bolsheviks did not know of his neutrality, Cehovsky presented himself to the commissar and asked him to forestall his attack until the legion had left the station. The commissar agreed because delay suited his plans. The temporary armistice, in fact, suited both sides, who connived to keep the echelon in the station for several days while they built up their forces.

Prolonged delay came on April 5 when the Soviet Government ordered a halt for the entire Czech caravan. The halt was dictated by the news that a Japanese battalion had landed in Vladivostok. Lenin and Trotsky feared this was the beginning of a Japanese thrust into Siberia, that the Japanese would enlist the Czechs along with the Cossacks to occupy Russian territory. But the truth was that Japan had sent troops ashore to protect the lives of its nationals, three of whom had been murdered by rioters the day before. There were thousands of Japanese in Vladivostok, and the anarchy that engulfed the city threatened them more than any other group. On April 25, as anarchy ebbed, the Japanese turned Vladivostok over to a soviet. Lenin and Trotsky, however, did not send the Czechs on their way.

The three-week delay, which proved almost intolerable for the waiting echelons, gave both the Allied Supreme War Council and the Bolsheviks time to think over the wisdom of sending the Czechs through Siberia. Having disbanded the Imperial Army, Lenin and Trotsky could count on only 50,000 Red Guards in Siberia to keep order against anti-Bolshevik partisans, of whom there were many thousands; organized Cossacks who moved at will; the Japanese and Chinese encroaching on Russian territory; and a small Allied fleet in the harbor of Vladivostok. Sending an armed Czech contingent across Siberia seemed now to the Bolsheviks as sensible as rolling a barrel of high explosives through a quickening brush fire.

When the Allied Supreme War Council saw another way to utilize the legion in Murmansk and Archangel, the Bolsheviks agreed and authorized diverting Czech troops still west of Omsk north. Omsk, on the Irtysh River, was roughly halfway between Penza and Vladivostok.

The order was relayed to the legion through the offices of Georgi Chicherin, Commissar for Foreign Affairs. No one, however, took the time to explain the reason for this change to the officers and men of the legion. The Czechs knew only that on Bolshevik orders half of their number were to proceed north, thus dividing the legion in two and rendering it even more vulnerable than it was when spread across Siberia.

The Czechs had good reasons to distrust Bolshevik intentions. Dozens of Bolsheviks had infiltrated the legion, most of them Czechoslovak Communists, and constantly agitated to separate the men from their officers. Trotsky publicly offered the opinion that the patriotic duty of all Slavs was to enlist as a Bolshevik force. Thus, the constant delays, extortion, endless subversion, the sudden change in direction, and the rapidly accelerating political strife had primed the Czechoslovakian Legion for a fight to save itself. On May 1, the legionnaires voted to send soldier representatives to a Congress of the Czechoslovakian Revolutionary Army which was to convene at Chelyabinsk on May 18, 1918.

Chelyabinsk was a lonely railroad depot on the rim of Siberia. Mounds of coal were heaped beside the railroad tracks rising almost to the height of the telegraph poles. A broad loading platform, the trainmaster's shack, and a tall wooden water tower marked the station. Around these landmarks were the cabins of the railway workers.

The town of Chelyabinsk, three miles distant, contained a great stone administrative building and an equally impressive stone arsenal. Nearby were barracks for the garrisoning of troops. These had been built by the Czar in anticipation of another war with Japan. A cluster of well-constructed wooden homes signaled the residences of the merchants and rich *kulaks*. Beyond them stretched the rude huts of the workingmen and peasants. Chelyabinsk served also as the center for one of the large prisoner-of-war camps which dotted the steppes.

On May 11, 1918, a twenty-van echelon of the Czech Legion drew into the depot and pulled off to one of the sidings. It ground to a halt not three feet from a freight on which Red Guards were waiting to load recently freed Hungarian prisoners of war, who were being repatriated under the terms of the Treaty of Brest-Litovsk.

The Czech train was pointed east, the Hungarian freight west. Both sets of soldiers, however, were bound for the same destination, the trenches of the Western Front.

The Czechs were a superbly disciplined and well-supplied force. They dug their slit trenches and latrines several hundred yards from the trains. They knew how to cook in the field. In the morning they did calisthenics, in the afternoon close-order drill. The Hungarians were casuals and soon made the Chelyabinsk siding fetid. Imprisonment had emaciated them, and they were subsisting on black bread, which they carried in the pockets of their greatcoats. Their morale was low: They knew they were going back to the living death of the trenches.

For three days the Czechs and the Hungarians kept out of each other's way, though politically they were mortal enemies. To the Czechs the Hungarians were the oppressors. To the Hungarians the Czechs were renegades, traitors to the empire. Then in the late morning of May 14, the Hungarian gondolas, fully loaded, slowly began to grind forward. One of the Hungarians, a Magyar named Malik, suddenly hurled a heavy piece of iron at a group of legionnaires. The missile struck a Czech soldier and killed him on the spot. Czechs swarmed aboard the Hungarian locomotive and brought it to a stop. Legionnaires invaded the gondola and demanded the miscreant. Since the Czechs were armed and the Hungarians not, there was little argument. Fellow soldiers pointed to the wretch. The Czechs threw him from the gondola and six legionnaires bludgeoned him to death.

Czech officers got the legionnaires back behind their vans. Red Guards waved the Hungarian locomotive forward. In this great war, which had claimed the lives of millions of men, this sad incident seemed of small consequence. But the Chelyabinsk soviet who had been governing the city since the October Revolution summoned the ten Czech legionnaires who had been on guard

duty at the time. When these soldiers voluntarily presented themselves, at the administration building, the soviet arrested them.
Understandably these men worried and their brothers—for thus
officers and men of the legion addressed themselves—worried
with them.

The echelon commander deputized two officers who on May
15 petitioned the soviet for the release of the prisoners. The soviet
arrested them, too. On the 16th, the Czechs deployed from the
station throughout Chelyabinsk, occupying the important streets
and intersections. One unit seized the arsenal. Four more companies surrounded the administration building.[3] That evening
Commissar Sadlutski wired Moscow:

> All the time [the Czechs] were demanding liberty for the
> prisoners. When I argued that their action was directed
> against the Soviet Government, they proclaimed they were
> not against it, but they wanted only the release of their men.
> To avoid bloodshed, and in view of the discipline of the
> Czechoslovaks and the unpreparedness of the Red Army
> I decided to free the prisoners. After this, the Czechoslo-
> vaks singing left the streets for their trains. We wanted to
> disarm them, but we were not strong enough. It is absolutely
> necessary to transport them to Siberia, since any further
> delay and uncertainty as to when they may go may, finally,
> provoke a strong rebellion among them. And to engage in
> a dispute with them while the movement of the Cossacks is
> not yet suppressed does not seem to be favorable. From
> Ekaterinburg it was decided they should not be disarmed,
> due to lack of forces which were sent to Orenburg and,
> further, to await decisions of the soviet in Moscow.[4]

Two days later several hundred legionnaires arrived in
Chelyabinsk from echelons along the length of the Trans-Siberian
save that none attended who had reached Vladivostok. Their congress was an innovation borrowed from the Russian soviets. "Soviets" were councils of soldiers, peasants, or workingmen which
proliferated after the abdication of the Czar. Up until now, the
Czechs' congress had determined only internal ends—military
organization, promotions, finances, and enlistment policies. Meet-

ing in Chelyabinsk, however, where an echelon had to resort to force to save itself, made the legionnaires aware that the fate of one might be the fate of all.

The most enterprising and eventually the most controversial of the legionnaires, Lieutenant Rudolph Gaida, dominated the sessions. A pharmacist, Gaida had been a medic in the Austrian Army until he deserted. An ideologue, a fierce anti-Bolshevik, articulate, the twenty-seven-year-old Gaida, who would be a general by July, had readied his own echelon for a fight and now exhorted the others. He had flashing blue eyes, an aquiline nose, "preferred force to negotiations, was unscrupulous in his desire for power, and was never satisfied by the complete execution of his task."[5]

The delegates, two from every echelon, met in the stone arsenal in Chelyabinsk. Among the outsiders who attended the congress was Ekaterina Breshkovskaya, the "grandmother of the Revolution," a woman who had followed Bakunin, suffered Siberian exile, and distributed thousands of copies of the *Communist Manifesto* and *Das Kapital* to peasants and workingmen. She was a symbolic figure to the old revolutionaries who emerged from the detritus of the October Revolution dazed, bewildered, unable to comprehend that Russian socialism had become not a people's cause but a totalitarian movement. Breshkovskaya's counterparts emerged in Archangel and Vladivostok, trying to capitalize on the profound change in Russia, succeeding only to the degree that Czech legionnaires, British Tommies, or American Yanks supported them. In this instance, the Czechs ignored Breshkovskaya's advice to send a delegation directly to Moscow.

One of the Czech officers read a telegram from Prokop Maxa and Jiri Klecenda which ordered ". . . all legionnaires to surrender arms to the Soviet authority because the Soviet Government took upon itself the task of protecting the Czechoslovaks. Those who do not obey are traitors and stripped of international status which they enjoyed as members of the Allied Armed Forces."[6]

Gaida took the floor and, waving a sheaf of messages, told the legionnaires his men had been monitoring the telegraph lines. In Russia, control of the railway line meant control of the telegraph lines. The Bolsheviks had reacted in panic to the news of the Chelyabinsk incident. The Cheka had arrested Maxa and Klecenda. Gaida read aloud a telegram from Trotsky to the commandant of the Red Guards:

> To supplement an earlier order I suggest that you immediately stop, disarm and disband all the trains and parts of the Czechoslovak Army Corps as remnants of the old regular army. From the present Czech Army Corps form the Red Army and the labor battalions. If you need help from Czechoslovak Communists contact the consulates of the Czechoslovak Social Democrats in Penza, Samarra, Petropavlovsk and Omsk. . . .[7]

Trotsky put into forced Labor

And another:

> All soviets are hereby ordered to disarm the Czechoslovaks immediately. Every armed Czech found on the railway is to be shot on the spot; every troop train in which even one armed man is found shall be unloaded, its soldiers shall be interned in a war prisoners' camp. Local war commissars must proceed at once to carry out this order.[8]

The Czechs were already convinced. This strengthened the conviction that they had no option but to fight their way through. To surrender their arms meant conscription in Red labor battalions or the Red Army. The legion believed that the Treaty of Brest-Litovsk was the profound betrayal of history. The Bolsheviks were handing Russia over to Germany, and this surrender would end once and for all the Pan-Slavic ideal of a congeries of independent states in eastern Europe protected by Mother Russia.

More than this, however, the legionnaires knew their lives were at stake. They were one and all deserters, renegades, and under the rules of war once they suffered capture they were summarily executed. Those who had escaped immediate execution were sent back to their small Czech villages and hanged in the square as an object lesson. They were toughened by an acute realization of their peril. Bolshevik threats did not make them pale. With an overwhelming roar, they voted to fight their way to Vladivostok.

They vested command of the legion in their own Provisional Executive Committee, which was composed of four members of the National Council, several of whom were traveling with the echelons; four enlisted men; and three regimental commanders. The legion obeyed orders only with the assent of this committee. The Provisional Committee put Captain Jan Syrovy in overall command.[9] Syrovy, an architect from Prague, had lost an eye at the battle of Zborov but was back with his men three days later, easily identified by his black patch. When Syrovy accepted and rose to address the delegates, one of them shouted, "The days of Zizka have returned."*

Syrovy chose a staff which, trusting to surprise, luck, courage, and initiative, took less than a night to draw up the campaign to advance twenty-six thousand legionnaires over a distance of three thousand miles. The line began in European Russia at Penza, a railroad terminal and switching station only three hundred miles southeast of Moscow, and proceeded east two hundred miles to the Volga River and another important railyard at Samara (present-day Kuibyshev). There were four thousand legionnaires in Penza and another four thousand in Samara. Syrovy's staff put these Czechs under the command of Captain Stanislaus Cecek. Cecek, who wore a clerk's mustache, had puffy cheeks and parted his hair in the middle, was well regarded for his absolute placidity.

From Samara the line stretched five hundred miles to Chelyabinsk, where Siberia begins on the eastern side of the Ural Mountains. There were eight thousand Czechs in the Chelyabinsk area. There were two thousand more Czechs between Chelyabinsk and Omsk, cities five hundred miles apart. A Russian, General Bruno Voitsekhovskii, took command of these ten thousand legionnaires. Between Omsk and Krasnoyarsk, a city on the Yenisei, five thousand Czechs were stretched along a distance of eight hundred miles. Krasnoyarsk was the easternmost penetration of the echelons. Rudolph Gaida assumed this command.

The legion was attacking not along a front but along an artery on which they were advantageously placed. The Trans-

---

* Zizka was the blind general who fought with Jan Hus against the Hapsburgs.

Siberian Railway was the aorta of Asian Russia. It was only along this artery that there were cities and warehouses and industry and garrisons. Russians who lived two hundred miles north of the rail lines or two hundred miles to the south never realized war had come to Siberia.

The campaign Syrovy produced called for Cecek's echelons in the west to close the gate at Penza, for Voitsekhovskii's echelons to secure the center, and for Gaida's eastern command to secure Irkutsk, six hundred miles from Krasnoyarsk. Once Irkutsk was in Czech hands, the westernmost echelons would begin leapfrogging toward it until all twenty-six thousand legionnaires were there assembled. Then the legion would proceed around the southern shore of Lake Baikal, moving as an integrated unit toward Vladivostok, another 1,500 miles away.

The orders issued on May 23 were that the attacks would begin on the 28th and 29th (for it took that long for some delegates to return to their commands).

Seizing Penza was instrumental to the success of the plan. The only way the Bolsheviks could pursue the legion or reinforce eastern garrisons was by rail. By taking and holding Penza, the Czechs denied the Bolsheviks the tracks leading east and kept them, momentarily at least, west of the Volga. Cecek sent the first units into the city on May 28. Prowling through the streets, scouting Bolshevik gun emplacements, Czechs scampered from cover to cover, making for the yards with its hundreds of idle freights.

While the Bolsheviks were not aware of the Czech stratagem, they knew they had to keep Penza. They tried to reinforce the garrison there with a trainload of troops bringing with them three armored cars. The train steamed into Penza on mid-morning of the 29th. Czech legionnaires dropped on top of it from viaducts and bridges, and when they had brought the train to a stop, more legionnaires streamed aboard from defilades. The Red commissar surrendered his troops. The Czechs offloaded the armored cars, one of which carried a small cannon, and by the afternoon captured the roundhouse, the telegraph station, and the signal points.

Having secured the yards, the legion began widening its perimeter in the city. From sandbagged roofs Red machine guns opened up. Bolshevik soldiers threw up street barricades. But inexorably the Czechs drove them back street by street. Cecek's men were in possession of some eighty machine guns captured from the Chelyabinsk arsenal. They moved to the north of the city to seal off a bridge over which the only counterattack could come. They took this bridge and held it against Red Guards, who were decimated when they tried to storm it on the evening of May 29. Minikin, the chairman of the Penza soviet, wired Trotsky, "We are at loss how to get out of the situation. . . . We cannot do without help from Moscow. I am stating it once again."[10]

Moscow was now in receipt of dozens of telegrams from stations that had been attacked. The Bolsheviks had no choice on the 29th but to pull back from Penza and let Cecek slam the door.

In the center Voitsekhovskii sent his echelons eastward. To take Kurgan, the station nearest Chelyabinsk to the east, the Czechs had to capture the bridge that spanned the Tobol River. The Bolsheviks had littered the bridge with immobilized locomotives past which the Czech echelons could not squeeze. The legionnaires called for a crane car from the Penza yards. Two days later it appeared. Bolshevik machine gunners zeroed in on it. The crane retreated. It tried again at night. Flares illuminated the bridge and again the crane car retreated. Four hundred Czechs, however, dismantled several of their vans to provide the lumber for a fleet of rafts. They dragged these several versts to the north. Intrepid swimmers among them got a cable across to the east bank so the others could be hauled over. A day later, Czechs attacked the bridge at both ends. It was theirs within hours. There was no resistance in Kurgan itself.

Gustav Becvar, the author of *The Lost Legion,* one of the few firsthand accounts of the war, had attended the congress as an enlisted-man delegate. From Chelyabinsk he made his way even farther east than Kurgan to his echelon at Barabinsk, where he reported to his commanding officer, Lieutenant Jiri Cehovsky. Cehovsky telegraphed the soviet at Omsk that he was about to proceed eastward and expected no interference. The Bolshevik commissar wasted no words. He wired back, "You are reaching for the sky. Surrender unconditionally."

Becvar saw the Russian telegraphist trembling with fright. Other Russians stared with wide eyes at Cehovsky. If the Czechs lost, these Russians would fare badly for having helped them.

"Send this," said Cehovsky. "The matter is settled."

Cehovsky's echelon numbered eight hundred infantrymen, most of them armed with single-action rifles. Coming toward them from the east was a Bolshevik armored train fitted with machine guns and field pieces and carrying 2,400 troops. The country was a typical steppe, as flat as a table, covered with high grass, to the south of the Czechs a dense birch forest. Cehovsky's legionnaires came up to Kastul, dropped from their train, blew up the bridge, and set up a skirmish line on the west bank of a sluggish stream.

The Red train consisted of an engine and two flat timber cars, one in front of the locomotive, the other behind, and dozens of vans. On the first of these timber cars were the field and machine guns, the crews securely protected by sandbags. The Bolsheviks directed a heavy fire at the Czech line and succeeded in driving the legionnaires back for repair crews to get at the bridge.

Cehovsky sent Lieutenant Skorinsky with a platoon that included Becvar in a flanking movement through the forest. Though this platoon successfully circled the Kastul station and came upon the Bolsheviks from the rear, they were spotted as they ran out onto the flat land. The Bolsheviks turned a machine gun in the water tower on them, and Skorinsky and his men dodged back into the forest.

During the night, the Bolsheviks spanned the bridge, and in the morning the armored train moved against the Czechs. Red infantry was deployed on both sides of the train and, despite Czech volleys, kept coming on. Cehovsky asked for help by wire and learned that the legionnaires nearest him were even harder pressed than he. But the same westward echelon had a field gun to lend Cehovsky if he could hold out until it arrived. The Czechs stuck. The field gun arrived. Its first shell, fired over the heads of the legionnaires, landed beside the second flat car. The next shell banged into the locomotive. Limping, the engine tried backing up, then, on a cant, stopped. The Czechs charged and the Bolshevik infantry withdrew across the bridge, turned, and fled. The legionnaires disengaged the ruined locomotive and attached their own to the Bolshevik train. Pursuing, they overran the Bolshevik contingent in a smaller station. Almost 1,000 Bolsheviks perished in this action, which they should have carried easily. The Czechs were battle-hardened, it is true, but what often gave them an advantageous *élan* in the early stages of the war was the knowledge that if they didn't win, they were dead men.

It wasn't until the fight was over that Cehovsky learned that the gun which turned the tide came to the battle with only six shells. Had its gunnery proved ineffective or had the Bolsheviks stood their ground the Czechs themselves would have had to flee.

Voitsekhovskii's echelons had mixed success, however. At Zlatoust, to the west of Chelyabinsk, a detachment of Red Guards crept up on an echelon. The Reds surprised the legionnaires, but these newly recruited Bolshevik soldiers were ill-trained and set up their machine guns too close to the Czech vans. When the Red commander ordered Czech Captain Muller to surrender immediately, Muller opened fire with an automatic pistol. Legionnaires rolled back their doors and, following one another, leaped from the vans onto the Red machine-gun crew. They wrested the weapon away and turned it on their attackers. On the other side of the van, a Czech platoon dropped and charged the second machine gun. Never stopping to reload their rifles, the Czechs were upon it before the gun mowed down their ranks. A half-dressed baker reached the emplacement with a heavy rock held overhead and, hurling it, felled the gunner. At the cost of twenty-five dead, seventy-five severely and five lightly wounded, the echelon dispersed the several hundred Red Guards.

But the position at Zlatoust was untenable. Red units had torn up the tracks in front of and behind the Czech train. The echelon, consisting for the most part of stretcher bearers, bakers, signal men, and the famous regimental band, which had led the parade to the Russian line, decided to march through the Urals. The legionnaires stripped their vans of materials needed for the march and set off with the two captured machine guns. By mid-afternoon, Captain Muller realized he would have to abandon most of his wounded to keep ahead of pursuing Bolshevik detachments.

Hoping to placate the Red Guards, Muller left behind plentiful food, medicine, and a cartload of boots. Without maps, the echelon plunged into the dense forest. They crossed a swollen mountain river by joining hands to form a living lifeline, though they had to leave behind the captured machine guns. The saddest loss was the small cart on which the band transported the bass drum. The drummer managed at least to save the drum skin by stowing it in his knapsack.

The band proved its utility later by trading a concert in a Baskir village for meat and bread. After four days of hard marching, Muller's men reached a small mining center where they connected with another echelon bound for Chelyabinsk. They had lost almost one hundred men, their drum and Lieutenant Zanaska, a schoolteacher from Prague who had stayed behind with the wounded. Only a few of these wounded survived to tell their comrades what had happened to the rest. The Bolsheviks had murdered many. When the legionnaires disinterred Zanaska from his shallow grave six weeks later for a proper interment, they found his arms and his feet had been hacked off.

On May 29, Gaida took Mariinsk, a depot between Omsk and Krasnoyarsk.* Mariinsk had been lightly defended, and Gaida expected a heavy attack from the east. Therefore he divided his echelon in two and put one half under the command of Captain Kadlac, once a plantation overseer for the Belgians in the Congo. Kadlac moved this wing several versts west and took cover.

The Bolsheviks sent a troop train from Krasnoyarsk to retake Mariinsk. Gaida's wing of the echelon put up a delaying fight against these reinforcements, then the legion vans began retreating westward. The Bolsheviks pressed them. Once the Red train passed Kadlac's position, the legionnaires tore up the tracks behind it. Gaida stopped and fought. The Bolsheviks backed eastward to regroup. When the Red train halted at the tangled tracks, Kadlac's men ambushed it. The legionnaires disarmed the Red Guards and turned them over to the citizens of the Chulmyn area who constituted for themselves a quickly improvised government, which

* Mariinsk is now Marinovka. I use the older name throughout because that was the name the Czechs used.

ordered the execution of the Red officers and sent the enlisted men home.

This was about as merciful as the fighting ever was. The Czechs had few provisions for prisoners of war, and the Bolsheviks were equally murderous when they took a Czech unit. One Czech company, beleaguered and running out of ammunition, committed mass suicide rather than face capture and torture. Another Czech company that did surrender was herded into its vans, the doors locked, and the vans set afire.

The Czech attacks were devastating because control of the railroads was *the* strategic objective of the Russian Civil War. Only by controlling the railroads could opposing forces transport troops, materiel, and food across the unending distances of Russia. The Trans-Siberian Railway was doubly important because it offered access to European Russia from the Pacific. The action of the Czech Legion in making itself the master of Siberia was to have momentous consequences. Its attacks against the Trans-Siberian remain to this day some of the most fantastic and incredible exploits in warfare. And the nature of the railway itself aided the Czech boldness.

The Trans-Siberian Railway reaches from the Ural Mountains, which divide European from Asian Russia, 5,000 miles to Vladivostok. It took two Russian Czars, Alexander and Nicholas, thirteen years and $250,000,000 to connect Moscow to the Great Ocean by uninterrupted rails. Considering that only nine months were devoted to its original survey, six of these when heavy snow masked the treacherous terrain, the Trans-Siberian Railway is an engineering miracle. It was laid to extract iron ore, precious metals, diamonds, oil, grain, timber, furs, and coal from Siberia to enrich the Czars as well as to transport grain and livestock to feed the industrial centers of Russian Europe.

Starting at Ekaterinburg, the city founded by Catherine the Great, the Trans-Siberian proceeds south to Chelyabinsk, then eastward to Omsk. Another branch slopes directly from Ekaterinburg to Omsk. From Omsk, the rails lead to Novonikolayevsk, Tomsk, Krasnoyarsk, Irkutsk, circumscribe the southern shore

of Lake Baikal, the deepest body of fresh water in the world, to
Chita. The line has two tracks and thousands of sidings so that
trains can reverse their direction without going all the way to the
terminals.

At Chita, the Trans-Siberian divides. One branch proceeds
for 1,000 miles through Manchuria before emerging again on
Russian soil at Ussurisk to drop easily southward to Vladivostok.
This branch, constructed as a short cut, is known as the Chinese
Eastern. It was laid to help the Czars exploit Manchuria with a
spur snaking down from Harbin to Port Arthur and Dalni, once
Russia's valuable Chinese concessions on the Liaotung Peninsula.

The importance of the Chinese Eastern diminished appreciably after Russia had to make peace with Japan in 1905, a peace
secured by surrendering Port Arthur and Dalni. Though Nicholas
kept control of the Chinese Eastern Railway, he realized he would
be hard put to defend it in the event of another war with Japan or
one with China. So in the same year he made peace, Nicholas
authorized construction of the Amur line from Chita, following
the crescent-shaped Amur Valley to Khabarovsk from which the
Trans-Siberian precipitously drops several hundred miles due
south to Vladivostok. This line was completed in 1916 and both
it and the Chinese Eastern were operating in 1918. Tons of war
materiel supplied by the United States and Japan had crossed
eastern Siberia on both these lines en route to the Eastern Front.
The Trans-Siberian had been a main supply artery for the Imperial
Army because early in the war German ships had blockaded the
Bosporus. The construction of this railroad, which on one occasion tumbled the value of the rouble and on another almost bankrupted the Imperial Treasury, was undertaken with the most
stringent economies. Its rails weighed forty-nine pounds to the
yard, half the weight which was the standard for American and
European rails. A heavy freight train on a curve crushed these
rails with every passage. The speed of the trains was always severely curtailed (even today a Diesel cannot exceed forty miles an
hour on the Trans-Siberian). In 1918, the embankments and the
roadbeds were inadequate. After a heavy rain, trains ran off the
track like squirrels.

These construction faults, however, aided the Czechs. Because of the many sidings, the legion suffered no delays in reversing the direction of one echelon to go to the aid of another. Because the rails were weak, ton upon ton of them were stockpiled all along the line as quick replacements. The Bolsheviks could not slow down the Czechs by ripping up the roadbeds because ties and rails were always near at hand. Huge pyramids of coal and wood were also stockpiled, and there were almost as many water towers as there were trains.

The Trans-Siberian traverses five of the world's deepest rivers—the Tobol, the Ob, the Irtysh, the Yenisei, and the Angara. Italian stonemasons had built the pillars for the bridges, pillars which still withstand the slamming shock of ice floes in the spring thaw and which proved impervious to Bolshevik dynamite.

The supreme economy—which guaranteed the Czech victory in 1918—was that the Trans-Siberian did not run from city to city. Russian engineers had spanned Siberia not from population center to population center but across the most felicitous terrain. At Tomsk, for example, once Siberia's largest city, the Yenisei was at its broadest. Therefore, the Trans-Siberian bridged the Yenisei where it narrowed, sixty miles to the south. The Bolsheviks had garrisoned only the cities in 1918. When the Czechs made their move along its actual route, the Trans-Siberian was there for the taking.

The Czechs seized upon a last great advantage in putting into commission the abandoned boxcars, gondolas, reefers, and passenger cars which lay like beached whales on the railway. The Czechs found over 200 locomotives in various states of disrepair, their boilers burst from the cold, their wheels cracked, or their gears rusted. An industrially skilled army, the Czechs cannibalized one to reconstruct several. The railway itself became the Czech entrepôt and arsenal. The correspondent of *The New York Times*, Carl Ackerman, who traveled with the legion, saw

> . . . hills and fields of munitions and materials, rotting, rusting, decaying and wasting. There is a hill of cotton shipped from the United States tucked under mounds of

tarpaulins. There are 37,000 railway truck wheels and
heavy steel rails in such quantities as to make it possible to
build a third track from the Pacific to Petrograd. There is
enough barbed wire to fence Siberia. There are field guns,
millions of rounds of ammunition, and a submarine; automobiles, shoes, copper . . .[11]

It took the Czech Legion a month to secure the line from
Penza to Omsk. After Penza, Cecek's western echelons seized
Samara and, to the north, Simbirsk, which gave the legionnaires
port cities on the east and west banks of the Volga. Voitsekhovskii's middle echelons secured the Trans-Siberia from Ufa to
Omsk. Securing the second third of the line, which stretched from
Omsk to Lake Baikal, took longer. Gaida directed this attack and
displayed immediately a thorough grasp of military necessities.
As his echelons moved east, he dropped off two- and three-men
detachments to serve as commissaries at every village and small
town. These commissary detachments catalogued the available
supply in the area, with the result that the Czech Legion never ran
short of ammunition, food, or transport even after long fighting.
The Czechs purchased what they needed. Prices in Siberia favored
this policy. Outside of the industrial cities and manufacturing centers, food was plentiful. At Chelyabinsk bread cost six roubles a
loaf; in Moscow, 350 roubles.

Gaida equipped the first of the Czech armored trains, the
Orlik (Little Eagle), which was to become as ubiquitous a symbol
of the Russian Civil War as the "Red Train" that transported the
Bolshevik commander-in-chief, Leon Trotsky, from one front to
another. The *Orlik* consisted of two flat cars each fitted out with a
turret resembling half an egg shell. The turrets revolved 360
degrees. On the same flat cars were quonset huts of steel sheath-
ing to protect the ammunition. Behind these cars was the locomotive and behind the locomotive a flat car, which transported a
cannon, originally a naval gun, bolted securely to the boarding. A
last freight car carried supplies.

Gaida's first significant victory after Mariinsk was the capture of Krasnoyarsk, a Bolshevik depot on the Yenisei River.
Moving east from Mariinsk, Gaida attacked with 1,500 men. He

coordinated this move with one by a Cossack unit under the command of Colonel Boris Usakov which moved upon Krasnoyarsk from Kansk, farther to the east. The Krasnoyarsk Bolsheviks split their forces as Gaida had hoped. Moving to meet forces east and west weakened Red defenses. Six hours after the battle began, Gaida and Usakov entered the city, rounding up two thousand prisoners and capturing large quantities of clothing and armaments. Many of the Red Guards, however, retreated south along the Yenisei River, where they regrouped into guerrilla bands, raided when they could—and waited.

Gaida turned around and moved west to attack Novonikolayevsk on the Ob, two hundred and some odd miles away. These were exquisitely timed and executed moves. Gaida had not only to maintain combat discipline and *élan* but he had to gamble that he could win in a hurry. A protracted battle meant serious supply problems, for it was by taking these depots and towns that he kept his legionnaires in food and arms. He had to gamble, too, that he would win without a devastating loss. He was, however, constantly replenishing his echelons wherever and whenever he could. After taking Novonikolayevsk, Gaida administered the oath of allegiance to the Czech Legion to a muster of former Czarist officers who had enlisted in the ranks of their own regiment under the command of Czech Lieutenant R. Marek.

This regiment fought with the legion when Gaida captured Nizneudinsk and Tulin, three hundred miles east of Novonikolayevsk, seventy-five miles west of Irkutsk. It was apparent by the beginning of July that Irkutsk would prove as crucial a battle for the legion as Penza. Penza closed the gate in the west. The capture of Irkutsk would open the gate in the east. The Bolsheviks began concentrating what troops they had in the city, realizing that if they could keep the Czechs west of Lake Baikal they would eventually starve them. Sooner or later, the Czechs would have to depend upon a supply line stretching along the Chinese Eastern to Vladivostok.

Gaida set about protecting his flanks. Beside the Trans-Siberian Railway, on its northern rails, runs the *Trakt,* the Great Moscow Road which also traversed the distance from Vladivostok to Moscow. Twenty-one feet wide, a swamp in the spring, a three-foot dusty trench in the summer, it offered the Bolsheviks areas in which to group for an attack.

Gaida organized several cavalry squadrons to patrol it. Legionnaires requisitioned horses from the countryside, quartering the animals in vans transformed into barns. Then he turned back to the work at hand aware that his men had only so much to give before exhaustion took over. Insects and snakes make Siberia pestilential in the summer. Czechs fought with faces and heads so misshapen by mosquito bites they could not wear their caps. Their wrists were always bloody and swollen. Snakebite was so prevalent that the legionnaires relied upon peasant remedies. While their food was adequate, it was plain and unvaried. Water discipline was rigid. Sleep was interrupted by guard duty. One defeat at the hands of the Bolsheviks and his men would become demoralized. Gaida had to go in and take Irkutsk as soon as possible before the Bolsheviks came out and took him.

The *London Daily Chronicle* editorialized on July 7 that "There have not been many pieces of purer luck for either side than that which has befallen the Allies in the matter of Czech control of the Trans-Siberian Railway." The recently founded *Pravda* in Moscow said, "The rising is spreading like a path of oil upon the water." *The New York Times* reported on the same day, "Lenin Is Ready to Resign" and that "Trotsky Denounces Red Guard Officers Who Refuse to Participate Against the Czechs." The Czech Army Congress declared: "In view of the continuous hostility of the Soviet Government toward us, we are ceasing to be neutral with regard to the internal strife within Russia. We shall support any provisional government in Siberia."[12]

NOTES

1. Margrete Klante, *Von der Volga zum Amur: Die tschechische Legion und der russische Burgerkrieg*. Berlin: Ost Europa Verlag, 1931, p. 132.
2. Kennan, *op. cit.*, p. 142.
3. For the narrative details of the legion: Henry Baerlein, *The March of the Seventy Thousand*. London: Constable, 1926. Rudolph Medek, *Anabase* and *Ostrove v. Bouri*. Prague: Vilamek, 1928. Gustav Becvar, *The Lost Legion:*

A Czechoslovakian Epic. London: Jonathan Cape, 1939. Rudolph Gaida, *Moje Pameti.* Prague, 1924.

4. Miroslav Fic, *The Origin of a Conflict Between the Bolsheviks and the Czechoslovakian Legion.* Chicago: Czechoslovakian Foreign Institute in Exile, 1958, p. 32.
5. Klante, *op. cit.,* p. 230.
6. Fic, *op. cit.,* p. 34.
7. Kennan, *op. cit.,* p. 152.
8. *Ibid.*
9. R. Gaida, *op. cit.,* p. 149.
10. Fic, *op. cit.,* p. 132.
11. Carl W. Ackerman, *Trailing the Bolsheviki.* New York: Scribner's, 1919, p. 142.
12. Fic, *op. cit.,* p. 34.

CHAPTER 4

SAMARA-OMSK-HARBIN-VLADIVOSTOK:

MAY 28–JULY 7, 1918

The never-ending steppe known as Siberia, the whole of which is north of Montana and the Dakotas, was notorious for the severity of its climate; and because of this severity it was even more notorious as a place of punishment and exile. Between 1800 and 1914, over one million murderers, rapists, thieves, religious dissenters, free thinkers, sectarians, political reformers as well as terrorists had crossed the Ural Mountains condemned to unremitting toil in the Czar's gold mines (which for unfathomable reasons the world referred to as salt mines). Those not condemned to hard labor were still condemned to unendurable loneliness in small steppe villages. Chita, for example, was founded by the officers who staged the Decembrist coup of 1825 and who spent the rest of their lives four thousand miles away from the gilded sophistication of St. Petersburg. And their descendants spent their lives condemned to the same deserted, lonely place.

But Siberia was also the one Russian province that never knew serfdom, not abolished in European Russia until 1861. Consequently, it lured settlers who wanted freedom from the manor. These settlers were joined by hardy adventurers and opportunists as well as a bureaucracy of thousands upon thousands of minor officials, petty administrators, and clerks.

Siberia remained the least industrialized area of Russia. Few of the factory workers along the route of the Trans-Siberian could be characterized as proletarians. Its population was tied to the land. The one place in the world somewhat like it was the emerging American West, which for many years was also far from the center of power in the east. The people of Siberia were self-reliant and independent. Like settlers of the American West, the citizens of Siberia had something to lose, their land if nothing else. They were the only mass of Russians who did have something to lose. They thought they could still keep what they had when the February Revolution deposed the Czar. They saw they could not keep it when the Bolsheviks took over.

Throughout the war, Siberia maintained its small prosperity. Its people were suspicious of the Bolsheviks when they made peace with Germany. They were mutinous when they realized the Bolsheviks were expropriating livestock, grain, and produce to feed the workers in the cities. The canny among them, the fierce, the independent saw their deliverance from Bolshevik expropriation when the Czech echelons started to pass across the steppes.

Even before the Czech Soldiers' Congress at Chelyabinsk, Gaida had sought out an underground group of Imperial officers and urged them to rise up immediately against the soviet, promising them the support of his echelon. "You just start in," he had boasted, "and we Czechs will take care of the Bolsheviki." After the war itself erupted in late May, Gaida began to coordinate his movements with many anti-Bolshevik groups.[1]

When the Czechs launched their attacks, which began on the afternoon of May 28, the anti-Bolshevik groups in Siberia leaped forward as miraculously fully grown as Athena when she sprang from Zeus's head. Wherever the Czechs loosened the not quite fastened grip of Bolshevism, Socialist Revolutionaries, democrats, and monarchists pried the Red hand from the lever of authority and established themselves. These anti-Bolsheviks were so multitudinous that they brought forth a galaxy of new governments. There were nineteen of these between Samara and Vladivostok by the end of the summer of 1918. In *The Japanese Thrust into Siberia*, James William Morley speculates, "It is extremely difficult to believe that anti-soviet elements in Siberia could have acted in such close coordination with the Czechs if at least some Russian Socialist Revolutionaries and others had not had an understanding with some Czechoslovaks."[2] Though often at cross-purposes with one another and often blunting principles for expedience, these governments held one goal commonly: an independent and autonomous Siberia.[3]

Four of these governments figured importantly in the career of the Czech Legion. The first was established on May 29 in Samara. Calling itself the Committee of Members of the Constituent Assembly, nicknamed the "Komuch" from an acronym of its initials, this government began to raise an army to fight along with the Czechs. It flew a red flag and its seventy members were Socialist Revolutionaries dedicated to realizing the radical reforms of the February Revolution.

Moving east to Omsk, former members of the Siberian Duma formed the Siberian Provisional Government. Thoroughly conservative, the Siberian Provisional Government wanted to restore the institutions and practices abolished by the Bolsheviks. It flew a green and white flag representing the forests and snows of Siberia. The government of Samara claimed authority over all of Russia, the government of Omsk over Siberia.

At Harbin, the headquarters of the Chinese Eastern Railway, General Dmitri L. Horvat, the road's general manager, also set up a government with himself as dictator. He titled his regime the Far Eastern Committee for the Defense of the Fatherland and the Constituent Assembly. To claim authority for a Russian government on Manchurian soil was anomalous. But Horvat wanted to keep the Chinese Eastern Railway from falling into the hands of Chinese and Manchurian war lords. Horvat found support for his government in a variety of Cossack armies; he found financing and advice from Japan and hesitant recognition from the Chinese Government, whose emperor felt that if the Chinese Eastern were to fall into the hands of any Chinaman that Chinaman might better be he.

The fourth of these governments was the Provisional Committee of an Autonomous Siberia, established at Vladivostok by Peter Derber, a Jew from Odessa. From its inception, this government lived in three railway cars at the station. While Derber's assumed authority commanded no obedience, his group sent telegrams to Woodrow Wilson three times a week.

These governments represented a genuine people's movement. All favored the convening of the Constituent Assembly, a democratically elected congress which the Bolsheviks had dismissed before it even came together. These governments were known as "White Governments," a term applied to all Russians of whatever sentiments who opposed the soviet in Moscow. The disorder and disarrangement which befell Russia after the February and October Revolutions nourished the mythic hope that a White general would save the Russian people as General Skobelev saved them in 1877 when he defeated the Turks as Plevna, leading a charge "clad in white, decked with orders, scented and curled, like a bridegroom to a wedding."[4] This was the ideal. In actuality, White governments wherever they existed were dependent upon foreign or external military authority to enforce whatever laws there were.

The 14,000 Czechs under General M. K. Dietrichs who had reached Vladivostok safely knew nothing about the congress at Chelyabinsk nor about its resolution to fight across Siberia. The firestorm along the Trans-Siberian Railway amazed and bewildered these legionnaires, but it did not bring them into action. There were many reasons why these Czechs made no commitments.

They understood their orders from Masaryk: Stay neutral and get out. These men were sensible soldiers. They were safe. They had a momentary haven. They knew they faced a difficult task in France.

They made no attempt to rush to the aid of their brothers because the odds were against them. While Syrovy, Cecek, Voitsekhovskii, and Gaida had cleared more than three thousand miles of track, the Bolsheviks held Irkustk in depth. Because the Reds held Irkutsk, they also commanded the tunnels around Lake Baikal. If the Reds blew one of these, they cut the legion in half forever and ever. Past Lake Baikal, the Reds controlled over one thousand miles of track along the eastern Amur Valley as far as Khabarovsk to the north. They were deployed in strength along the track from Khabarovsk south to Nikol'sk, only forty miles above Vladivostok. To go to the aid of the legion by this route meant the Vladivostok echelons had to wage as desperate a war in the Maritime Province as their brothers were waging in Siberia. The Chinese Eastern which stretched across Manchuria was controlled by Horvat, the Cossacks, the Japanese advisers, and the Chinese Army. To proceed by this route meant fighting equally desperate.

In addition, the legion in Vladivostok did not have the independence of movement their brothers had along the Trans-Siberian. Vladivostok had become a multinational city in which the legion was not the only disciplined and organized force. There was an Allied fleet in the harbor, which consisted of the USS *Brooklyn*, flagship of the United States' Asiatic fleet under Admiral Austin M. Knight; the British cruiser *Suffolk* under Commodore John Payne; the *Awami, Asahi,* and *Asage,* a Japanese squadron commanded by Admiral Kato Kanji; and the Chinese warship *Hai Jung.* Each of these ships could train its guns on the city and each carried a complement of marines.

There was also a sizable force of Red Guards who were barracked in an old fortress on one of the city's promontories. Nominally, in fact, the city was in Bolshevik hands. Red Guards patrolled the outlying areas and the railroad. Czechs patrolled only the railroad terminal and the dockside area. It was possible that the Czech Legion would have trouble fighting its way out of Vladivostok let alone fighting along one thousand miles to the westward interior.

These echelons were also reluctant to fight because they were dependent upon the Soviet Government for supplies and food.*

* Until March 1918 the Czechs subsisted on Russian and Ukrainian credits. Only when the Germans began overwhelming these territories did Allied representatives in Russia realize the legion's need for money. The Supreme War Council had authorized the French consul in Moscow to pay out credits in Russian roubles from local French reserves, a fact seized upon in later Bolshevik propaganda. *Cf.* John Bradley, *Allied Intervention in Russia* (London: Weidenfield and Nicholson, 1968).

None of these conditions, however, absolutely discouraged Czech resolve. They were men of courage, good soldiers. Certainly they would go if there was a chance they could get out and get there in force. And there were Allied officials in Vladivostok interested in getting them out and getting them there.

To their detriment, the Bolsheviks did not destroy the telegraph lines between Irkutsk and Vladivostok. News filtered into this seaport city about the Czech action along the Trans-Siberian. The news was sparse and incomplete. If there were six correspondents between Samara and Vladivostok there were a lot. But they were enough to convey the importance—and success—of the Czech war. General J. Lavergne, chief of the French Military Mission to Russia, wired his government from Vladivostok via Tokyo that the presence of the Czech forces along the Trans-Siberian could well be utilized for intervention. A variety of American officials from Admiral Knight through John K. Caldwell, American consul at Vladivostok, apprised Washington of the news. British Embassy personnel were uniformly enthusiastic about employing the Czech Legion. All of these men were advising their governments without competent intelligence reports and without any clear ideas of their respective governments' determined policy.

Nevertheless on June 20, General Lavergne received orders issued through the French Minister for War to instruct the Czech Legion in Siberia to hold its position along the Trans-Siberian Railway. It was the first direct order in which Allied intervention in Russia specified a military goal.[5]

Holding in Western Siberia was an extraordinarily difficult task for Syrovy. The legion had begun fighting to get out of Siberia. The echelons under Cecek, Voitsekhovskii, and Gaida were cut off without avenue of supply or retreat as long as the Bolsheviks held Irkutsk. The military truth was that the Czechs could not hold part of the Trans-Siberian unless they held the whole in a continuous line from the Volga to Vladivostok. It was obvious to any military man that Dietrichs' echelons in Vladivostok would have to open up that avenue.

Admiral Knight, Commodore Payne, General Lavergne, and

Admiral Kato unilaterally constituted themselves a military council and explained their plans to General Dietrichs: that the Czech
forces rise up, sweep the Bolsheviks out of Vladivostok and
Nikol'sk. One small force of Czechs would speed north to occupy
Khabarovsk. The larger force would go directly over the Chinese
Eastern to help the legion west of Irkutsk seize the railway. Once
secured, the Trans-Siberian would facilitate the westward transportation of Allied forces to establish the anti-German front in
Russia.[6]

Dietrichs explained what was needed: arms, supplies, rolling
stock, medicine—and protection for his rear in Vladivostok.
These discussions took place aboard the *Brooklyn* between June
21 and June 23. On the 23rd, Knight wired Washington that "The
Czech is now ready to cooperate with Allied movements against
German activities in Siberia for the re-establishment of the Eastern Front."[7] On the 26th, the Allied consuls in Vladivostok recommended that their governments supply the Czechs with arms,
ammunition, supplies, and an accompanying military force to
assist the Czech actions.[8] On the 27th, Admiral Kato asked the
Japanese cabinet for authority to begin this distribution to the
legion.

The deck log of the USS *Brooklyn* notes that the *Asahi* sent
six boatloads ashore at 4:00 P.M. on June 27 and that at 8:25 of
the same evening the Czech commander-in-chief came aboard to
confer with the American consul.[9] Later Lavergne and Commodore Payne came aboard with Kato. The British promised to order
up a battalion of the Middlesex Regiment from Hong Kong. General Lavergne said that a French battalion was on its way from
Indochina. Admiral Knight promised that within days his government and the Japanese would reach an agreement whereby both
would send in armed detachments. And without waiting for cabinet authorization, Kato informed Dietrichs that his government
would soon come to the "fundamental decision to treat the Czechs
as an Allied army."[10]

At 10:00 A.M. on June 28, a Czech company drew up before
the building that housed the Vladivostok soviet. Its captain deliv-
ered an ultimatum to the commissar. If the Bolsheviks did not sur-

render their arms by 10:30 A.M., he could not answer for the consequences. The commissar said, "Come and get us." At 10:30, the legionnaires opened fire. A squad rushed the building, blowing open the door. The Czechs hurled grenades. A platoon rushed in. Red Guards and Bolsheviks, shaken and dusty, came down the stairs with their hands above their heads. Elsewhere in the city, a Czech unit broke into the telegraph office. A battalion, moving along the waterfront, began shelling the Bolshevik fortress with mortar shells. The surprise here was complete. The Bolsheviks hoisted the white flag and surrendered to the legionnaires.

In the harbor, Admiral Kato's warships steamed with screaming sirens on four Russian destroyers. Japanese marines boarded these and spiked their cannons.

By the evening of the 28th, the Czechs owned Vladivostok and had arrested and interned not only members of the Vladivostok soviet but the members of the Regional Bolshevik Committee. On the 29th, the Allied consuls recognized the Provisional Government of Autonomous Siberia headed by Peter Derber. Czech echelons began chugging out of the city. They charged the Bolshevik forces at Nikol'sk. The legion took heavy casualties on July 1 and 2. The enemy was entrenched and determined. On July 3, Dietrichs brought up another two echelons. These breached the Bolshevik defenses. Admiral Kato, however, had to dispatch an emergency medical squad to remove and treat the wounded. Admiral Knight ordered the American Red Cross unit in Tokyo to transfer to Vladivostok. He ordered army doctors in Cavite in the Philippines to form a unit for service in eastern Siberia. From the makeshift hospital on the wharf at Vladivostok, the admiral took aboard seventy badly wounded Czechs who needed surgery.

The Czechs turned a ninety-degree angle at Nikol'sk, moving toward the maelstrom to rescue their companions in the west. One more obstacle was in their path. Arrayed against them at Grodekova was a Cossack force led by Ivan Kalmykov, part of the 1,000-man army of Dmitri Horvat. Horvat had taken advantage of the Czech coup on the 28th to move from Harbin across the border to Grodekova on Russian soil. To assert the authority of his government, Horvat refused to allow the Czechs passage across the Chinese Eastern unless they traveled in support of the policies of his own Far Eastern Committee for the Defense of the Fatherland. These policies included restoration of the monarchy under a constitution and the return of lands to their Imperial owners.

Dietrichs told Kalmykov simply that the Czechs did not cooperate with political elements. His echelons had steam up. They were moving within the next ten minutes. Kalmykov spurred his horse and prudently led his Cossacks back into Manchuria. These Cossack horsemen watched the echelons glide by. So on July 7, Dietrichs' forces crossed the Russian border at Grodekovo on their way through Manchuria, the vanguard of the warring powers of the Western world.

NOTES

1. Kennan, *op. cit.,* p. 163.
2. James William Morley, *The Japanese Thrust into Siberia, 1918.* New York: Columbia University Press, 1957, p. 241.
3. John Albert White, *The Siberian Intervention.* Princeton: Princeton University Press, 1950, p. 25.
4. Richard Luckett, *The White Generals.* New York: Viking Press, 1971, p. xvi.
5. Morley, *op. cit.,* p. 243.
6. *Ibid.,* p. 247.
7. Kennan, *op. cit.,* p. 392.
8. *Ibid.*
9. Deck Log of the USS *Brooklyn,* 173.3. National Archives, Washington, D.C.
10. Morley, *op. cit.,* p. 252.

CHAPTER 5

THE WESTERN FRONT:

JULY 15–AUGUST 10, 1918

For a variety of reasons, Ludendorff's four hammer strokes never quite knocked out the Allies. The fifth never fell at all because on August 8, two thousand British cannons began a surprise bombardment against the German front at Amiens as 450 tanks came upon the German line like a beast out of the jungle "August 8 was the black day of the German Army," wrote Ludendorff. "The Army had ceased to be a perfect fighting instrument."

On August 10, John J. Pershing announced the formation of the United States First Army.

The war in Europe was ending. Men did not realize how quickly it would end, but they knew it would end where the bravest and the best always insisted it would end—in the trenches of the Western Front. Sadly, another war was swelling far from these trenches in France.

CHAPTER 6

SIBERIA:

JULY 12–AUGUST 31, 1918

The orders of the Allied Supreme War Council to the Czech Legion were to conduct "holding operations" along the length of the Trans-Siberian Railway. The Czechs presumed that the arrival of Japanese and American forces in Vladivostok in the fall would mean relief.

For the westernmost Czechs the holding operation meant a push north from Samara and Simbirsk to Kazan, as important a Volga port as St. Louis is a Mississippi port. Cecek, the commander in the west, saw that if he did not occupy Kazan in force, he exposed his flank to Bolshevik attack. Kazan was four hundred miles from Moscow, a potential staging area for great attacks by either the Reds moving east or the Allies moving west. Its capture would additionally pose a serious blow to the Bolshevik regime by denying food and raw materials to the Red Army beginning to come together on the west side of the Volga behind the Urals.

Cecek told his echelons to

> notify all the brothers that, in conformity with the decision of the Congress of the Army Corps and our National Council and in agreement with the Allies, our Legion has been made a vanguard of the Allied forces in Russia.[1]

The legion, Cecek went on, would move on Kazan and stay there until the Allies arrived and re-created an anti-German front.

But Cecek and the legion's higher command knew the move was also a knife thrust at the Bolshevik heart. Kazan was within the industrial perimeter the Bolsheviks believed inviolate.

On July 12, Cecek opened the attack with 14,000 legionnaires and eight thousand Whites mustered by the Komuch Government of Samara. The Bolsheviks had not had time to prepare an adequate trench system to halt the Czechs. But they fought bravely and stubbornly in the outlying areas and in the streets of the suburbs. Just as William Tecumseh Sherman took Atlanta by constantly flanking its defenders, so the legionnaires constantly flanked the Bolsheviks moving ever northward around the city until it was completely invested. Kazan is on the east side of the Volga and the Reds could no longer supply themselves from the west bank. On August 6, the Bolshevik regiments fled across the river. Czechs flooded into the city. Cecek wanted the railyards secured immediately. He wanted the materiel the Reds had abandoned. He got this (which was sparse enough), but the quick move by a Czech company into the yards claimed for the legion one of the most valuable and unlikely prizes ever to fall to an enemy in war.

Legionnaires, smashing open the doors of boxcars, boarded one freight and discovered it contained the gold reserves of the old Czarist government. A dozen legionnaires stood in amazement at the sight of gleaming bullion in a crate they had pried open. They ripped apart dozens more. Gold enough to satisfy the cravings of a Midas.

A year before, when it seemed likely the Germans might take St. Petersburg, the officials of the Provisional Government's Treasury had crated the bullion in a twenty-car freight and moved it to Samara, then by barge to Kazan. Its location was forgotten during the Bolshevik takeover. No one remembered where the gold was save the two old assayers who faithfully kept registers of the quantities of the gold and lived in the boxcars with their families

The Czechs determined the gold was worth $333,000,000 or 650,000,000 roubles. Besides the gold there was 100,000,000 roubles in paper "Romanovs," currency which still held its value even in Red areas. There were also Nicholas' and Alexandra's gold, platinum, and silver stocks as well as assorted crowns, jewels, and a priceless collection of porcelain.

The disciplined Czechs were no looters. They did not even dispossess the venerable assayers. The legion sent the gold train to Chelyabinsk, the gold still crated, the paper money still bound, the porcelain statuettes still sleeping in excelsior. The Komuch Government claimed it. The gold train guaranteed a new government economic ascendancy over all others.

To the Czechs the great prize was the port city of Kazan. By taking it they had cut the Volga in two. They had incidentally seized the commercial vessels of the Volga fleet, and on one of the trawlers they discovered the Bolshevik codes.

The holding operation ordered by the Supreme War Council also meant the middle echelons of Czechs around Chelyabinsk had to attack north to take Ekaterinburg, another point on the Bolshevik perimeter crucial to both sides If the Reds kept this city they could cut the Trans-Siberian. One branch of the railway dropped south from Ekaterinburg to Chelyabinsk while another branch sloped east all the way to Omsk. By resupplying and reinforcing the Ekaterinburg garrison over interior lines, the Bolsheviks could mount an attack down either of these two branches.

The middle echelons were under the command of Voitsekhovskii, who moved out of Chelyabinsk on July 2. It took his echelons three weeks of bloody fighting to get 200 miles north to Ekaterinburg. Casualties were heavy. Medics and cooks had to fill in on the line. The fighting took place at the small stations, which were soon reduced to rubble by hand grenades, the furniture inside smashed to matchwood. The platforms were littered with bodies strewn grotesquely. Often these way stations changed hands several times.

"This is the law of civil war. Kill all of the wounded of the enemy camp," instructed M. I. Latsis, who had assumed charge of the secret Cheka.[2]

The farther north along the branch Voitsekhovskii pushed, the harder the Bolsheviks resisted. The campaign, it seemed, might be stalemated sixty miles south of Ekaterinburg. The Reds were bringing over artillery which could drive the Czechs back to their starting point. Voitsekhovskii needed quick help. He asked Gaida for several echelons from Omsk. Gaida sent them. They steamed up the slope against Ekaterinburg. Voitsekhovskii ordered his own echelons to mount a do-or-die charge from their positions.

This converging attack convinced the Bolsheviks that Ekaterinburg would fall. What worried the Bolsheviks even more than the fall of the city was that by taking it the Czechs would free Czar Nicholas and his family, who were held prisoners in the Dom Impatiev, formerly the home of a wealthy Ekaterinburg professor. The Bolsheviks feared that in Nicholas the Whites would have a figure around whom they could rally. Therefore, on the night of July 13, the Ural soviet voted to murder the Czar. Four nights later, on July 17, in the cellar of the white stone dom, Bolshevik executioners ended the possibility of Romanov succession with a hail of bullets which wiped out the entire family. The executioners then carted the bodies to a mine at Koptyaki fourteen miles outside of Ekaterinburg. Here the bodies were consumed in a pyre. The ashes were thrown into a mine shaft. On the 18th, the Soviet Presidium announced only the execution of Nicholas.

On July 26, the Czech Legion occupied Ekaterinburg. At the Dom Impatiev they found one of the Czar's dogs whimpering for his master. The cellar, scrubbed clean, nevertheless gave evidence of a massacre with its bullet-pocked walls and floors. Officers of the legion checked out the rumors. Newspaperman Carl Ackerman reported on the extinction of the royal family shortly after the Czechs found the pyre and the mine shaft.

The key to the entire holding operation lay with Rudolph Gaida, who had to capture Irkutsk. Without Irkutsk, the Czechs did not control continuous passage along the Trans-Siberian. Without Irkutsk, the legionnaires marching from Vladivostok under Dietrichs could not join the echelons under Cecek, Voitsekhovskii, and Gaida. Without Irkutsk, eastern Siberia was no man's land.

A cosmopolitan city of 130,000, Irkutsk lay on the east bank of the Angara River. It guarded the railway approaches to Lake Baikal, which is ninety-five miles long and fifty miles wide, shaped somewhat like a hockey stick with the blade pointing west. On the southern shore of the lake, on the bottom of the blade, were a series of thirty-nine tunnels carved through precipitous cliffs. As long as the Bolsheviks held Irkutsk, they controlled these tunnels. Squeeze here and the Trans-Siberian was broken in two.

The Bolsheviks could have blown these tunnels in June and once and for all have separated the western echelons of the legion from those of Dietrichs in the east. But they would have separated western from eastern Siberia at the same time, an economic hardship Moscow found unendurable. The Bolsheviks chose to fortify Irkutsk, hoping to stop Gaida here. If they failed, they intended to blow the tunnels before Gaida could reach them.

Gaida moved his echelons out of Novo-Udinsk in early July and steamed to a position two miles west of the New Irkutsk Station. From here Gaida sent the Barnaul Regiment at night on foot south of the city. The Barnaul skirted Irkutsk, keeping out of sight by marching through a heavy forest, and once east of the city came upon a wharf which services a lumber yard on the Angara. The regiment awaited the arrival of the *Siberiak,* an icebreaker the Bolsheviks had fitted out as a gunboat. When it docked, the legionnaires ambushed its crew and transformed the *Siberiak* into a troopship hauling rafts laden with armed men. The convoy made its way easily downriver (for the Angara flows north) to come upon Irkutsk from the rear.

On the morning of July 11, Gaida put the armored-train *Orlik* into action against Irkutsk from the west while the Barnaul Regiment opened fire from the east. The Bolsheviks thought they were caught in a nutcracker. In freights and flat cars the Red garrison fled east along the tracks of the Trans-Siberian, past the withering fire of the river-based Barnaul. On July 12, the Czechs entered Irkutsk, Gaida leading the triumphal parade astride a gigantic black horse. The populace, relieved that the city had been spared devastation, lined the wooden sidewalks cheering the legionnaires who marched behind a band without a drum.

The capture of Irkutsk did not, however, resolve Gaida's problem of getting around Lake Baikal. Though badly clawed, the Bolsheviks had taken positions around the tunnels and were preparing to blow them up to halt the advance of the Czechs. Czech intelligence confirmed the existence of a freight train loaded with dynamite parked in the yards of the Baikal Station where the lake feeds the Angara River.

Gaida realized he had to get the dynamite before he could attack the tunnels. The Bolsheviks had torn up some of the track between Irkutsk and the Baikal Station, so he could not support a frontal attack with artillery from the *Orlik*. But he had to move fast, for the Bolsheviks were drilling holes in the rock walls of the tunnels.

He was elaborate. And he was canny. And his timing was exquisite. He sent three regiments south from Irkutsk who attacked at Kultuk, a station on the tip of the hockey blade. Bolsheviks rushed from Baikal and other points to meet what they thought was an attack in force. But it was a diversionary move.

A fourth Czech regiment had left Irkutsk and crossed to the north bank of the Angara. The men scaled the mountains to descend on Listvinichnoe, a small fishing village that was directly above Baikal Station on the lake. Sliding down the mountain, they rolled into Listvinichnoe and drove its surprised defenders into the water.

Then by raft, rowboats, and launch—whatever they could expropriate—the regiment crossed south to the now deserted Baikal Station. The legionnaires made their way quickly to the railroad yard and lit fuses under the dynamite train.

The roar was heard in Irkutsk. The concussion demolished Baikal Station and its wharves, leveling the ground in a mile-wide perimeter. Fishermen were blown from their boats. The wooden huts of peasants sank as though an invisible weight had collapsed their roofs. The lake itself heaved. Great waves dashed against the cliffs. Masses of rock plunged into the water. The railway tracks leaped and writhed, twisting themselves into fantastic shapes. The station and warehouses were smoldering heaps of masonry. Debris rained for minutes. Parts of the bodies of railway personnel were scattered among the wrecks.

The Bolshevik commander at Kultuk realized he had been had. Though he was sorely pressing Czechs to his front, now he had Czechs moving upon his rear. The stratagem had robbed the Red commander of the chance to blow the tunnels *en masse*. If he were going to blow any of the tunnels, he had better get at it now. So he pulled his men back through the tunnels to the last of them at the Sliudianka Station. As the Reds retreated, they tore up the tracks behind them.

Gaida had his tunnels, but it was slow work moving through them. The Reds commanded the water by virtue of two large ships which bombarded the Czech work gangs and advance parties. These ships were the world-renowned ferry *Baikal,* large enough to transport whole freight trains, and the *Angara,* an ice-breaker, the largest ever built. Smaller ferries served as Bolshevik consorts. The cannons on the *Baikal* and the *Angara* forced the Czechs to work on the rails only at night. Even then it was death-defying work.

Against the fleet, Gaida dispatched the *Siberiak,* to which he transferred one of the cannons from the *Orlik*. But the *Siberiak*'s first shot put it out of commission: The cannon's recoil sent it crashing through the deck into the hold.

The labor gangs laid their rails in the tunnels by day and between the tunnels at night. By July 21, they had proceeded almost to Sliudianka, which marked the last of the tunnels. Here the tracks curved left and right so that the *Orlik* moved like a sidewinder. Once the legionnaires took Sliudianka they were almost home free. A small patrol of ten men, commanded by newly promoted Lieutenant Becvar, preceded the armored train. Becvar described what happened next:

> First of all I agreed with the train commander the usual signals for passing orders at a distance—"stop," "go," "fast," "slow," "shoot." Cautiously we pressed forward, constantly on the watch for signs of the enemy. From the Bolshevik side there came no shot nor sound. Presently, the sun came out, and with the silvery lake on our left, and the beautiful forests on the slopes to our right we could have been having a grand time had it not been for the circumstances of our march. This we guessed was much too good

to last. And we were right. Suddenly a loud bang sounded
from somewhere ahead. The echoes rolled loudly through
the hills. We rushed forward. Soon we saw a column of
smoke and dust rising high in the clear air. When eventually
we arrived at the scene of the explosion our hearts sank low
indeed. There was no tunnel anymore. The rails just ran
into a mass of rock and huge stones. The armored train was
now useless. For the Legion to advance without repairing
the tunnel would be to invite destruction, for on that narrow
lakeside trail we could not do without the support of our
armored train.[3]

The Czechs were stopped. Behind the demolished tunnel, the
Reds began to prepare a defensive position to deny the legion passage across Trans-Baikalia. This was a last-ditch defense. The
Bolsheviks could not fight along the Chinese Eastern Railway for
fear the Chinese would intern them, and they could not move
north along the Amur Line because the area was controlled by
anti-Bolshevik Cossacks.

Clearing the tunnel should have taken the Czechs several
weeks, but Gaida detailed 300 German prisoners of war for the
shoveling, and he found unexpected and crucial aid from Colonel
George H. Emerson, the American commander of the Railway
Service Corps, which Woodrow Wilson had sent to Russia several
months before. Emerson was not a stranger to the Czechs. During
June, he had tried to negotiate armistices between the legion and
the Bolsheviks at various stations along the Trans-Siberian. He
had failed. In the process, however, he had become a Czech partisan. When the Bolsheviks blew the Sliudianka tunnel, Emerson
on his own authority hurried the heavy machinery, the cranes,
bulldozers and backhoes, and most importantly more dynamite,
which eased Czech efforts to clear the ruined passage.[4] Emerson
later insisted that the heavy machinery came from captured Bolshevik stores.[5] Gaida said the equipment was marked "Made in the
U.S.A."

George F. Kennan believes Emerson's principal motive was
to preserve the railway intact. "In this respect his attitude typified
the unquestioning fidelity to technical purpose and the high-

minded impatience with the domestic-political conflicts of other nations which have marked the American mind in all ages and which often made it difficult for Americans and Russians, in particular, to understand each other's preoccupations in the distracted year of 1918."[6] Whatever else it was and whatever else it meant, Emerson's gesture was the first overt act of American intervention. Certainly it was propitious for the Czech Legion. Gaida was through the Sliudianka tunnel within a fortnight. The legion cleared it only to the height that a locomotive could squeeze through, laying new tracks atop old rubble. By August 6, the Czechs were about to round the eastern shore of Lake Baikal, moving on the last of the Bolshevik defenses.

Again, Gaida planned a frontal and rear attack. He sent a battalion across Lake Baikal on barges towed by the repaired *Siberiak*. These troops left Listvinichnoe at dusk and before daybreak were ashore on the eastern rim. A heavy mist enshrouded them as they made their way down to Mysovaya, where they took to the mountains and positioned themselves to deliver enfilading fire on the tracks below.

Three Czech regiments astride and riding on the *Orlik* moved past Mysovaya and against the Bolshevik defenses. The Bolsheviks opened fire. The Czechs began to give way, slowly at first, then in a hurry. The Bolsheviks pushed forward, suckers for the gambit. As the Czech attack apparently collapsed, the Bolsheviks pursued. Bolshevik cavalry and infantry accompanied by three armored trains went through Mysovaya. The legionnaires on the cliffs and in the mountains began firing. As the Bolsheviks halted and turned to defend themselves, the *Orlik* whipped down on them again. The Czechs and the Bolsheviks fought through a day and a night until the Czech marksmanship convinced the Reds their position was untenable.

By this time, a Czech detachment had cut the rails behind the Bolsheviks. In retreating, the Reds had to abandon their armored trains. The Bolsheviks made one last try to deter the legion. At Tankhoi they sent a van of explosives hurtling down the tracks toward the *Orlik*. The Czechs quickly detached a flat car to intercept it. The explosion devastated the few peasant huts nearby and blew away the vegetation. The Bolsheviks finally withdrew from the Trans-Siberian Railway. Gaida took Verne-Udinsk a few days later and turned eastward from Lake Baikal to meet the forward echelons of Dietrichs' Vladivostok force, which began arriving in Chita on August 15.

Now the Czechs were the masters of Siberia.

The French Minister of War gave field command of the legion to Jan Syrovy on August 28. Surrendering his post, Deitrichs became chief-of-staff. To the legionnaires this shift was a clear indication that Czech independence was near. An army of Czechs could take orders from a Russian, but a Czechoslovakian army, the defender of a new republic, could not.

The skirmish that finally secured the Trans-Siberian from Kazan to Vladivostok took place at Nikol'sk in late August. Nikol'sk was forty miles north of Vladivostok, the point at which the Trans-Siberian turned at a right angle toward Manchuria. Dietrichs had left a rear guard at this point to make sure no one cut off his supplies. This rear guard had pushed farther north past Lake Khavka and taken up positions at Kraevsk. The Bolshevik guerrillas along the Ussuri River attacked Kraevsk on August 3 and by August 20 had pushed the Czechs back to Nikol'sk. If the Bolsheviks took Nikol'sk they severed the lifeline.

Coincident with the Bolshevik attack was the arrival of the 25th Middlesex Battalion from Hong Kong, the first Allied unit to reach Siberia.* The Middlesex Battalion, which was composed of troops invalided from other fronts, was commanded by Lieutenant Colonel John Ward. He debarked to the strains of "Rule, Britannia," which the Czech bandmaster confused with "God Save the King." The British wore pith helmets and couriers wheeled bicycles.

Colonel T. A. Robertson, the British Military Representative at Vladivostok, asked Ward to commit his battalion to the line at Nikol'sk. The Czechs needed reinforcing until the Japanese forces arrived.

* It was also sent from Hong Kong to Korea in 1950.

Ward's men lacked such niceties as mosquito netting and artillery. The lack of cannon bothered Ward less than the former, for the mosquitoes, he wrote, "could suck your blood through a thick blanket as well as if you had nothing on at all." Nevertheless, Ward took 500 infantrymen and forty-three machine gunners forward, intending to use them only defensively and in reserve. These Tommies did little actual fighting, though at Nikol'sk some wandered into the path of incoming Bolshevik shells. What Ward did to save the day for the legionnaires was to bring forward artillery by which heavy Red attacks were repulsed. Ward found the artillery aboard the *Suffolk*. He persuaded Commodore Payne to part with two 12-pounders and brought these up by train. The *Suffolk*'s artificers came ashore to repair several more guns. With this artillery, the Czechs stabilized their line.[7]

Japanese gunboats traveled up the Ussuri to fire on the Reds on August 25. On the same day, several Japanese battalions came up and, joining with the Czechs, drove off the Bolsheviks who threatened Nikol'sk.

By August 31, the Czechs controlled the whole of the Trans-Siberian. Gaida, now a general, had turned his echelons westward and with those of Dietrichs was speeding to establish a Ural Front. The vanguard of the Allied intervention was ready for the big push. Russia, however, is a place that swallows ventursome vanguards whole.

NOTES

1. Fic, *op. cit.,* p. 54, and Matamey, *op. cit.,* p. 293.
2. James Bunyan, *Intervention, Civil War and Communism in Russia: April–December, 1918.* Baltimore: Johns Hopkins Press, 1936, p. 232.
3. Becvar, *op. cit.,* p. 146.
4. Gaida, *op. cit.,* p. 101.
5. George H. Emerson Papers, *U.S. Advisory Commission of Railway Experts to Russia* 74064-10V. Hoover Institution of War, Revolution and Peace, Stanford, California.
6. Kennan, *op. cit.,* p. 288.
7. John Ward, *With the Die-Hards in Siberia.* New York: George Doran Co., 1920, pp. 23–43.

CHAPTER 7

LORD OF THE EAST:

SEPTEMBER 2, 1918

Major General William S. Graves, commander of the combat-ready 8th Division at Camp Fremont, received "Eyes Only" orders on the morning of August 2 that directed him to take the first train out of San Francisco to Kansas City, where he was to report to the Secretary of War at the Baltimore Hotel. Graves got the last remaining coach seat on the noon train but did not reach Kansas City for two days because of the delays en route. A redcap met him at the Kansas City station and said a Mr. Baker was in the waiting room.

Newton D. Baker, who had been inspecting military installations at Fort Leavenworth, hoped by meeting Graves halfway between Washington and San Francisco to have the time to explain the general's new assignment: Graves was not going to France; he was going to Siberia. But now Baker had only a few moments in which to hand over a sealed envelope with Woodrow Wilson's *aide-mémoire*. Baker said, "This contains the United States's policy in Russia which you are to follow. Watch your step. You will be walking on eggs loaded with dynamite."

William Sidney Graves was a tall, well-set, fifty-three-year-old West Pointer who became a soldier after being outwitted as a horse trader in and around his native Mont Calm, Texas. He had chased Indians, fought in the Philippines, and served recently as

Secretary to the United States General Staff. He wore rimless glasses, affected a Pershing mustache and was a humorless man in a profession noted for humorless men. Peyton March, who had recommended Graves to Newton D. Baker, knew he was self-reliant, well trained, intelligent, and that he had common sense and a self-effacing loyalty. Peyton March and Newton D. Baker were also to learn that Graves was capable of rigorous restraint and had a moral indignation with a low boiling point.

Graves, of course, did not want to go to Siberia; he wanted to take the 8th Division to Europe. But he got working on the expedition right away. While changing trains at Omaha he determined on 250-man provisional companies, wired Washington for advice on clothing, and ordered his adjutant to make sure the men picked from the 8th Division came from each of the forty-eight states: If there were heavy casualties, Graves didn't want them all from the Pacific Coast.

By August 10, Graves had detached 5,002 men from the 8th which included forty-eight sergeants and ninety-six corporals, thirty-nine first and twenty-four second lieutenants. Each of the lieutenants was ordered to obtain an alarm clock. The entire command was ordered to load up with handkerchiefs, face and laundry soap, and as much tobacco as each could carry. Graves and his command left San Francisco on August 15 aboard the *Sheridan* and *Thomas,* converted cattle ships. He reached the Bay of the Golden Horn on September 1, where he merged command with 3,011 officers and men of the 27th and 31st Infantry Regiments who had left Manila for Vladivostok three weeks before. Graves's 9,014 Americans joined 70,000 Japanese, 829 British, 1,400 Italian, and 107 Ammahese troops under French command.[1]

During the Pacific crossing, Graves had studied Wilson's *aide-mémoire* closely. He knew, for example, that he was not bringing Yanks to Siberia to fight German prisoners of war, for he was familiar with the reports of William B. Webster of the American Red Cross and British Captain W. L. Hicks, who had assured the Allies correctly that there were no armed German prisoners of war in Russia. He knew he was not coming to reopen an Eastern Front in European Russia. He knew he was not to interfere with the sovereignty of Russia, for the *aide-mémoire* clearly forbade any intervention in Russia's internal affairs. The seventeen days it took Graves to cross the Pacific gave him the time to make up his mind about his orders, and for the next nineteen months that Graves remained in Siberia he never changed it. The general believed he would best serve his country's interests by waiting until it was apparent which faction the Russians wanted to form a government and then turning Siberia over to it.

American troops underwent no customs or quarantine delays, a telling sign to Graves. His Yanks were disembarking in a country which virtually had no government. On September 1, Graves and his staff searched the city for a suitable headquarters. They decided on the German Mercantile Company Building in the center of Vladivostok, which was large enough to house the units of headquarters command as well as serve as an officers' barracks. The Russian landlords said the rental was worth $8,000 a month, but considering that the Americans were the occupants they wanted only $6,000. The astute Graves detailed one of his staff to check on recently passed municipal ordinances. He soon learned that landlords in Vladivostok could increase rents only by 50 percent above the previous lease. The United States, explained Graves, could not legally pay more than $750 a month. Take it or leave it. The landlords took it.

Vladivostok, called by the Russians the "Lord of the East," is built on several hills, some of which descend to the waterside. The city much resembles San Francisco. In 1918, its cobbled streets were crowded with uniformed soldiers and sailors of the Allied nations. Mixing with them were thousands of officers of the Imperial Russian Army who came out of hiding resplendent with jewels and medals.

The trolleys were crowded to suffocation. *Droshkies* with one horse between the shafts and another running by the trace sped by constantly. The horses endlessly turned their heads from one side to the other, which made Graves at first suspect too tight a bit; but he learned later they were protecting themselves against wolves.

Everywhere Chinese and Korean coolies shuttled, carrying upon their backs a yoke on which they transported mattresses, trunks, cupboards, and cordwood. The marketplaces offered piles of tanned hides, fish, butter, bread, and hams. The breakdown of the Russian rail system had momentarily produced a glut in Vladivostok. Soon enough this would turn into a scarcity when an additional 250,000 refugees jammed in beside the 100,000 who normally lived there.

Surrounding the entire city were the vast dumps of military stores, plus more than three thousand cars, their tires still deflated.

On September 2, Graves went across the city to call upon Lieutenant General Otani Kikuzo, the Japanese commander and the ranking Allied officer in Siberia. General Otani had posted the following order two weeks before:

> I have the honor to inform you that I have been appointed Commander of the Japanese Army at Vladivostok, by his Majesty, the Emperor of Japan, and that I am entrusted unanimously by the Allied Powers with the command of their armies in the Russian Territory of the Far East. I hope with all my heart that our armies will work together for the common aim.[2]

That he had a superior officer who was Japanese was news to Graves. He found General Otani a far from inscrutable Oriental. Short and wiry, the Japanese general was completely bald, wore a khaki tunic with silver buttons, and affected a monocle.

Otani, who spoke perfect English, told Graves he had been the military cadet chosen to attend Ulysses S. Grant on his trip through Japan in 1879. He had presented himself, saber at the salute, and carried it thus until Grant said he had better put the pin away before he stuck someone with it.

Graves smiled.

Otani said that the United States State Department had notified him of his overall command. Graves replied that the same State Department had not informed him of this arrangement. While he wanted to cooperate with Japan, he had no orders to place his troops under the command of a foreign general.

Otani shrugged and the matter never came up again.

Matter of factly, the Japanese general proceeded to the next item, the Allied plan of operations. Otani wanted to order the entire force north to take Khabarovsk. After succeeding in this, the Allies would advance west with massive reinforcements to engage German war prisoners who threatened the Czech Legion.

Graves asked Otani where he got his information.

Again Otani shrugged.

It was obvious to Graves that Otani expected neither obedience nor compliance with his orders. In that moment Graves intuited Japanese policy in Siberia: It was to keep strong forces apart, as Otani was keeping Allied forces apart, by insisting that if they united they would have to unite under Japanese command, and to encourage the proliferation of weak forces behind whom the Japanese could screen their aggrandizement.

Japan was in Siberia ostensibly to transform the Maritime Province into a buffer state against the possibility that a German victory would mean a German presence in the Far East. In actuality, Japan was in Siberia in the hope of expanding her burgeoning empire.

American historians such as Pauline Tompkins and A. Whitney Griswold have argued that the Wilson Administration "inevitably" and "rightfully" went to Siberia to restrain the Japanese.[3] If true, the United States indulged a paradoxical policy, for the Japanese could not have undertaken their ambitious program without the financial and material support of the United States. Japan had fought three wars for expansion on the Asian mainland in thirty-eight years, two with China and one with Russia, the last of which, despite victory, brought the empire close to bankruptcy. By 1916 Japan was one of two creditor nations in the world—the other the United States—but she was barely a creditor. Her economy was delicately balanced and could not have supported a broad military effort without the infusion of dollars and industrial materials from the United States. Empire was a necessity for Japan because her population, mostly urban, was utterly dependent upon foreign commercial and industrial sources of wealth.

World War I had given her the "opportunity of a thousand years." The European colonizers in Asia and China had unaccountably retreated to their metropoles to fight a civil war that had so far lasted for four years. Japan had been able to enlarge her empire easily at the expense of Germany. So far, she had gained the most of any Allied nation with the least expenditure of lives and money.

All that kept Japan from moving at will in the Far East was the foreign policy of the United States. The United States was still the one Western power that could fight and win in the Pacific. The United States insisted on the "open door" policy by which it meant it would trade and develop in the Far East and Asia where other nations traded and developed; and it insisted on enjoying a "most favored nation" status by which it meant it demanded the same concessions and privileges as the colonizing power.

The two revolutions in Russia in 1917 were therefore a godsend for empire. Intervention gave Japan the chance to take over the whole of the Sakhalin Islands to the north with their oil resources (the southern half of these islands had been ceded to Japan by the Czar in the Treaty of Portsmouth which ended the Russo-Japanese War). Japan also wanted economic control of the Maritime Province, which would yield to her island industry vast timbering tracts, 2,000,000,000 tons of coal, and other minerals in the Amur River basin, easily transported down the Ussuri to Vladivostok.

But Japan realized she had to move fast before the Bolsheviks consolidated their power. She had to stake out her claims before the Western colonizers returned to the East to continue the development of Asian and Chinese markets. Thus it was that Japan said yes to the request of the Supreme War Council for intervention. The Japanese made it clear they had no intention of mounting a military expedition that did not add to imperial expansion. They just as clearly indicated they would not venture past Irkutsk. The Japanese General Staff calculated that an expedition past Irkutsk would have to include every Japanese soldier, would take at least three years to reach Chelyabinsk, would require 107,000 railroad guards, and would necessitate quadrupling and then quadrupling again the rolling stock. In the meantime, Japan's other interests in eastern Asia would go unprotected.

Japan and the Allies, therefore, were working at cross-purposes. The Allies hoped to establish a White government that would unify Siberia and speed Russian soldiers to the Eastern Front. The Japanese wanted to keep Siberia in disunity until they themselves could establish a puppet government that would exchange territory for stability and order.

To stay in Siberia, the Japanese implemented a two-fold policy. They flooded Siberia with Japanese soldiers. They subsidized the Siberian Cossacks.

Thirty-eight thousand Japanese soldiers lined the route from Vladivostok to Manchouli, a small depot inside the Manchurian frontier where the Chinese Eastern connected with the Trans-Siberian. Another 22,000 occupied the Ussuri line from Vladivostok north to Khabarovsk. Twenty thousand more controlled the Amur Railway from Khabarovsk to Chita. These soldiers had carved out a triangle inside of which was the core of Siberia's treasure.

In Mukden, the Japanese established a school to teach the Russian language and Russian railway operations to their own engineers. They believed the future of Siberia lay in control of the roadbeds. They sent gun- and torpedo boats to every navigable stream and river in eastern Siberia. The army recruited Japanese priests from the Russian Orthodox Church in Japan, which had a congregation of 37,000. Most importantly, the Japanese introduced their own currency in both small and large denominations and made it a capital crime to refuse to honor it.

When General Graves realized the strength the Japanese had deployed along the railways, he saw that he would have to spread his own forces meagerly to make the American presence known. When he questioned Otani on the need for 70,000 troops, Otani pointed out that the Americans numbered almost 10,000 and that America looked on the Czech Legion as its own army. Therefore the disparity in numbers was not as great as Graves supposed.

Graves had too much sense to argue that the Japanese had 30,000 armed and desperate anti-Bolshevik Cossacks. In fact, it was their reactionary politics that recommended the Cossacks to the Japanese. Japanese military men did not comprehend the differences between Mensheviks and Bolsheviks, between Socialist Revolutionaries and Social Democrats. Socialism in any form was an anathema in Japan. That the Cossacks were anti-Socialist was more important to the Japanese than that the Cossacks were also barbaric, primitive, and their numbers too few to have much impact as a movement. The Cossacks would fight Bolsheviks. And the Cossacks were eager to sell out to a foreigner.

The Cossacks were governed by cliques, just as Japan itself was governed by cliques. Dealing with Cossack cliques was easy. The Japanese had simply to bargain with the ataman. Save that he is elected, the Cossack ataman corresponds in all respects to the Arabian sheik: His power is absolute, he speaks for the tribe, and he leads the men into battle.

Descendants of the Russian and Ukrainian serfs who fled servitude in the sixteenth and seventeenth centuries, the Cossacks inhabited the desolate border steppes of Russia. Here they were forced to defend their settlements against a panoply of invaders who thought them easy marks. After a century and a half of determined resistance, they had become such fierce and tenacious fighters that one of the Czars began to organize them into a splendid and efficient cavalry by granting them special privileges. By the beginning of the twentieth century, the Cossacks constituted not only an elite fighting force but also a profoundly reactionary nucleus in a Russia torn by dissidence.

Even before their landing parties came ashore at Vladivostok, Japanese military missions were recruiting atamen with promises of money, arms, training. They subsidized the Amur Cossacks led by Colonel Boris Nikitin, the Ussuri Cossacks led by Ivan Kalmykov, and the Trans-Baikal Cossacks led by Captain Grigori Semenov. Of them all, Semenov best served Japanese interests. He was disciplined, brutal, and pathologically criminal.

A stocky man with puffy cheeks, a handlebar mustache, and eyes that glittered like an animal's, Semenov was the son of a Russian father and Buryat Mongol mother. He was born in the Cossack village of Kurenzka in 1891 and received a commission in the Imperial Army in 1909. He served along the Ussuri River until 1914, when he was sent to the Eastern Front. There he formed a lifelong attachment to Baron Ungern-Sternberg, a Russian of Baltic-German extraction who served ever afterward as a devoted adjutant. Kerensky sent both Semenov and the Baron to Trans-Baikalia to raise volunteer military units for the Provisional Government. After the Bolsheviks took power, however, Semenov kept his agents circulating in Cossack border villages. He mustered a motley unit of 556 officers, civil officials, Mongols, and Chinese. To outfit themselves, this band raided Bolshevik posts and rustled horses wherever they found them along the steppes.

For a while, the British supported Semenov with 10,000 pound sterling a month, which encouraged more recruits. But Semenov would not stay put nor would he let the British reorganize and train his men. The British dropped him, which made him easy pickings for the Japanese. Semenov met their military mission in Harbin, boasting that he commanded two thousand troops at Manchouli. He described himself as a man without politics whose one consuming cause was restoring order in eastern Siberia. He needed two thousand rifles, twenty machine guns, six mountain guns, two six-inch artillery pieces, ammunition, and 250,000 roubles to advance on Chita immediately. Once he gained Chita, he promised to move on Irkutsk.[4]

The Japanese decided to help him in March 1918, and they transported arms and ammunition as well as a headquarters company and a general staff to his outpost. When Semenov moved from Manchouli in the summer of 1918, he was overwhelmingly successful solely because the Czechs had cleared Trans-Baikalia of effective Bolshevik opposition. Semenov quickly established himself at Chita, another key junction between the Chinese Eastern and the Amur line of the Trans-Siberian. His Cossacks claimed tribute from every train proceeding westward. They turned the area into a witches' cauldron of murder and mutilation. The longer the civil war lasted, the more Semenov and other Cossacks gave vent to blood lust. But they followed Japanese instructions to the letter and were everywhere recognized by Whites as no more than Japanese puppets. Through Semenov's depredations, the Japanese realized one of their principal aims: to prevent the establishment of any strong and united White Russian authority that could block their exploitation of the region's temporary anarchy.

The Japanese supported 70,000 soldiers in the field and a dozen Class A fighting ships that cost the empire over one billion yen. Five hundred million yen were sent to Semenov.[5]

The Japanese were only one of the many complications Graves encountered. Soon after he had set up his command, Graves met Gaida, who had come to Vladivostok accompanied by General Erwald Paris, then the senior French officer in Siberia. Gaida, flushed with his success, described his ambitions for establishing an Eastern Front.

"I thought it advisable," wrote Graves later, "to tell him not to expect American troops to go west of Lake Baikal, as he was being used by Allied representatives to do what he could to get each nation to send troops west."[6]

Gaida was disappointed, cruelly disappointed. He made this cruel disappointment public, asking newspapermen why had Allied promises become the promises of women, promises written on water. Graves had to reply that he himself was a soldier. He was sent to Siberia not to keep promises but to follow orders.

This statement prompted a strong reaction from Dr. Raymond Teusler, the head of the American Red Cross in Vladivostok. Dr. Teusler was a cousin of Mrs. Woodrow Wilson, which, he said, gave him secret intuition. He told American newsmen that while he was aware that Graves's response to Gaida was the announced policy of the United States, he, Teusler, was sure Graves would hasten troops westward if the Czechs needed reinforcement.

Graves made no reply. He did, however, wire the War Department that foreigners were attaching great importance to Dr. Teusler's intuitions which they might not attach if he were not the First Lady's cousin.

Graves had also to educate his own soldiers as to their purpose. The troops had received no information as to why they had come to Siberia. Some Yanks thought they had come to aid the

Czechs, some to recapture German and Austrian prisoners, still others that they were to march to the Eastern Front. There was widespread belief in the American contingent that they had come to Siberia to crusade against the Bolsheviks. When Graves learned that an American officer had arrested a Russian simply because he was a Bolshevik, he posted the following:

> Whoever gave you those orders must have made them up himself. The United States is not at war with the Bolsheviki or any other faction of Russia. You have no orders to arrest Bolsheviks or anybody else unless they disturb the peace of the community, attack the people or Allied soldiers. The United States Army is not here to fight Russia or any group or faction in Russia. Because a man is a Bolshevik is no reason for his arrest. You are to arrest only those who attack you. The United States is only fighting the Bolsheviki when American troops are attacked by an armed force.[7]

This policy brought a murrain of criticism on America in eastern Siberia. The Allies charged that the Yanks were pro-Bolshevik and the charge plagued and annoyed Graves for the rest of his life. "This is the thinking," John Albert White remarks in his book on the intervention, "so characteristic of a confused and warring world which hated neutrals only a little less than enemies."[8]

The neutrality Graves maintained, which he believed implicit in his orders, was eventually to slip from his grasp, partly because on the September day Graves posted his order American soldiers half a world away though still in Russia were locked in a bitter fight with Bolsheviks. Virtually under the polar ice cap, Yanks were digging snow trenches to save themselves from Red artillery bombardment.

The central truth of the American intervention was that it was not one policy in one place at one time but a variety of policies in a variety of places at a variety of times. Intervention was never continuous but episodic. The reason for this perhaps is that Russia geographically is a behemoth. Gaida and Graves were in Vladivostock, but they were talking about two different wars. And there was a third war of which both were ignorant, but that war left dead men on the Arctic tundra.

NOTES

1. A. Whitney Griswold, *The Far Eastern Policy of the United States*. New York: Harcourt, Brace and Company, 1938, p. 235.
2. William S. Graves, *America's Siberian Adventure, 1918–1920*. New York: Peter Smith, 1941, p. 34.
3. Pauline Tompkins, *American-Russian Relations in the Far East*. New York: Macmillan, 1949. See also Griswold, *op. cit.*
4. Morley, *op. cit.,* p. 227.
5. *Ibid.,* p. 4.
6. Graves, *op. cit.,* pp. 84–85.
7. Betty Miller Unterbarger, *America's Siberian Expedition: A Study of National Policy*. Durham, N. C.: Duke University Press, 1956, p. 90.
8. White, *op. cit.,* p. 233.

Czech armored train. Notice camouflage.

Czech armored train.

The 31st Infantry parades past American headquarters in Vladivostok on
November 11, 1918.

Wharves and docks of Vladivostok congested with war supplies.

Street scene in Vladivostok.

Machine-gun company of 31st Infantry takes its mess in the field.

Village of Suchan. Mine No. 1 in the foreground.

Machine-gun company of 31st Infantry tracking Bolsheviks around Suchan.

Typical railroad station on the Trans-Siberian Railway.

Mule skinners rodeo in Kharbarovsk.

Colonel George Emerson and John
Stevens.

U.S.S. *Brooklyn* in background,
H.M.S. *Suffolk* in foreground, Bay
of the Golden Horn, 1918–1919.

Bolshevik prisoners of war on their
way to execution.

Japanese troops load heavy artillery in the Amur Va

CHAPTER 8

ARCHANGEL:

JULY 30–OCTOBER 13, 1918

Neutrality was what America wanted in Siberia. War, however, was the pledge she had to pay to enter North Russia, war without assent or declaration.

Archangel is four thousand miles from Vladivostok, about the distance between New York City and Nome. It would be foolish for an invader to believe the citizens of Nome would have to fight without the help of New Yorkers. But in 1918, the Allies thought there was a way to invade a foreign country as a friend. The friendship worked for a while in Vladivostok. It did not work at all in Archangel.

The invasion got under way on the night of July 30, 1918, with HMS *Tay* and *Tyne*, subchasers escorting armed trawlers; the HMS *Nairana*, a cruiser with a seaplane launch; HMS *Attentive*, a light cruiser; the French *Amiral Aube*; and the American *Olympia*. The fleet, under the command of British Rear-Admiral T. W. Kemp, left Murmansk bound for the White Sea. Behind it on the 31st steamed the troop transports *Stephans, Asurian, Westborough,* and *Kassala,* accompanied by four more armed trawlers and convoyed by the expropriated Russian destroyer *Lieutenant Sergeyev.* Aboard these transports were 1,500 Allied troops, which included an infantry brigade of Royal Scots, the French 21st Colonial Battalion, a brigade of Canadian artillery, members of the Italian Military Mission, a company of Serbian infantry and 51 sailors, and three officers from the *Olympia* chosen for their marksmanship.[1]

The commander of the expedition, Major General Frederick C. Poole, one of His Majesty's most experienced soldiers, was aboard the converted yacht HMS *Salvator*. Poole was bold and confident about his mission. His orders from the Supreme War Council directed him to secure "bridgeheads into Russia from the north from which forces can eventually advance rapidly to the center of Russia."[2] By obeying these orders, French and British war leaders expected Poole to achieve two results. From Archangel, he was to march four hundred miles south and join his forces with the Czech Legion at Viatka. The juncture of these two Allied armies would pose a threat to Germany. Poole's bridgeheads also might convince Russians to depose the Bolshevik regime. It will be noted that these results were not the results Woodrow Wilson anticipated in his *aide-mémoire*. Yet given the times and the attitudes that characterized those times these were desirable results.

Poole failed. The intervention at Archangel was to become the classic template of how and why intervention sometimes fails. Intervention at Archangel failed because of insufficient military force to accomplish objectives and inefficient politics which failed to augment the military force.

Reciprocally, one failure sapped strength and resolve from the other. General Poole was leading those behind him into a wilderness—indeed, a biblical wilderness where the winter sky was a frozen hell and the tundra with its unending swamps and impenetrable forests a valley of the shadow of death. These soldiers aboard the transports and the Americans who would soon follow them were to wage war for ends which could never be realized, by means which could never ennoble, and for reasons which were beyond comprehension.

The odds for Allied success in such a venture were initially long odds. But they were made more favorable by the fact that the invasion could be mounted from Murmansk, the Russian port to which the British had come several months before, expressly at Bolshevik invitation.

At one point in the peace negotiations at Brest-Litovsk, Trotsky feared the Germans wanted more than the Bolsheviks could give. Throughout Russia the German advance continued, endangering several newly established soviets. One of the most vulnerable of these soviets was that at Murmansk. The Germans had sent a division to Finland, where with White Finns they threatened capture of this Barents Sea port. Once in possession of Murmansk, the Germans could mount an attack on St. Petersburg over the 600-mile-long Murman Railway. Trotsky advised the Murmansk soviet to accept any and all assistance from the Allies.

The Murmansk soviet asked the British to put ashore a detachment of Marines from the HMS *Glory* on March 6. Three hundred and seventy more British Marines went into garrison at Murmansk in April and May. In addition to the *Glory,* the British and French cruisers *Cochrane* and *Amiral Aube* with several tenders rode at anchor in the harbor protecting Russian warships.

Located just below the Arctic Circle, Murmansk is an ice-free port warmed by the Gulf·Stream as it sweeps by the Kola Peninsula. It is a war-built city, hurriedly thrown up as a terminus for the Murman Railway laid at British instigation. In its own way, this line was as miraculous an achievement as the Trans-Siberian. Begun in 1915 by Goriatchovsky over seemingly bottomless tundra, it was built by German prisoners of war and one hundred thousand conscripted Russians. The bones of thousands of these men became part of the roadbed when they died of exposure or malnutrition. This flimsy, single-track railroad stretched from Murmansk due south to St. Petersburg. It was just beginning to transport thirty-five hundred tons of war supplies every day from Britain to the Eastern Front when the October Revolution halted its operations. The fifty thousand workers in Murmansk would have starved and frozen to death if the British had not begun supplying them with food and clothing in the early winter of 1918. Trotsky's directions were superfluous to the commissars at Murmansk: There was no way they could survive if the Allies didn't help them.

But once the Bolsheviks ratified the Treaty of Brest-Litovsk, Red leaders began to cool toward this foreign presence in the north. Other alarums about Allied intentions worried Trotsky and Lenin. When they learned on May 24 that the USS *Olympia* had steamed into Murmansk harbor carrying Major General Poole and another seven hundred soldiers of all ranks, the Red leaders ordered the Murmansk soviet to banish the Allies. The commissars in Murmansk replied that the Allies simply would not depart, that they were defending the region from the incursions of Finns and Germans, that they were feeding the local population and clothing them. Promptly, the Bolsheviks condemned these commissars to death as outlaws and traitors.

Victims of a dilemma, the Murmansk commissars hastened to conclude a unique agreement between their soviet and representatives of the three Allied powers. On July 6, British, American, and French consuls recognized the Murmansk Regional Soviet as the supreme authority in the Murman. The Allies pledged to defend the area and disclaimed any desire to separate the region from the Great and Undivided Russia of the future.[3] This agreement provided Woodrow Wilson with a quasilegal basis for the intervention. It provided Britain and France with a crucial staging area for the more important thrust from Archangel south. The Murman Railway ran only to St. Petersburg. But the railway from Archangel connected directly with the Trans-Siberian. Strategically this was the easiest way to resupply and reinforce the Czechs. That the British intended more than the re-establishment of the Eastern Front is evidenced by the careful planning that went into the evacuation of the Allied ambassadors and the coup the British worked in Archangel to coincide with Poole's invasion.

The Allied diplomatic personnel were in Vologda, a provincial town three hundred miles due east of St. Petersburg and four hundred miles due south of Archangel. The ambassadors and their staffs had withdrawn here in February when the Germans menaced St. Petersburg. On July 25, British intelligence warned the doyen of the corps, Ambassador David R. Francis of the

United States, that General Poole would leave Murmansk for Archangel no later than August 1. Francis saw that it was important that he, the Italian, Chinese, Japanese, and Brazilian ambassadors as well as the French and British embassy staffs get out of town while the getting was good. Francis arranged for a train to transport these men to Archangel on that very night.

Francis had become increasingly concerned while in Vologda at the continuous removal of stores from Archangel by the Bolsheviks. The Bolsheviks neither paid nor promised payment. Francis had made several representations to Moscow for the retention of these stores, which consisted of acres and acres of barbed wire, stands of small arms, pyramids of shells of all calibers, great parks of artillery, motor trucks, field kitchens, ambulances, railroad iron, coils of precious copper wire, and the interminable rows of metal pigs—the alloys essential for artillery production. Francis was afraid that these stores piled in Archangel would fall into the hands of the Germans when the Bolsheviks removed them. The Bolsheviks, however, failed to satisfy Francis' requests. Irritated, he urged the United States State Department to undertake a military intervention to save them. Francis saw Bolshevik expropriation as theft. This hardened him and blinded his reason as to what his government expected of him. His government wanted Francis to safeguard its interests, which are not necessarily its property. Poole's invasion and the impending coup that was to pave the way for the Allied expedition were good news to Francis, although both were occurring too late to recover the stores spirited away in the past months.

The diplomats reached Archangel on July 26. Wheedling, cajoling, and finally bribing, they negotiated the charter of two vessels to transport them across the White Sea to Kandalaksha on the western shore. One hundred and thirty-two Allied diplomats together with some seventy British and French residents sailed from Archangel on July 28. Francis was determined to return in ten days to a democratic, free, and honest Russia.

The coup, instigated and financed by the British, had a short-range and a long-range purpose. The short-range purpose was to immobilize the Bolsheviks so that Poole could get his force into the city; the long-range purpose was to free the northern provinces of Bolshevik control so that a White government, using the Allied expedition as a cadre, could rally an anti-Bolshevik army to wage war against the Reds.

Archangel was governed by a soviet that derived its power from the presence of an Extraordinary Evacuation Commission come to remove the military stores. Accompanying the Extraordinary Commission were several shore batteries, eight hundred infantrymen, a machine-gun company, and two battalions of untested troops. The batteries particularly and the machine-gun company that perpetuated the Red grip on the city were capable of repelling an invasion. Archangel lay twenty-five miles up the Dvina River on the northern bank. The river flowed north. Shore batteries easily controlled the channel, which narrowed precipitously to a width of no more than five hundred yards. Shore batteries could sink the transports of the Allied fleet at will. The terrain to the north of Archangel offered no advantageous roadstead to an invader. Poole had to come up the river through the channel to Archangel or not come at all.

The British Foreign Office asked its consul in Archangel, Douglas Young, to arrange a coup that would depose the Bolsheviks, thus silencing the shore batteries. With typical British aplomb, Young complied. He enlisted the services of an opportunist and adventurer named George E. Chaplin (whom the Allied soldiers called "Charley"), formerly a commander in the Imperial Russian Navy, a dark, wiry man with a mercurial temperament who spoke perfect English. Chaplin easily enlisted a counterrevolutionary cohort from the five hundred ex-Czarist officers who had gravitated to Archangel since the October Revolution.

Chaplin and these conspirators staged a mock uprising on July 21 in and around Shenkhurst, a populous village to the south which drew the machine-gun company and the eight hundred battle-tested infantrymen out of Archangel.

On August 1, when Chaplin heard the guns of the *Attentive* open up to the north, his men began killing Bolsheviks and commissars wherever they encountered them. Panic was epidemic. The Extraordinary Evacuation Commission summoned the gunners and their crews from the shore batteries to help staunch the flow of blood in the city.

The timing was exquisite. Poole could not put into Archangel until the coup succeeded, but the coup could not transpire until his small army was able to support it. Poole opened the conflict by attacking Mudyug, the northernmost island which defended the approaches to Archangel. There were two batteries on Mudyug, one emplaced to the north, the other to the south, the two firing sixteen six-inch guns. The *Attentive* and the *Nairana* zeroed in on these. The northern battery surrendered when the British bracketed it with shells, but the southern battery returned fire, one of its shells hitting the base of the *Attentive*'s forward funnel, wrecking the boiler room below. The *Attentive* withdrew and, once out of range, recommenced fire. These British seamen had had four years of war in which to perfect what was already their creditable gunnery. The shells were coming in on target. The *Nairana* launched its two seaplanes, which strafed the Bolshevik gunners. The Mudyug's power magazine blew up and the Bolsheviks deserted their post. Boarding a tug, the Reds sped toward Archangel, the seaplanes pursuing them. British Marines immediately debarked from the *Attentive* in power launches and, after encountering some scattered opposition on Mudyug, secured the island by nightfall. Mudyug was the first successful combined air-sea-land operation in the history of warfare. The sight of seaplanes coming in on Archangel convinced the Bolsheviks remaining in the city that overwhelming Allied supremacy was moving upon them. In disorganized retreat, they gave up the city to what was essentially a minuscule force.

On that same August 1, seventy-five miles to the west of Archangel at Onega, the Russian cruiser, *Archangel Michael,* manned by British seamen, opened fire on the Bolshevik detachment, headquartered near the city's one wharf. Expert gunnery again convinced the Bolsheviks that resistance was useless. They abandoned Onega when a British infantry company, sent down from Kem, attacked their rear. At very little cost and in record time the Allied Expeditionary Force had not only taken Archangel but secured its western flank on Onega Bay.

The region to which the Allies had come was almost as large as the combined area of France and Germany. Archangel Province is 330,000 square miles of tundra and thick fir forests through which six rivers cut to the sea, the largest of these the muddy Dvina.

North Russia was not industrialized, and consequently it was free of the radical proletariat who in St. Petersburg and Moscow made the Bolshevik Revolution happen. The northern population engaged in fishing, trapping, and farming, with some manufacturing at Archangel. The Russians grew oats, rye, barley, potatoes, cabbage, and flax. There were 60,000 people in Archangel and perhaps 350,000 in the province. The latter lived in villages along the rivers, their villages often no more than a mile apart. Each village was marked by a church, usually the only building that was painted, and soldiers looking up or down the rivers could see several of these churches at once. Peasants and farmers lived in log huts that in structure and design resembled the log cabin of the American frontier save that the Russian hut was chinked with moss and the American cabin with mortar. It is a region of steamy heat in summer and sub-zero cold in winter. Beginning in October, the nights begin to lengthen until by January they are almost twenty-four hours long.

The chief resource of the area was timber. British consuls, generals, and foreign correspondents never tired of noting that outside of Archangel there was enough timber to pay the whole of Russia's war debt.

The invasion fleet had a safe and uneventful passage up the channel to Archangel. At 8:00 P.M. on August 2, General Poole, clean-shaven, tunic bemedaled, boots glistening, riding crop thrashing the air, disembarked from the *Salvator* and came ashore. Men, women, and children lined the quays and riverbanks to cheer his arrival although the American consul, Felix Cole, noted that none of them was workingmen or the children of workingmen but instead the bourgeois, mercantilist, and property-owning aristocrats. The city was festooned with streamers. On the wharf the pipes of the Royal Scots whined as Poole inspected the colors.

On hand to greet him was the new government of the Archangel Province, a pro-Allied government. The so-called Supreme Administration of the Northern Region was headed by Nikolai K. Chaikovsky, a sixty-seven-year-old world-famous Socialist. Chaikovsky had been making his way to Siberia when destiny in the form of British intelligence agents advised him to get to Archangel as quickly as possible. Chaikovsky disguised himself from the Bolshevik Cheka by the simple expedient of shaving off his long, flowing beard by which he was universally recognized, and once in Archangel Consul Douglas Young put him in contact with George Chaplin. Chaplin told him about the coup and the need of the Allies for a "business" government. Before Chaplin moved, Chaikovsky had assembled a phantom cabinet, secretly printed proclamations, and drawn up a municipal constitution. Chaikovsky spoke flawless English. He had lived in Independence, Kansas, between 1875 and 1879 where he tried to found an evangelical sect. He had spent another twenty years in London expounding Socialist doctrines. As he stepped forward to greet General Poole, he was realizing the millennium, the dream of the oppressed and downtrodden for their rights and security.

But that was as far as the dream went. Once the handshake was concluded, General Poole curtly ordered Chaikovsky to haul down all the red flags in the city. Poole knew the Bolsheviks flew red flags. He did not know that the red flag was also the age-old symbol of the Socialists. When the bewildered Chaikovsky and his ministers protested, Poole curtly informed them that he was the commander-in-chief of the Allied forces in North Russia, which was now under martial law. He did not want red flags flown.

The British hand was now out of the velvet glove and it was an iron fist. Whatever authority the Supreme Administration of the Northern Region wielded over Russians derived from the presence of an Allied military presence, a fact General Poole did not want anyone to forget.

Frederick C. Poole was a distinguished soldier, an expert artillery man who had spent thirty of his forty-nine years in the army. He had fought in Tirah, then in the Boer War, where he won the Distinguished Service Order, next in Somaliland, and finally on the Western Front, where he was mentioned in the dispatches three times. An optimist, his first cable from North Russia to the War Office was that he was "cheerfully taking great risks." He saw a problem and went at it, though he was no detail man. One must wonder, however, if his enthusiasm in this instance did not overwhelm his military training and good sense.

Poole was a soldier playing politics and eventually doomed to play them badly. He was an Englishman setting up as a viceroy where no viceroy was needed. One of his subordinates complained that Poole treated Russians rather as a housemaster treats a couple of his prefects; they must realize their responsibility and act for the good of the house. Ambassador David R. Francis said the British had been bullying Hindus for so long they did not know how to respect the feelings of Socialists.

The first of the Allied forces to see action in North Russia were the American sailors from the *Olympia,* who came ashore on August 3 to serve as embassy guards. Twenty-five bluejackets were detailed to the railroad yards under Ensign Hicks. Here they came across a wood-burning locomotive with a full boiler of water. Getting up steam, the sailors hooked on two flat cars, mounted their machine gun on the forward one, and decided to give chase to a Bolshevik unit that had just left the yards.

In a furious rattling race, the sailors drew upon the rear of the fleeing "Bolos"* and began exchanging pot shots. The chase continued for thirty miles due south on the railroad until a hot box forced the sailors to a halt. This gave the Bolsheviks time to burn a bridge to cover their retreat. The sailors were prepared to wade into the river and across the other side until the Bolos, who had the chance to entrench, directed a withering fire in their direction. Not only did the Bolsheviks have plenty of ammunition but were professional about expending it. The sailors ducked under the flat cars for cover. Bolshevik fire did not slacken. Ensign Hicks took

* "Bolos" for "Bolsheviks" derived supposedly from a Yank who remarked on seeing a group of Red prisoners that they looked like "Bolo wild men." But the British staff used "Bolo" in their very first reports, and "Bolo" for "Bolshevik" is characteristic of the British, who called Livorno "Leghorn" and Firenze "Florence" and pronounced Don Juan "Jew-an" because they didn't know any better.

U.S. Sailors
First in Action in north Russia.

a bullet in the leg, the first casualty of the Allied Expeditionary Force. Wisely, the sailors decided not to charge but to hold the position. Unwittingly, but importantly, they had established the "Railroad Front" in North Russia and they continued to hold it for the next thirty-two days along with the French and a few Tommies.[4]

Here the war stalled.

Poole rushed the French Colonial Battalion down the railway hoping it could brush by the Bolshevik defenses. The poilus, however, veterans of four years of trench warfare, were duly cautious about charging machine-gun emplacements. They began the advance first by circling the Bolshevik left flank, then the right flank, then waiting for the center to drop back. This was a time-consuming process where speed was essential. When the Bolshevik center did drop back, it dropped back into a prepared defensive position impervious to the day-long fusillade of the *Olympia*'s sailors.

General Poole's primary purposes were to take Vologda, a city four hundred miles due south of Archangel through which the railway passed. He had also to take Kotlas, which was five hundred miles southeast of Archangel on the Dvina River. By taking and holding Vologda, Poole denied the Bolsheviks the opportunity of reinforcing the northern region by rail. By taking Kotlas, he could use the rails to link his force with the Czech Legion at Viatka, still farther to the southwest.

As soon as he had sent the French down the railroad, a plumb line to Vologda, Poole sent the Royal Scots up the Dvina River. Two weeks after he had landed, the Royal Scots informed Poole they had taken Bereznik, a town that commanded the junction between the Vaga and the Dvina rivers. Here Bolshevik resistance stiffened. Though ill-trained and badly organized, the Bolos turned on their pursuers, aware at last that no expanding invasion was upon them. They needed no extraordinary intelligence to tell them Poole was stretching his lines of communication taut.

Poole did not have the artillery to dislodge the Bolsheviks from either of these two fronts. He had only two sections of French 75s; one brigade numbering 487 men of the Canadian

Field Artillery firing three-inch shells; one 55-millimeter and one 77-millimeter howitzer along with guns removed from the *Attentive* and the *Olympia* which were fitted onto an armored train. There were also some isolated White Russian units with artillery. Poole put them together as best he could, but he could not blast out an advance.

By this time Poole was aware that the further he penetrated on the Railroad Front and along the Dvina the more he was moving his forces apart. It was as though he had put each on the opening blades of a pair of scissors. The more progress each made, the less each was able to support the other.

Poole needed more men. He went to Chaikovsky of the Supreme Administration whom he had deputized to recruit two regiments of Russians. Chaikovsky confessed his new government had so far enlisted only one hundred men. The Supreme Administration considered a draft undemocratic. At this moment Poole must have stopped taking great risks cheerfully. He was, after all, attempting to invade an expanse as large as France and Germany with fewer than two thousand men. The hope of achieving his military objectives quickly was doomed.

But Poole made the best of it. He set up the Slavo-British Legion and called for volunteers. The Slavo-British Legion wore British uniforms, used British weapons, and took orders from British officers. Though eventually this legion numbered twelve hundred men, it was of no use to Poole in August.

Poole always kept under his own command the entire services of supply—medical, training, commissary, ordnance—which inhibited the formation of locally mustered Russian forces. Poole also insisted that Chaikovsky's Supreme Administration administer rather than govern. Where the Supreme Administration wanted to carry out the reforms of the February Revolution, Poole only wanted it to organize the province for a life-or-death struggle with the Bolsheviks. This did not help recruitment.

The French tried to emulate the British in Archangel by setting up a unit of the Foreign Legion, which at best attracted two hundred Russians. As August drew to a close, Poole knew he would have to wait for Allied reinforcements before venturing farther. These reinforcements consisted of Americans of the 339th Infantry Regiment, one battalion of the 310th Engineers, the 337th Field Hospital, and the 337th Ambulance Company.

John J. Pershing selected the 339th for North Russian duty principally because its commanding officer, Colonel George Evans Stewart, had served in Arctic Alaska. A second reason was that the regiment, newly arrived in England in July as part of the 85th Division, was conveniently encamped along the London-Aldershot Canal in Surrey.

These doughboys were sweltering through the worst heat wave in England's history when the rumor spread through camp that the regiment was bound for duty in cool Murmansk. Within the week, the rumor was fact when the troops turned in their Enfield rifles for the Russian "long gun" of American manufacture. They promptly discovered that the sight was calibrated in Russian paces instead of yards and that it jammed in the midst of extended rapid fire. They drew twenty-four Lewis guns and fifty Colt machine guns, also of Russian pattern. They drew a winter issue of overcoats, fur hats, and Shackleton boots designed by the famous Arctic explorer. However, the men found soon enough that the Shackleton boot was heavy, slippery, and, when the snow was wet, damp. They were also to discover that no matter what their clothes, once they were wounded they froze to death. They drew one thousand pairs of skis, 5,500 snowshoes, and 7,500 moccasins for ski use. The quartermaster also included fifty long cross-saws and fifty ice tongs for water supply in North Russia.

The 339th and its support units added up to a total of 5,500 officers and men. They boarded the troopships *Tydeus, Nagoya,* and *Somali* at Newcastle-on-Tyne on August 27 bound for the Murman coast.

When they were four days at sea, influenza became epidemic. This scourge of World War I put some five hundred men of the 339th on sick call, one hundred of whom would not live to see Russia. The sick bays were small, and the medics could not provide beds for all the victims. Men with temperatures no higher than

102 degrees lay delirious on makeshift bedding on deck. Medicines were quickly exhausted. In the midst of this disaster, Colonel Stewart received orders to make for Archangel instead of Murmansk and to put the 339th under the command of General Poole.

On September 4, the American North Russian Expeditionary Force came up the Dvina to dock at Bakaritza. On the south bank of the river, Bakaritza was called the "Brooklyn of Archangel" by the Yanks. A chilling rain drenched the topside troops, whose first impression of the place was gleaned from the appearance of the muddy, bandaged collection of sailors from the *Olympia* standing on the nearest dock.

At 4:00 P.M. on September 5, the 2nd Battalion disembarked at Smolney Quay in Archangel and encamped in nearby Smolney Barracks.

Immediately afterward, the 3rd Battalion came ashore at Bakaritza and entrained for the Railroad Front.

On September 7, the 1st Battalion loaded itself and its equipment on two barges, which proceeded up the Dvina River towed by tugs.[5]

Medical personnel began unloading the sick and the dead on the 7th. The only space available for the influenza victims was at the Russian Red Cross Hospital, which had double-decked pine board beds with neither mattresses nor linen. While Lieutenants Lowenstein and Danziger did their best for these desperately ill men, Major Jonas Longley, the battalion's chief medical officer, asked the British for help. The British agreed to take the American officers into their hospital. Before he would make a distinction between sick officers and sick enlisted men, Longley said he would establish his own hospital, an action which the British staff informed him was forbidden. Longley contacted Mr. C. T. Williams, deputy commissioner of the American Red Cross Mission, and explained what he needed. Williams promptly turned over what he had—which was considerable. Five Red Cross trains made up of from eighteen to twenty-five cars containing tons of supplies had been sent by the American Red Cross to Archangel before the Bolshevik Revolution. A dozen volunteer workers had accompanied this materiel, of whom two were nurses who forthwith volunteered for army duty when Longley asked.[6]

Longley detailed some doughboys to scrub and whitewash an unused brick building near the Archangel waterfront. He stripped the transports of all bedding and cots and began moving his sick to a place where they could get well. He also hoisted the American flag over his hospital. A British officer told him this was in violation of Poole's orders; Poole apparently liked only the Union Jack. Longley promptly assigned two armed Yanks as guards at the flagpole. Longley was the only soldier to win the argument with Poole about what flag a unit would display.

The British attempted more than symbolic action. They promoted subalterns to lieutenant colonels and made colonels and generals out of captains. British sergeants held the temporary rank of major. British personnel always outranked the other Allied commands. Poole was confident that the intervention would become a large-scale Allied operation and he wanted to be sure that he and the British controlled it. He also wanted to insure that the British controlled the White government in Archangel and here, in trying to set up a military dictatorship more congenial to British aims than Chaikovsky's Supreme Administration, he overreached himself regrettably.

Poole connived with Chaplin, who was now the Military Commander of the Russian forces in the North. Both despaired of Chaikovsky's ability to raise an army to fight the Bolsheviks.

Accordingly, Chaplin again assembled a cohort of ex-Czarist officers and quietly surrounded the building where the ministers and Chaikovsky lived—which happened to be directly across the street from Poole's headquarters, surprisingly deserted on the night of September 5. Chaplin and his conspirators broke in upon the members of the Supreme Administration and arrested them at gunpoint. They hurried the protesting Chaikovsky and his government to the waterfront, dumped them into a motor launch, and sped them to a monastery on Solovetsky Island in the White Sea.

Before dawn Chaplin had posted a proclamation on buildings, lampposts, and on public transportation which announced the demise of the Supreme Administration.

But Chaplin had not deposed the Supreme Administration entirely. Two of Chaikovsky's ministers had escaped. They spent the early dawn publicizing the fate of their colleagues. They, too, prepared a proclamation, which condemned Chaplin and warned that ex-Czarists intended to restore the monarchy.

Chaplin had contrived his coup to coincide with the arrival of the Yanks so that they would be blamed for it rather than the British. This devious ploy ran afoul of American Ambassador David R. Francis, who had returned in late August to Archangel with the other ambassadors—Joseph Noulens, France; Nobile Pietro Tomasi della Toretta, Italy; and F. O. Lindley, British High Commissioner for North Russia. These four diplomats believed that if the Allies wanted to control North Russia it was absolutely necessary to see to it that North Russians had a government they regarded as their own.

The four men were on the steps of the town hall reviewing the newly arrived 339th on the morning of September 6 when Poole apprised them that there had been a revolution the night before.

"The hell you say!" cried the surprised Francis. "Who pulled it off?"

Poole told him Chaplin had.

Francis stormed up to Chaplin and demanded an explanation. Chaplin explained to the angry Francis that the Supreme Administration was in General Poole's way, that there was no need for any government in Archangel.

Francis abrogated the coup. He was the most influential of the ambassadors and they followed his lead. He told Poole to rescue the kidnapped ministers and to place Chaplin under close arrest. Francis quickly drew up his own proclamation to the effect that the Supreme Administration still lived.

There were three proclamations up at the same time. There was Chaplin's, that of the ministers-in-hiding, and the ambassadors'. As Francis put it later, to say the population of Archangel was confused "inadequately expresses the condition of their minds."

When the workingmen of Archangel began reading these proclamations in broad daylight, they called a general strike. Peasants and moujiks, some of them armed with scythes, others with old blunderbusses, came into the city to save the Supreme Administration. These Russians found the Yanks running the streetcars, and while they had no objection to the free ride they wondered just what the Allies were about.

Chaplin took refuge aboard a British ship where the returning Chaikovsky could not get at him. Chaikovsky again governed but the Supreme Administration had been dealt a mortal blow. The Allied ambassadors insisted Chaikovsky set up a more "conservative" administration. He did, calling his new government the Provisional Government of the Northern Region. But the high hopes of using the intervention to establish a representative White government directing an aggressive army had been seriously deflated. "If Vologda had been reached in the first few weeks," concluded a United States Naval Intelligence Report

> and a large part of the territory which the Supreme Administration represented had been freed from Bolsheviks, everyone, that is the Government and the Military Authorities (and I might add the Ambassadors) would have had sufficient sphere of action to attend to, without interfering with one another. As it was all were cooped up in Archangel and continually in each other's way. No wonder that they clashed.[7]

The paradox with which the Allied military force had to contend was that only a Socialist government could command the loyalty of the North Russians, but the Socialists were averse and incapable of getting together the army needed to depose the Bolsheviks.

Politically, Major General Frederick Poole was an ignoble failure. Militarily, however, he was a decisive and canny tactician. He was increasingly aware that as the blades of his scissors opened between the railroad and the Dvina Front, he was presenting an opportunity for an enterprising enemy. An enemy who could drive a wedge between the two points could wipe out either. The one barrier that would impede the enemy's movement was the Emtsa River, which ran east and west, curving like a snapping bullwhip. However, if the enemy followed the road which ran from

Plesetkaya to Kochmas to Avda to Kodish, he could cross the river at this last point and fall upon either the flank of the railroad or the Dvina Front. Poole saw that the Allies would have to take Kodish.

He saw also that he was weak at Bereznik on the Dvina. Bereznik was vulnerable to a Bolshevik attack coming down the Vaga. If the enemy took Bereznik, he cut off Allied troops to the south. So Poole understood he would have to send a small expedition up the Vaga to secure Shenkhurst and the river towns south of it.

Poole gave up the idea of taking Vologda before the winter. Instead, he determined to take Plesetskaya, which was halfway between Vologda and Archangel. To take Plesetskaya would deprive the enemy of a key rail and road center. Poole planned on a multicolumned attack.

The area was large and the terrain troublesome, the available force limited. Yet Poole anticipated the moves the Bolsheviks would make, and though the Allied force was numerically inferior and often barely equipped, their deployment blunted Red attacks and saved the strategic situation. Before winter set in, Poole held Onega in the west, established a front below Obozerskaya on the railroad, held Kodish on the Emtsa, Shenkhurst on the Vaga and Toulgas on the Dvina.

On September 5, the 21st Colonial Battalion bulled its way to Obozerskaya on the Railroad Front. When the 3rd Battalion of the 339th detrained the next day, they went onto the line just south of the depot.

Obozerskaya was the largest station between Plesetskaya and Archangel. It was a crux of passable trails which cut the forest east and west. The depot was marked by a tall water tower, used by the artillery spotters, and surrounded by several ramshackle huts once used by railway workers. In a widening perimeter were the log cabins of the Russian lumbermen and moujiks. Beside the rails corded pine waited to feed locomotives. The Yanks used these to build barricades to defend their position.

In a drizzling rain, the Yanks marched from their boxcars

through Obozerskaya to Verst 466. (A verst was .66 of a mile or 1,164 yards. Each verst on a Russian railroad was marked on a post, the numbers running from the south to the north.)

Major Charles D. Young led the battalion and brought them to parade rest south of the water tower. He had the bugler sound "Officers' Call," but the conference was interrupted by a gesticulating French major. Young stared uncomprehending until an explosion made clear what the Frenchman wanted to say: The area was under Bolshevik artillery fire. The Yanks broke formation and took shelter in the forest, where the swamp water reached to their knees.

When the Bolsheviks lifted the barrage, the Yanks griped at Young's orders, which forbade them making fires. One hundred yards away, the Americans could see the poilus drying their clothes on sticks and poles held near the flames.

Two days later, Bolshevik airplanes dropped bombs on the Yank position. As one plane circled for its return, it stalled and glided to earth, crash-landing about two hundred yards from a Yank outpost. Major Young, mistaking the Bolo markings for British, ran toward the crumpled aircraft shouting, "Don't shoot. We are Americans." The two Red airmen were not so shaken that they couldn't direct a burst from their machine gun at the charging major. Young disappeared into the moss in a fast, shallow dive. The pilots cleared their cockpits and dashed for the woods. An intrepid patrol of six Americans cautiously advanced to claim Young's body. Young, though covered with moss, was far from dead.

Two days later, the major was relieved. He spent the rest of the intervention as provost for the 339th, meting out harsh sentences at court-martials.

On September 11, two platoons of M Company encountered an enemy patrol seven versts south of Obozerskaya. The Yanks chased the Bolsheviks, signaling for the men behind them to advance. The Railroad Front moved forward to Verst 464. On September 16, the Bolsheviks counterattacked with machine guns and grenades. L Company beat the Bolos off, supported by two platoons from I Company and artillery fire from the big gun on

the armored train. In the fight, the 339th took its first casualties—
three killed and two wounded.

This was the nature of the war on the Railroad Front. Small
unit action which won minor gains, surrendered some of the gains
to counterattack, then came back to consolidate the advance.

"All patrols must be aggressive," ordered British colonel
Sutherland. "It must be impressed on all ranks that we are fighting
an offensive war." The little French and American graveyards in
Obozerskaya grew larger with each passing week.

Farther east, Poole sent a force of Royal Scots and White
Russian infantry along the Emtsa. These troops secured Emetskoe,
Tiogra, and Seletskoe, but the Bolsheviks turned them back before
they reached Kodish. This determined defense made the capture
of Kodish all the more imperative.

Poole decided to attack it from the rear by sending out a
detachment from the Railroad Front. He chose K Company of the
339th commanded by Captain Michael Donohue, nicknamed
"Iron Mike" by his men.

Along with a medical detachment of nine, Donohue took off
to the east on September 7. He made five miles the first day, thirteen the second, and by the third day realized he was lost. Donohue spent the fourth day trying to find out where he was. On the
fifth, he ran into Lieutenant Gardner, sent out from Obozerskaya
to find him. Gardner had twenty men and four Lewis guns. He
also had new orders for Donohue. Donohue was to skirt Kodish
to the north, for the Bolsheviks had reinforced the town, and make
for Seletskoe.

Donohue reached Seletskoe and got his men and Gardner's
machine guns into position in time. The machine guns poured such
galling fire into the attacking Bolos that the Red infantrymen
assassinated their commander in order to break from it. The Bolos
then retreated to Kodish.

The battle sapped both sides. The CO of the Royal Scots
anticipated renewed Bolo attacks. He ordered his and Donohue's
men to withdraw. The command began pulling back to Tiogra.
However, a last British reconnaissance patrol discovered the Reds

were evacuating Kodish. The patrol hurried back with this information. The British corporal passed through now abandoned Seletskoe, whose natives were trailing behind the Allies with everything from the samovar to the cow. The patrol caught the tail of the retreating column in time to see some Yanks setting fire to a bridge. "I say, old chaps," the British corporal called across, "wot's the bloody gaime?"

So the column of Royal Scots and Yanks turned and went back into Seletskoe. The Russian natives turned with them.

The Yanks and the Royal Scots improved their defenses at Seletskoe and prepared to move again on Kodish. Company K— the men claimed the "K" stood for "Kodish"—was reinforced by the Machine Gun Company of the 339th. Captain William Cherry also brought over 149 men of L Company from the Railroad Front. Using rafts, K, L, and the Machine Gun Company crossed the Emtsa below Seletskoe and gained a toehold on the south bank. But the Bolos beat them back, and artillery and machine-gun fire pinned the Yanks down for a week. They were half on the bank and half in the water and began to weaken from exposure. Their feet were so swollen they dared not remove their shoes for fear they could not get them back on. Lieutenant Charles Chappel was killed while leading a platoon, the first American officer to die in North Russia. Finally Donohue ordered his men back across the Emtsa to its north bank.

The key to Poole's entire campaign in North Russia was the force on the Dvina River, the eastern blade of the scissors. Poole thought he would have to take Kotlas on the Dvina before winter so that he could move from Kotlas to Viatka in the spring and join up with the Czechs. He had reached Bereznik, 150 miles southeast of Archangel. Kotlas was another 250 miles away. At Bereznik he had a force numbering 600-odd Royal Scots, 110 White Russian infantrymen, the company of Serbs fleshed out with thirty-six Polish and thirty-eight Lithuanian volunteers. He had one section of eighteen-pound guns from the Slavo-British Legion and some other ill-assorted guns scoured from Archangel.

Against him were a 2,000-man Bolo regiment and batteries

of field guns on the east and west banks of the river which would
have to be silenced before a movement south got fairly underway.
The Reds also had a variety of gunboats—armed river steamers
and converted pleasure craft—which outnumbered the four British gunboats and two river monitors.

The 1st Battalion of the 339th started upriver as reinforcements on September 7, transported by barges towed by old wood-
burning tugs. Pushing against the strong Dvina current made the
going slow. One Yank swore he saw the same church on three suc-
cessive mornings. This journey through the widening Dvina took
six days. Companies A, B, C, and D reached Bereznik on September 13, where they buried two of their number who had succumbed
to influenza.

Leaving A Company to guard Bereznik, B, C, and D moved
south to relieve the Royal Scots, who had advanced to Chamova.
The Yanks were in the line on the night of September 16. In the
early morning mist, a Bolshevik gunboat shoaled near the shore,
opening fire on two unsuspecting Scots who thought it an Allied
supply ship. The Americans, roused from sleep, formed a skirmish
line and began spraying the Red craft with rifle fire. The gunboat
moved out of range and, mooring by a mid-river island, shelled
the position with its heavier guns. Captain Coleman of D Company sent doughboys to collect rowboats and was preparing to load
them for an amphibious attack when a British gunboat rounded
the curve of the river. British gunners threw one shell into the Bolshevik boat, setting it afire, and the boat began lumbering upriver,
the Yanks chasing it along the shore. The Bolo soldiers along the
riverbank who witnessed the shelling retreated with the listing
Bolo gunboat. The Yanks took off after them.

After tramping for two days, the Yanks came nearly to
Seltzo, which was protected by a waist-deep swamp. Now the
Bolsheviks made a stand. Captain Coleman reached Yakolevskaya, a village wharf north of Seltzo, which offered a road leading
over the marsh. The Reds flooded it. D Company was 1,500 yards
short of its objective when the Bolo machine guns, rifles and pom-
poms, and rapid-firing artillery throwing one-inch shells made
them go underwater. Coleman ordered C Company forward. Cap-

tain Fitz Simmons got his 234 men deployed in the woods and, after dark, B Company under Captain Thomas Boyd came up with them. Advance through the swampy terrain was impossible.

Without maps, with no artillery support, the officers and men huddled together, trying as best they could to dig in without drowning. Their position outside Seltzo worsened when Russian artillery began zeroing in and gunboats desultorily fired into the darkness. The Yanks wanted to know where Lieutenant Colonel James Corbley, the Battalion CO, was and what plans he had to help them.

Corbley was in the rear for good reason. He had expected that sooner or later his men would encounter well-prepared Bolshevik defenses and he would need artillery for an assault. On this cold wet night, Corbley was helping bring up the guns of the Slavo-British Legion—a difficult task, for the horses were slipping in the mud, which reached to the wheel hubcaps. The horses strained and collapsed only to be whipped to their feet again.

In the meantime, the 1st Battalion took a heavy shelling. They had already lost several men when a patrol, sent out to reconnoiter, ran into a Bolo machine gun, which wiped it out. At dawn Captain Coleman decided to pull back without Corbley's okay. Then the toiling horses and White Russians appeared. The Russian gunnery officer knew his business and he laid down a telling barrage on the gunboats and on Seltzo. The houses in the village began to collapse, and one of the gunboats nosed down in the river. The artillery kept up the firing all day until 5:00 P.M., when Corbley ordered a charge through the swamp. Shrieking, the Yanks ran forward, luck with every one of them, for the Bolsheviks were abandoning Seltzo. The 339th rushed into the streets of the town, shortly to discover they were no better off than before. The artillery could not cross the swamp. Red gunboats shelled the village and Russian howitzers again raked the position. The *droshky* caravan could not cross the swamp and the lake with needed ammunition and food. Corbley saw that his line was over-extended. He pulled the troops back to Yakolevskaya.

The Dvina Front was a third face of war. It was characterized by fierce fighting with a variety of weapons, alternate advance and retreat and daily casualties. When the two contending forces met, they met with everything they had. The Yanks, the British, and the Canadians were always to give as good as they got, but they gave it with the growing knowledge that the Bolsheviks had more men.

Once his force moved south toward Kotlas, Poole realized Bereznik had become vulnerable. If the Bolsheviks came down the Vaga and took Bereznik, they cut Allied supply and communication lines. The Vaga, a deeper and swifter river than the Dvina, flowed into it at a forty-five-degree angle a few versts south of Bereznik. At this junction, the Vaga was a hard river to defend, for its banks were steep bluffs, sometimes rising to a height of fifty feet. Poole decided to defend the Vaga farther south. On September 16, two platoons of A Company under Captain Otto Odjard (called "The Viking" by his men) went up the Vaga in a paddleboat christened *Tolstoy*. Company A, which called itself the "Horse Marines," proceeded toward Shenkhurst, the second largest city of the province, which they took on September 17 without firing a shot.

Located on a high bluff with good soil, Shenkhurst was comparatively dry even in the wettest weather, and its three thousand citizens were prosperous anti-Bolsheviks. Knowing this, the small Bolshevik unit had fled the city at the news of the Allied advance. Shenkhurst had been a summer resort for Moscow aristocrats. It had more churches than any other town in Archangel as well as sturdy brick buildings, six schoolhouses, a monastery, a seminary, a sawmill, a shipyard, and the only adequate supply of food in North Russia. Its populace turned out *en masse* to greet the *Tolstoy,* and when A Company's remaining two platoons came upriver two days later, the small detachment of the Slavo-British Allied Legion which came with them was considerably swelled by Shenkhurst enlistments.

On September 19, Odjard and Lieutenant Harry Mead continued south along the Vaga to find the enemy. At Rodvino, a Bolshevik pom-pom scored a direct hit on the *Tolstoy,* which made a right-angle turn in midstream and headed for the Bolshe-

vik position on the shore. Anticipating the Pacific atoll invasions
of World War II, Company A clambered over the side and
splashed through the water to overrun the enemy. Odjard was able
to move from Rodvino to Ust Padenga and decided from there to
take on Puya, another of the river towns so small that General
Peyton C. March complained they couldn't be found even on
detail maps. At Puya, the Bolsheviks were ready for Odjard. While
Red defenders engaged Odjard's front, another Bolshevik detachment cut across his rear. Surrounded, Odjard audaciously ordered
a bayonet charge forward that caught the Bolsheviks off guard.
Company A took this forward position, then turned to deal with
the enemy at their backs. These Bolsheviks melted away, as they
often did. The Vaga was defended by the Bolsheviks Poole's
kindest dreams envisioned—Bolsheviks made helpless by a disciplined force, intimidated by an aggressive enemy. But deep to
the east, west, and south of the Vaga were Bolsheviks fit to popu-
late a nightmare, Bolsheviks coming north from other fronts,
toughened by other battles, ready to obey seasoned leaders. The
Soviet Government fought a war on many fronts: against a White
Army and the Czechs in Siberia, against Ataman I. A. Dutov along
the Volga in the south, against General I. Denikin along the Don,
and against General N. N. Yudenich in Poland. As the Reds stalemated these other offensives or beat them back, they transferred
troops along their interior lines to deal with emergencies elsewhere.

Company A could not hold on to what it had won. With the
approach of winter, the Vaga's water level began to lower. The
steamboats and supply tugs could not reach Rodvino and Puya.
Odjard pulled his men back to Ust Padenga, the farthest penetration thereafter of the Allied Expeditionary Force.

In his headquarters at Archangel, Poole hung a map of North
Russia which had a curve sweeping from the western shore of the
White Sea to the eastern shore, fully five hundred miles in the
round, longer by one hundred miles than the Western Front. But
the curve was manned at only five points: at Onega, on the railroad, outside of Kodish on the Emtsa, at Shenkhurst on the Vaga,

and on the Dvina. To help establish this curve, the Yanks had so far expended thirty men killed in action, another seventy-six wounded, of whom eighteen would die.

Poole and his small Allied force could not bear a stalemated war. A prolonged static period would allow the Bolsheviks time for an offensive build-up. Poole thought his best bet was to get between the enemy and his base at Plesetskaya, about 110 miles due south of Archangel on the Railroad Front. If Poole could get behind the enemy on the railroad, destroy him, he could have Plesetskaya for the asking. Once he occupied the town, he denied the Bolsheviks an important staging area for spring attacks.

He planned to accomplish this in early October with a three-pronged attack. A column would move south from Onega along the Onega River and come upon the Bolshevik rear from the west. The troops on the railroad, aided by a flanking movement, would attack directly to the front. The force on the Emtsa would take Kodish, then proceed southeast to join with the Onega column.

On October 1, Company H, commanded by Captain Howard Clark, moved upriver from Onega toward Chekuevo. Clark was reinforced by a machine-gun platoon under Lieutenant Clifford Phillips and a detachment of ninety-three Cossacks. But after passing through Chekuevo, Clark's column ran into serious trouble. Clark had a hard time moving his supplies by *droshky,* and he lost many hours having to repair cut telegraph lines. At Kaska, ten miles below Chekuevo, he ran into seven hundred well-entrenched Bolos. Clark ordered a quick assault by his 350 troops. The Bolsheviks had machine guns. This show of fight convinced the White Cossacks to desert. H Company dug in as well as it could, and Lieutenant Phillips' machine guns kept the Bolos at bay. Clark saw that his situation was untenable, and he extricated his Yanks that night, withdrawing north to Chekuevo. Poole's western column had failed.

The eastern column, which was to take Kodish and come down the road to join the western one, got under way also on October 1. To L and K companies of the 339th, Poole added a unit of British Marines and a section of Canadian artillery. L and K companies crossed the Emtsa east of Kodish at Shredmarenka and proceeded westward, coming within one thousand yards of Kodish. Two platoons of this force circled a swamp to come upon Kodish from the south. At the same time, the British Marines came over the Emtsa to the north. K and L companies attacked at dawn when the Canadians poured shells into the city. The well-planned assault drove the Bolsheviks out.

The Kodish force, however, found it could not advance. Stronger, more defensible Bolshevik positions halted the Allies only a few versts west of Kodish. Poole's eastern column had failed, too.

On the Railroad Front, M Company and two platoons from I as well as a detachment of engineers were to work their way around the Bolshevik lines to the east and blow up the tracks, stranding the Red armored trains. At the moment the tracks were blown, French and Americans were to commence a frontal assault supported by 75-millimeter cannons.

When Captain Joel Mead of M Company brought to Colonel Sutherland's attention that there were no maps to guide the circling Americans through the forest, the British officer replied airily, "You Yanks can manage somehow."

M and I companies moved through a cutting in the woods last blazed during the reign of Peter the Great. Since darkness descended early, Mead quickly discovered his men could not trace their way by notched trees and posts, most of which had rotted years before. Soon the detachment found itself in a huge swamp. Search blindly as they might from left to right, the Yanks could not find firm footing. They wallowed forward, many of them foundering and forced to abandon their equipment. The swamp finally led to a lake which could not be crossed.

Mead saw that his force could not reach its objective on time, let alone collect itself for an attack. He ordered the men to retrace their steps. Corporals Grahek and Getzloff, timbermen from northern Michigan, took the point, and slowly the two companies slogged their way back. Nearing their starting point, Mead heard the French 75s opening up on the Bolo positions.

The frontal assault by the French did remarkably well. The initial attack dislodged the Bolsheviks and the poilus moved down the tracks to Verst 458, where they crossed a railroad bridge. They dug in on the south side to prepare for the Bolo counterattack.

Savagely the Bolsheviks came at them. Major J. Brooks Nichols, now in command of the Yank 3rd Battalion, saw the French must give way. Hurriedly, he equipped Headquarters Company with some Stokes mortars and sent it forward. These clerks and typists leaped in beside the French and, though inexperienced, nevertheless started lobbing shells with some effect.

Mead and his bedraggled men were just exiting from the forest. Brooks ordered them forward. As they hastened down the tracks, Colonel Sutherland began shelling his own position. When Major Nichols finally got through, screaming at Sutherland to move his fire forward, the colonel telephoned for another quart of whiskey before correcting his coordinates. Worried that he had wiped out his command, Sutherland ordered a general withdrawal. Nichols and the French line commander, Victor Alliez, countermanded the order on the spot. The American-French contingent was holding and it held during the night. In the morning, the Bolos withdrew even farther down the tracks.

Colonel Sutherland, whose headquarters were in a blue railroad car at Verst 466, complained to Poole that the attack failed because of the inexperience of the Americans. The battle had gained a little less than three miles at the cost of two dead Americans and seven Frenchmen. More than thirty, however, had been wounded.

Simultaneous with these attacks on the Railroad Front and Kodish, British gunboats steamed up the Dvina. The 1st Battalion of the 339th kept pace on shore. This time, the Yanks got through Seltzo. Captain Thomas Boyd of B Company led the way and started his men still farther south toward Puchaga, an heroic journey, for the countryside was an avalanche of mud. The Bolos had massed at Puchaga. Boyd took some casualties in tentative probes and decided to wait until the rest of the battalion caught up before attacking.

In the morning, the doughboys of B Company awoke to discover the British gunboats were gone. They had withdrawn downriver during the night without a by-your-leave because the Dvina was beginning to freeze and the British captain dared not let the ice lock his boats in place.

Without the guns of these boats, however, Boyd was defenseless and so, for that matter, was the battalion. The Bolos knew as much. Boyd sent his wounded back with one platoon and waited with the two others to cover the retreat. When the Bolsheviks came out of the Puchaga, Boyd started back. Red artillery began to devastate the line of march. Boyd moved the men into the river and worked down, moving from one near-shore island to another, hoping the Bolos never got in front of him. B Company got back safely to Seltzo, where the battalion received orders from Poole to work still northward to Toulgas on the east bank.

In these first ten weeks, the war had been lost. By mid-October there was no chance the Allies could realize their objectives with the forces on hand. These forces were not strong enough to push to Vologda to threaten Moscow nor to advance to Kotlas to join the Czechs. The Allies were unable to recruit Russians to help augment their force. To succeed in their original plan, the Allies would have to enlarge their own forces many times over— which would, of course, make intervention more than intervention. To bring in the forces the Allies needed would be to activate a full-fledged war, the last thing the Allies wanted.

Many Allied statesmen knew the war was lost. One of them was Secretary of State Robert Lansing, who had cabled Ambassador Francis:

> No gathering of effective forces is hoped for. We shall insist to the other governments, so far as our cooperation is concerned, that all military efforts in northern Russia be given up, except the guarding of the ports themselves and as much country around them as may develop threatening conditions.[8]

Despite this definition of the American role, which was dispatched to Ambassador Francis in late September, the Yanks were fighting deep in Russia and would continue to fight deep in Russia —because Ambassador Francis sent them there.

A sixty-eight-year-old self-made millionaire, Francis had
served as mayor of St. Louis, governor of Missouri, and Secretary
of the Interior in Grover Cleveland's second administration. He
was silver-haired, handsome, garrulous, and willful. He had been
Wilson's ambassador to St. Petersburg since 1916. Other diplomats thought him a naïve rustic. He had indulged a scandalous
liaison (which the State Department ordered him to end) with
Madame Matilda de Cram, a suspected German agent.

What made him a power in Archangel was that Archangel
was the frontier and Francis was at home on it. A mayor has the
city council to check him, a governor the legislature and a cabinet
secretary the Congress or the President. But an ambassador thousands of miles from the State Department has no one and nothing
to restrain him save his own good sense and his willingness to
understand U.S. policy. Francis was determined, forceful, and
ruthless—witness that he had ended Chaplin's and Poole's intrigue
within the hour. By undoing the September coup, he had made the
Allied ambassadors—himself, Noulens, Toretta, and Lindley—
the actual government and administration of North Russia. When
the workingmen of the city went out on strike, Francis warned
them he would not tolerate civil strife at the rear or the front. "If
there is a gun to be fired," he said, "we will participate in the firing
ourselves if we have to kill Russians."

Ambassador Francis hated Bolshevism. He called it a "mon-
ster" and a "vicious incubus" and a "plague." He had witnessed the
spiriting away of the vast military stores at Archangel by the Bolsheviks and he considered this thievery.

When the Americans landed, Francis had wired Secretary
Lansing:

> I shall encourage American troops to proceed to such points
> in the interior as Kotlas, Sukhona and Vologda as at those
> places, as well as Petrograd and Moscow, are stored war
> supplies which the Soviet Government, in violation of its
> promises and agreements, transferred from Archangel.
> Furthermore I shall encourage American troops to obey
> the commands of General Poole in his effort to effect a
> junction with the Czechoslovaks and to relieve them from

the menace which surrounds them; that menace is nominally Bolsheviks but is virtually inspired and directed by Germany.[9]

Instead of interpreting policy which was set forth in Wilson's *aide-mémoire*, Francis was devising policy. Wilson's cautious and limited intervention could not afford a David R. Francis, especially a David R. Francis who had control of American forces. General Peyton March had foreseen the danger of giving an ambassador— a political and not a career diplomat—control of American forces and had drawn up orders directing Colonel George Stewart to resist Francis' intercession. But Woodrow Wilson at the behest of the State Department countermanded these.

By October 13, the Allies had not only lost the war but had failed tragically even to understand why they were in North Russia. Had they come to reopen the Eastern Front? To protect military stores? To depose Bolsheviks? They failed at all. The tragedy was it cost lives even to fail as badly as they did.

NOTES

1. Leonid I. Strakhovsky, *Intervention at Archangel*. New York: Howard Fertig, 1971, pp. 13–14.
2. E. M. Halliday, *The Ignorant Armies*. New York: Harper and Brothers, 1960, p. 24.
3. Kennan, *op. cit.,* pp. 371–76.
4. In the main, I depend on four accounts of American action in North Russia. The first three are eyewitness accounts. Joel E. Moore, Harry H. Mead, and Lewis Jahns, *The History of the American Expedition Fighting the Bolsheviki: Campaigning in North Russia, 1918–1919.* Detroit: Polar Bear Publishing Co., 1920. A Chronicler (John Cudahy), *Archangel: The American War with Russia*. Chicago: A. C. McClurg Co., 1924. Dorothea York with the cooperation of Sergeant Edward McCloskey *et al., The Romance of Company A.* Detroit, 1923. The definitive account of the expedition is the already cited *Ignorant Armies* by Halliday.
5. Details of troop movements are drawn from "Operations Summary, 339th Infantry," Stewart Papers, USMA Special Collections, West Point, New York.
6. "Report on American Red Cross Activities in North Russia," *RG 120, American Expeditionary Force, North Russian Historical File,* 23-17.3. National Archives, Washington, D. C.
7. Strakhovsky, *op. cit., Appendix III*, p. 273.
8. David R. Francis, *Russia from the American Embassy, April 1916–November 1918.* New York: Scribner's, 1921, p. 270.
9. *Ibid.,* p. 274.

CHAPTER 9

SIBERIA:

SEPTEMBER 5–NOVEMBER 11, 1918

The plan by which an Anglo-American force would move south from Archangel to hook up with the Czechs at Viatka was never a sound plan. It did not take into account the incredible distances to be traversed, the difficulties of terrain and climate to be overcome, and the intransigence and opposition of the enemy. But when Poole sent the 339th down the railroad and along the Dvina, the plan—at least on the map—still looked like a good plan. On the day the Yanks landed in Archangel, the Czech Legion attacked Volsk with numerical superiority and took it. Volsk was a Volga port north of Kazan on the east bank of the river. It was three hundred miles due south of Viatka. The capture of Volsk was the highwater mark of Czech penetration.

In early September the Czechs were fighting along a front that measured over eight hundred miles, extending from Samara to Kazan and Volsk, then looping along the foothills of the Urals to Ekaterinburg. A total of 65,709 troops, of whom sixty thousand were Czechs, held this precarious front. South of Samara the front was held by three thousand Cossacks arrayed in a dozen armies. A Cossack army sometimes constituted no more than a general on horseback and a squadron on foot.

On September 5, strongly reinforced Red Army divisions counterattacked along the Volga. Commanded by Trotsky, these divisions bypassed Volsk and fell on Kazan. These were no Red Guards or passionate Bolsheviks; these divisions were the nucleus of the Worker-Peasant Red Army which Trotsky was mustering. When Trotsky opened the counterattack against the Czechs this army numbered 331,000. By the end of 1918 it would number almost 1,000,000.[1]

The Czechs could not hold Volsk nor Kazan against this force, and they abandoned both on September 10. The Red Army pursued them. On September 13, it took Simbirsk. In seesaw battles along the Volga, the Red Army constantly established its supremacy in men and materiel. In October, nine thousand Czechs evacuated Samara when twenty-five thousand of the enemy began to flank them. There was no way to reinforce the Czechs. Resupply was a tortuous and protracted process. The Czechs had to retreat to save their lives. But every step backward represented a diminution of Allied prestige in Siberia. Every step backward by the Czechs made more futile the fight of the Anglo-American force in North Russia.

Britain's ambassador to Japan, Sir Conyngham Greene, appealed to the Emperor of Japan to send his troops to the Volga:

> To give no further help to the Czecho-Slovak forces would seem to His Majesty's government to be a grave mistake on political, economic and military grounds. They are also deeply sensible of the point of honor involved. Happily, they are informed by their military advisers that there is no technical military reason to render such decision necessary. The British government is confident the Japanese, as loyal Allies, will not withhold their hearty cooperation.[2]

The Japanese cabinet replied that grave military dangers awaited any expedition that ventured past Lake Baikal. The Japanese thought the Czechs should withdraw of their own accord to Omsk or any other place of safety rather than take the risk of further fighting. When the British also importuned the United States, Robert Lansing replied that "The ideas and purposes of the Allies in Siberia and on the Volga Front are ideas and purposes with which we have no sympathy. We do not believe them to be practical or based on sound reason or good military judgment."[3]

The British took pains not to inform the Czech leadership of the Japanese and American decisions. The Czechs fought on, believing their defeats were only temporary, to be reversed when the Allies arrived. Allied representatives conveyed not the promise of but the plans for a massive intervention. Carl Ackerman in *The New York Times* of January 1, 1919, described how French officers assigned to the legion constantly pumped up visions of an Allied-army-in-becoming. The French Military Mission to Russia officially designated the legion as "the advance guard of the Allied Army."[4]

The Czechs therefore had every right to expect relief and reinforcements. In seizing the Trans-Siberian Railway, they had obtained the right-of-way for the prosecution of the war. That fight had been a costly one. The legion was exhausted from six months of continual fighting during which they suffered nine thousand casualties. According to General Rudolph Gaida, they had lost almost one-quarter of their original force. The legionnaires were to find out in subsequent months that the number-one killer was tuberculosis, which ravaged the exhausted and the undernourished.

When the Reds retook Simbirsk in October, a growing number of Czech legionnaires began to lose heart. Their nerve had not failed, though their nerve was shaky. They knew they had been lied to and quite rightly they suspected they would be lied to again. They wanted to leave the front.

The symbol of Czech disillusion was the suicide of Colonel Josef Svec on October 28, the day Czechoslovakia became an independent republic by a bloodless revolution in Prague. An inspirational commander, Svec was about to become a general and assume duties as Gaida's executive officer. Svec had spurred his echelons on to battle after battle with the promise that help was on the way, that if the echelons would fight one more time alone, the next time they would fight beside multitudes. The crisis came when the man of conscience could not rally his men again with these promises, for he knew they were false. Svec's legionnaires, their weariness bone-deep, refused to leave their vans when he ordered an attack. In his own van, Svec gave up and put a pistol to his head.

White Russians also contributed to diminishing Czech morale. Rudolph Medek described how wealthy Russians escaped danger by bribing railway officials to attach their private coaches to eastbound echelons. While the legionnaires deployed to defend Kazan, ex-Czarist officers went to the races. The government at Omsk included a Minister of Marine not because the Whites maintained a few gunboats on the Irtysh but because thousands of former officers of the Imperial Navy had sought refuge in the city, where they lounged in the cafés and night clubs, drinking and womanizing, somehow hoping the Czechs would put their world right again. These White officers wore epaulets as big as ironing boards, and "the jingle of the Russian spur," wrote an English officer, "is as noisy as a vigorously shaken tobacco tin with a marble inside." In one of the port cities the Czechs occupied, a sign in the public park prohibited dogs and soldiers.

The day after Svec's suicide, the Czech National Council complained to the government at Omsk:

> Among others, the detachment under Krasnilikov [a Cossack general] has not been to the front since it was at Kirensk in the month of August. The detachments under Semenoff, Anenkov and Kalmikov are all at the rear. They are wanted at the front. We have a right to ask for them.[5]

The Czechs braved not only constant danger but also constant hardship. They were poorly supplied. Though the Allies shipped the legion an immense amount of equipment, food, and uniforms, much of this materiel never reached its destination. Graft and corruption among White Russians depleted Czech supplies as fast as such supplies were shipped. A British supply officer wrote that thousands of winter coats, destined for the front, went over to the Reds with White soldiers in them.

On November 10, the Czechs staged a gigantic military parade at Ekaterinburg at which the legion received its national flag and the regiments their colors. On a snow-covered field, domed mosques and cathedrals in the background, eighteen thousand Czechs drew up in formation, General Syrovy and Allied representatives taking the salute. The huge acreage was ringed by Russians in greatcoats, babushkas, and boots. At one corner of the field bulked the tragic Dom Impatiev, its bloody secret now given to the world. The British decorated three hundred officers and men of the legion. General Syrovy read aloud a telegram from King George, who promised Britain would always honor the Empire's obligation to the Czechs.

Lieutenant Gustav Becvar remembered the event:

> When the formalities of the official welcome were concluded, the men of the Middlesex Regiment marched off along the snow-up railway toward the front line. They had brought a band with them and after still more welcoming ceremonies the detachment lined up behind our armored train and the British national anthem was struck up. Hardly had the final strains of "God Save the King" died away than the enemy started vigorously to shell that part of the line from which the music had come. . . .
>
> Smartly the British detachment marched back to the station, smartly they entrained, and as smartly the engine whistled and drew them out of the danger zone on their return to Omsk, leaving the Bolsheviks in a thoroughly nasty frame of mind which they proceeded to vent on us.[6]

So on Armistice Day, Becvar's regiment plowed back into the forest seeking to bring their own artillery to bear on the canonnading Reds. The Middlesex Regiment was never near action again.

Colonel Ward explained that the bitter cold made British military operations quite impossible. Moreover his orders prohibited any engagement beyond the port of Vladivostok unless approved by the War Office.

Prominent in the line of march at Ekaterinburg was General Gaida, who was followed by a retinue clad in uniforms resplendent with gold and braid. General K. B. Sakharov, a White Russian who despised the Czechs and loathed Gaida, nevertheless brought himself to ask, "Who are these jokers?" "Jokers" is a literal translation.

"This is my escort," answered the vainglorious Gaida.

"Those are snazzy uniforms," said Sakharov. "Did you think them up yourself?"

"No," said Gaida. "I copied them from the uniforms of Nicholas' bodyguard. These men are my Caucasians."

"From the Caucasus?" asked the incredulous Sakharov.

"No," said the confident Gaida. "I put these Caucasians together here. I got the material from war booty." And with that he rode off.[7]

But Gaida rode off to battle while Sakharov entrained for safety.

NOTES

1. White, *op. cit.*, p. 83.
2. Richard H. Ullman, *Anglo-Soviet Relations, 1917–1920*. Vol. 1: *Intervention and the War*. Princeton: Princeton University Press, 1961, p. 265.
3. *Ibid.*
4. Peter Fleming, *The Fate of Admiral Kolchak*. New York: Harcourt, Brace and World, 1963, p. 83.
5. Quoted by Baerlein, *op. cit.*, from the National Council's *Official Journal*, p. 215.
6. Becvar, *op. cit.*, pp. 186–87.
7. K. B. Sakharov, *Die tschichischen Legionem in Siberien*. Berlin-Charlottenberg: Henriock-Verlay, 1930, p. 178.

CHAPTER 10

LORD OF THE EAST:

OCTOBER 1–NOVEMBER 11, 1918

The intervention at Vladivostok did not fail as cruelly as the intervention at Archangel or the Czech intervention along the Trans-Siberian Railway because it did not attempt an impossible military objective. In some respects it cannot be said to have failed at all, though it did not secure any Allied interests. The intervention at Vladivostok had neither unanimity of purpose nor unanimity of policy. The British and the French came to Vladivostok to thwart Bolshevism; the Japanese came for annexation; the Americans came to guard military stores, rescue the Czechs, and keep order until the Russians made their own decision. In the beginning, the American forces had more trouble with their Allies than they did with the Bolsheviks.

General Alfred Knox was in command of all British forces in Siberia. Knox was also invested with proconsular authority by His Majesty's government. He announced that he was in Siberia to organize the Russian Army, which would fight Bolsheviks. Therefore the British forces claimed all the supplies at Vladivostok as well as complete control of their distribution.

General Graves disagreed. He said his orders were not to give a shirt to one Russian faction lest another charge the United States with a breach of neutrality.

The French insisted that the Czech Legion was nominally

under their command. They demanded of Graves that he supply Cecek and Syrovy with funds.

Graves replied that he had no authority to supply a foreign army with American money.

The Japanese diplomatic and military personnel promised Graves they would comply with both the letter and the spirit of the agreements they had entered into with the United States.

Graves was to confess that "I was slow to come to the conclusion that the Japanese representatives still believed in and practiced 'oriental diplomacy'—which in plain language means deception."[1]

Nor was there agreed-upon policy within the American establishment. The State Department and the War Department were at loggerheads over the issue of intervention. The State Department relied upon its consuls and officials—Ernest K. Harris, consul-general at Irkutsk, John K. Caldwell, consul at Vladivostok, and Paul S. Reinsch, minister to Peking. These men had quickly understood the threat of Bolshevism to the Allied war effort. This fear guided their thinking and made the defeat of Bolshevism paramount. State Department consuls and representatives always saw one last ray of hope in any White cause and always urged one more intervening effort.

General Peyton C. March had spoken for the War Department in opposing the intervention. William Graves echoed this. When the State Department point-blank ordered Graves to alter his estimates of the situation, Graves said he would not. And when the State Department forbade him to offer any more of his estimates, Graves informed Baker and March that if the State Department wanted to rely on Ernest K. Harris, it could. He himself could not.

The two regiments that undertook the Siberian intervention —the 27th and 31st Infantry—were Regular Army regiments. The 31st Regiment was, in fact, the one army regiment that had never served on American soil. Neither of these regiments was disbanded when the intervention ended, as the 339th was disbanded.

The 31st Regiment was on duty in Luzon on December 7, 1941, and the 27th was on duty in Oahu.

The 27th was the one Siberian regiment that briefly engaged the Bolsheviks in September 1918. When the Japanese came to the rescue of the Czechs at Nikol'sk and began driving the Bolsheviks north through the Ussuri Valley, the 27th tagged along as the strategic reserve. On September 7, contingents of Japanese and American troops entered Kharbarovsk. Companies E and F of the 27th turned west to pursue the Reds along the Amur. But once he was satisfied there was no danger of the Bolsheviks coming down the Ussuri to threaten Vladivostok, Graves ordered the Yanks to break off.

Some Yanks went into garrison as far west as Chita. Many were in garrison around Vladivostok and in towns along the Ussuri as far north as Khabarovsk, all of them unaware in October of the fierce Siberian winter that awaited them.

Virtually all of Siberia is north of the United States and one half of it is above the 60th parallel. The cold constantly preoccupied the men. It is an Arctic cold, a midnight cold as one of the men put it, as deadly and merciless as the clamping paw of an enraged polar bear. The windless air increased the danger of frostbite, for the men were not aware of its incipience. A soldier could spit and see it ping from the frozen surface. A number of soldiers had fingers, toes, and in some cases feet amputated because they passed out drunk in weather 40 degrees below zero. A young American lieutenant stationed at a remote village in the Amur Valley saw wolves approaching his command post. Before he fired his .45 into the snowy night, he realized the wolves were gray-coated Russian soldiers crawling through the blizzard because their feet had frozen.

In the fall and spring, the mud along the Ussuri Valley was knee-deep. One afternoon during the changing of the guard, the new guard in Khabarovsk was actually mired while passing before the old, and the officer had to disband it on the spot so the men could extricate themselves.

There were the usual hardships for the troops and some unusual ones as well. Water was always in short supply. Along the railroad to the west, the garrisons relied on the officials of the Chinese Eastern to supply tanks. To the north of Vladivostok, the soldiers often had to melt and chlorinate snow. Throughout Siberia, execrable sanitation was the rule. There were no sewerage systems. There were rarely pavements and never storm drains for the streets, though most of the cities were electrically lighted. The garrisoning of troops therefore presented diplomatic problems for the junior officers of the command, who, in true American fashion, insisted on the absolute in sanitation. Graves himself found it an impossible task to convince a Chinese, Japanese, Italian, or Russian officer that because of American sanitary regulations he could put only 150 men in a building into which they would put from three to five hundred.

At Yevengka, a village of three hundred people on the Ussuri, Private Emanuel Reichart, now a New Rochelle, New York, surgeon, remembered that D Company of the 31st Infantry went on forced hikes three times a week despite the hazards of the weather. The men ate frozen beef and hardtack. They tired of both, so the mess sergeant bought a haunch of bear at Spassko. After one experiment, the mess sergeant went back to frozen meat and hardtack and the doughboys waited until spring to bury the bear.

But the enlisted man soldiered and, in fact, soldiered with the best of them. The Allied forces in Vladivostok staged a contest in November 1918 to determine the acme of military composure. Each of the British, Canadian, Czech, Chinese, Italian, French, Japanese, and American commands forwarded a non-com adept at soldierly bearing, ability to tear down and reassemble rifle, pack, and equipment in the quickest time, and furl his national colors. The American entry was Corporal Noble Rust, later a police chief in Trenton, Kentucky.

"Everything went fine in the contest," wrote Rust, "until the turn of the Czech soldier came. He demonstrated his rifle and pack but that boy was a crack corporal of grenadiers and proud of it. He jerked one of those potato-masher grenades off his belt and had it half taken down when about five officers grabbed him and told him they understood hand grenades fully and to hang 'er back on his belt. He came pretty near breaking up the show."[2]

The men soldiered and invented and passed along the typical Yank tall stories. The kitchen range at Vladivostok, they boasted, was ninety-two feet wide by 135 feet long and required eighteen firemen to keep it hot. There were nineteen cooks and seven hundred KPs who mashed potatoes with a pile driver and ground coffee with a 250-hp Liberty motor. They hauled garbage from the kitchen on railroad cars and the KPs went from place to place on roller skates. The mess sergeant used a motorcycle and shouted recipes through a megaphone. Steam shovels moved eggshells. Eighteen KPs with bacon rinds strapped to their feet skated on the griddle to keep it greased. The men also insisted that Lake Baikal was so deep that fishermen had to play out their line on winches. Fish hatched weighing eighteen pounds. When one was hooked and brought to the surface it came from such depths that it exploded, thus cleaning itself.

While the Yanks could accommodate the cold and the hard duty with good humor, what many of them could not accommodate were the atrocities perpetrated by the Japanese and their henchmen, the Cossacks. Many of the Yanks went through the same disbelieving disgust when they witnessed the results that later Yanks experienced in liberating the Nazi death camps. The rapacious and pathological pair, Semenov and Kalmykov, were wanton murderers. Russian women, for example, would beg the lieutenant at a small railway garrison to save their husbands or their children and when the lieutenant rushed to the Cossack camp he would find men and children already dead. Frightened refugees told stories of unutterable excesses during Cossack raids.

Colonel C. H. Morrow of the 27th Infantry heard these stories. He reasoned that his authority along the Ussuri and the Amur extended to keeping the peace and therefore dispatched investigating teams to establish the extent of Cossack raids. One of these teams—which included Vice-Consul Henry Fowler of Chita, Lieutenant E. Davis of the 27th, Japanese Lieutenants Fuji and Koda, and French officers H. Marland and Delatour de Jean —passed through Bobinka collecting evidence of a bloody rampage by one of Semenov's commanders, General S. Levitsky. Wrote Lieutenant Davis:

> A dozen corpses with their hands cut off were lying heaped in a pile half destroyed, all the bodies more or less cut up by saber wounds. The greater part bore many wounds made while living by saber blows, particularly on the face and back. All the corpses were burned. Many bore traces of having been burned while still alive. For the last observation it must be admitted that the greater part, severely wounded only, must have died of asphyxiation as an inspection of the wounds show not one was immediately fatal.

A Yank intelligence officer described the Gordyevka massacre perpetrated by Kalmykov:

> I found that the floor of the room these men were beaten in was covered with blood, and the walls in the room were all splashed with blood. The wire and loops of rope that were used around the men's necks were still hanging from the ceiling and covered with blood. I also found that some of these men had been scalded with boiling water and burned with hot irons, heated in a little stove I found in the room.

General Graves found the report incredible and ordered the officer before him. The young lieutenant begged, "General, for God's sake, never send me on another expedition like this. I came within an ace of pulling off my uniform, joining these poor people, and helping them the best I could."

Whenever Graves protested to the Japanese, General Otani invariably replied that the forces under his command had no responsibilities in controlling Cossack behavior. The outraged Graves asked Consul Harris once if he could think of a crime Ataman Kalmykov had not committed. While the general found Semenov's cruelty unspeakable, he still thought Kalmykov the more wretched. On his orders from headquarters, Semenov's men whipped and raped and burned and plundered. Kalmykov enjoyed murdering with his own hands.

The Japanese themselves were more restrained, but their idea of justice was sometimes repugnant to the Yanks. The epitome of their Siberian justice was witnessed by Lieutenant Sylvian Kindall, executive officer of Company C, 27th Infantry, who published his Siberian diary in 1945.[3]

Near Spasskoe was a small mill village with two heavy stones in the stream through which grain was daily crushed. While the Russian women lined up with their *droshkies* to await their turn, the men repaired to a vodka house, where they sang the plaintive and wild songs of the Siberian steppes. One Saturday night, a Japanese patrol broke into the house and made captive three men and two boys. They bound the hands of these Russians behind them with rice-straw thongs and marched them to a railroad car near the Japanese camp. On Sunday, they moved these five men down the track. Russians followed; American soldiers too. Kindall could determine no reason for the arrest unless the Russians had protested Japanese rudeness.

The Japanese prodded the prisoners with rifles, moving them to a wide space where five shallow graves had been scooped out. Each prisoner was forced to his knees before one of these and made to bow his head upon his chest. A cordon of Japanese sentries with fixed bayonets kept the circling Russians and the anxious Americans back.

A Japanese officer stepped forward and precisely and slowly measured the distance to one of the bowed heads with his saber. Then he tapped the saber delicately on the bowed Russian's neck. Beads of sweat poured down the Russian's face, but he bore the suspense with a calmness and a fortitude. The Japanese officer leaped into the air, bringing the blade through the neck as he landed. The body tumbled forward, blood spouting. Japanese soldiers jeered at it and prodded it so that the corpse lay straight in the grave. An orderly stepped forward with a white cloth and wiped the blood from the saber. The officer proceeded to execute the remaining four Russians. Some of the five were still trembling in their graves as Japanese soldiers started piling dirt atop them. The Japanese sentries drove the crowd from the scene and a small detachment mounted guard on the graves.

There was, however, another look and feel to Siberia, a strangeness and a newness captured by the letters and diaries of other soldiers. One of these was Captain William S. Barratt, who was amazed at the size of the compound in which he was housed in Khabarovsk. It could accommodate 100,000 troops, and it was one of many which had been strung across Siberia by the Czarist regime in anticipation of another war with Japan.

A Japanese division was stationed nearby, and Barratt learned that the soldiers had their *Yoshiwara,* or public women, with them. The whores were quartered in town near the barracks area. Each Japanese soldier was issued a monthly ration of *Yoshiwara* tickets which he could use for love, or sell, or gamble with.

Nor had Barratt ever seen such a proliferation of churches in every village and city. Not long after his arrival, Barratt betook himself to the massive church in Khabarovsk whose chimes he heard so often. "Russian churches," he wrote, "all have pear-shaped domes, ranging in number from one to five, seven or more, representing the apostles. I bought a candle when I entered which was lighted and which I held throughout the service. The congregation stands, there being no seats. The altar is ornate with other candles and the choir sings continuously. There is very little in the way of a sermon. People line the walls praying before their favorite saint's picture."[4]

Barratt counted only three automobiles in Khabarovsk, all of which belonged to Ataman Kalmykov. Colonel Morrow used a *droshky.*

The more he traveled, the more Barratt liked the Russians. He grew fond of the food and noted that everyone took a nip of vodka with every bite. He bought Russian roubles at ninety to the dollar, and a good meal cost twenty-five roubles. He ate fresh cabbage, potatoes, cucumbers, raw fish, caviar, goat cheese, egg specialties, and also drank *kvass,* which was distilled from sweetened and fermented bread crumbs.

As a courier, he met Madam Semenov in Nagasaki. She confided in him that she visited Japan once a month to deposit gold in the banks.

Barratt found the Russians vainglorious. Even the garbage collectors in Vladivostok and Khabarovsk were fancifully uniformed. For all their posturing, the Russians remembered in self-inflicting wounds to shoot themselves through a loaf of bread, which prevented the powder from infecting the mutilation.

"The rapidity with which spring comes on," Barratt noted in his last entry, "is astonishing. It comes overnight and the hills and fields are filled the next day with berries—wild berries grow everywhere—blackberries, blue berries, huckleberries, strawberries. To go berrying is to go *yagedi*."

The first American officer of the Siberian Expedition to try to comprehend something of the political and economic situation in Russia was Colonel Edwin Landon, whom Graves dispatched to the west almost as soon as the troopships berthed. Landon traveled ten thousand miles over the Chinese Eastern and Trans-Siberian railways with five junior officers, two Red Cross officials, and three American businessmen. He went as far as Ufa. Forty-five days later, Landon returned to give his commanding officer a connected account of conditions in Siberia.

Landon was prophetic in sensing the disaster that was soon to descend upon the land. The peasants, he wrote, were using up capital.[5] They had money but little to spend it on. There were great accumulations of grain, hay and horses and cattle in enormous numbers, but the Russians had gone on with another planting even though they had yet to dispose of the last two crops. There were many railroad cars but not enough locomotives. The coal mines were still in operation, but production was low. Cotton sat in the fields while soldiers lacked clothes.

There was not only economic dislocation but dislocation serious enough to herald economic collapse, chaos. Colonel Landon doubted the White Russians would save Siberia. The Russian officer was *sui generis*. "The generals and the colonels are all older men, 45 to 50. They appear to be earnest and busy. The lower ranks are very young, triflers and incompetents. The streets and cafes are filled with officers at all times of the day. There are no non-coms. No officers are ever seen working with the men, drilling them or conducting classes. The staffs of the generals are enormous. But office hours at headquarters are from 11:00 A.M. only until 2:00 P.M."

Lieutenant Benjamin Dickson was a recent West Point graduate in 1918 attached to the Engineers. He made extensive commentary on Siberia in letters to his father. He got badly sunburned in September, discovered in the hospital that Hungarian wine cost only eighty-five roubles a bottle, and sympathized with the enlisted men who complained that the Red Cross and YMCA sold them articles in Siberia that had been donated in San Francisco.

For his father's amusement, Dickson copied out a decree issued by the Free Association of Anarchists:

> The private possession of women is hereby abolished (between the ages of 17–32). The decree does not affect women with more than five children. The birth of twins will be rewarded by a bonus of 200 roubles. Women who spread venereal disease will be severely punished.[6]

Dickson was youthfully impressed by Harbin, supposedly the wickedest city in the world. He was not so blinded by its vice that he did not observe farms covering the landscape as far as the eye could see. He counted forty churches in Irkutsk, walked paved streets, ate at the one good restaurant, where he bought an omelet the size of a saddle.

The Russians, he wrote, could not understand why the *Amerikanskis* shaved so much and washed so often and why they bothered at all to brush their teeth. The Japanese, however, were as sanitary as the Yanks. Dickson described their peculiar marching step that indicated severe discipline and good training. The Czechs easily beat the Americans at soccer. But the Americans outclassed them in boxing.

Dickson met a Semenov captain with blood on his tunic from executions. From Irkutsk he wrote, "Bolshevik prisoners come through here in terrible shape. Wounds are terribly infected and typhus and dysentery are only too general. The Whites put fifty prisoners in a long boxcar, lock the doors, feed the prisoners scant bread and water, let the dead lie in the cars, strip the men half naked in a season when nights are chilly. The Russian is a strange bird. He transports these wretches for three thousand miles and then shoots them."

Only one American soldier ever came in contact with the notorious German prisoners of war. He was Russell C. Swihart, Company E, 31st Infantry, who was detailed in October 1918 to supervise a work gang made up of Germans who had been incarcerated in a foul prison camp near Vladivostok. General Graves released them for more useful activities. In this instance, Swihart was to oversee the Germans loading cord wood cut on Russian Island, which is in the middle of Golden Horn Bay. Corporal Swihart and two PFCs left the wharf at Vladivostok with their charges who numbered 150 at dawn on October 1.

The company mess, however, forgot to provide the three Yanks with a noontime meal. The Germans, who had their own cook, had stew. Hungrily Swihart and the two PFCs watched. Handsomely, the Germans invited them to share.

The launch did not reach Russian Island until well after dark. The pilot could not find the pier. Germans and Americans were soaked getting ashore and all had a long hike to the barracks. In the morning, captors and captives began loading the wood on scows. Over the next few weeks, the Germans and the three Yanks became friends. Swihart even escorted some of the prisoners to a party at the Red Cross orphanage on the island. The PFCs bought rings made from Russian coins by a skilled metalsmith who had been a POW for three years.

One morning, the power launch appeared. An American lieutenant hopped ashore with the news that an armistice had been signed in France.

"If the war is over, why can't we go home?" asked some of the Germans in good humor.

"You can't go home because we can't go home," said Swihart.[7]

The Yanks and the Germans had a long wait. Many a girl next door would be married before any of these men saw home again.

NOTES

1. *Final Report of Operations,* 21-33:6. Historical Files of the American Expeditionary Forces in Siberia, 1918–1920. National Archives, Washington, D.C.
2. Noble Rust, "The *Wolfhounds* Pick a Winner," *The American Legion Monthly,* September 1934.
3. Sylvian Kindall, *American Soldiers in Siberia.* New York: Richard R. Smith, 1945.
4. William S. Barratt, "The Diary of a Russian Wolfhound," TS Russia S56 B16. The Siberian Collection, Hoover Institution.
5. Colonel Edwin Landon, "Report on Trip Through Western Siberia and Eastern Russia." VW Russia, USL 259. The Siberian Collection, Hoover Institution.
6. Benjamin Dickson Papers. Special Collections, USMA Library.
7. Russell C. Swihart, "German Prisoners of War in Siberia." Joseph Longueven Papers, 74060-10v. The Siberian Collection, Hoover Institution.

CHAPTER 11

ARCHANGEL:

OCTOBER 14–NOVEMBER 16, 1918

October 14 was one of the hallmark dates in the history of the Allied intervention in North Russia. It was the date of the last free election in Russia's history and the day on which General Poole was recalled to England.

Of the 21,000 voters in Archangel, only 8,000 cast ballots. They returned thirty-two Socialists, twenty-six Bourgeoisie, and two Jews to the City Council.[1] This division represented a fundamental split in the North Russian constituency. Chaikovsky's Socialists wanted to press on with the reforms of the February Revolution, while the Bourgeoisie were a conservative faction who wanted the restoration of the monarchy. There was no compromising between the two of them. They would hang separately before they would hang together. This division, of course, foredoomed the White military effort.

General Poole was recalled because Ambassador Francis had informed the State Department of Poole's interference in Russian affairs. The State Department had cabled the British Foreign Office that in the event of subsequent interference, "the United States shall be compelled to consider withdrawal of American troops from British superior demands. . . ."[2] The British War Office ordered Poole home ostensibly to confer on the future of his North Russian forces.

Poole guessed what was up. He called upon Chaikovsky, whom he had tried to depose a few weeks before, and asked that beleaguered old Socialist to write London requesting his return. Chaikovsky found the visit acutely embarrassing, though he confided in Ambassador Francis that he sent the general off with a letter of thanks.

Poole was succeeded by Major General William Edmund Ironside, one of the most efficient officers ever to serve His Majesty. Thirty-seven years old, Ironside had been an officer since 1899, fighting through the Boer War, serving in India, then on to the Army Staff College before taking command in 1916 of the 99th Infantry Brigade in Flanders. General Ironside, DSO, CMG, KCB, Croix de Guerre with palms, Legion of Honor, later Baron of Archangel and Ironside, was six feet four inches tall with wavy brown hair, clear blue eyes, and weighed 240 pounds. When he came ashore at Archangel, a British sailor at the colors involuntarily exclaimed, "Lor' lomme, I wouldn't want 'im to 'it me." Ambassador Francis was so impressed that he cabled the War Department that Ironside—he called him "Ironsides"—was a direct descendant of the last Saxon king as well as an accomplished aviator. Ambassador Noulens described the new Allied commander as a *"magnifique geant."*

The War Office had chosen Ironside not only because he was a versatile and brave field commander but also because he was an excellent staff man, able to assimilate and direct the enormous administrative tasks that go into the planning of a campaign. He was also an extraordinary linguist, fluent in eleven languages, including Russian.

He brought with him an additional three thousand British troops, all of them, in B-1 category, men invalided home from the Western Front, supposedly fit only for garrison or light guard duty. Ironside in typical British fashion did not suspect that one or two or even three wounds affected a man's devotion to duty or his ability. In describing his command, he proudly noted, for example, that the long-range guns were under the command of Hilton Young, who lost an arm at Zeebruge, and that the river vessels were under T. Edwards, who had lost an eye in the trenches, and that the front-line guns were commanded by Major C. I. Graham, who had escaped from a prisoner-of-war camp despite his limp. He thought it a signal honor that the 21st Colonial Battalion had lost half its complement at Verdun.

He found the Americans, however, inexperienced. This was evident, he said, with the first company he visited. The doughboys were lined up, peering through the forest with their arms at the ready though they had cleared no fields of fire. Ironside explained this need to the company commander, suggesting that the captain post sentries while the rest of the troops fell to.

"What? Rest in this hellish bombardment?" asked the Yank. The shelling was only desultory and took place hundreds of yards away.

The Americans had a lot to learn, concluded Ironside, "but like all troops of good heart, they shook down to their task."

After a tour of the fronts, Ironside saw that the expedition was in serious straits. The Bolsheviks were far from collapse; in fact, they were growing stronger. The Reds taken captive were no longer from partisan or guerrilla bands but from military units. It was obvious to him that he could not take Plesetskaya on the railroad nor Seltzo on the Dvina. If he were to hold Archangel over the winter, which were his explicit orders—"no joke that," Sir Henry Wilson had warned—and save the expedition from becoming another Gallipoli, Ironside would have to give up the campaign to meet the Czechs and dig in where he was. Even to hold onto his present positions was a risky and tedious operation, for all transport had to be shifted from water to land and from wheels to sleighs.

The troops could not entrench in the frozen tundra, so Ironside began fortifying the curve of his front with log blockhouses constructed by the 310th Engineers. Though only in battalion strength, the 310th constructed 316 log blockhouses, stoutly reinforced with timber. Flat-roofed with gunnery ports for the machine guns and loopholes for the rifles, these redoubts studded the curve in North Russia as parapets studded the trenches on the Western Front. In front of each blockhouse, the engineers cleared a field of fire. Each blockhouse was emplaced so that it could support its neighbor. The 310th built dugouts where they could and lined them front and rear with heavy logs and constructed 273 machine-gun emplacements. The defenses proved impervious to frontal assault and artillery barrage, though a direct hit could demolish a blockhouse. During the black winter, fierce Bolshevik patrols probed, looking for weaknesses. There were none.

Ironside also simplified the problems of command. The Dvina and Railroad forces had penetrated to a distance where communication between the two was impossible. Poole had kept relays of officers in busy transit trying to keep a rein on both. Ironside resolved to put each force under a commander who was to make the tactical decisions on his own. He chose British Brigadier R. G. Finlayson for the Dvina Front. Then Ironside paid a personal visit to American headquarters to confer with Colonel Stewart.

Stewart had a lot of complaints about British management. Administering troops split into various units was difficult, their proper supply impossible. Nor could headquarters maintain proper lines of communication with the dispersed commands.

Ironside broke in here to explain that the dispersion of troops was a military and political necessity. Because it was necessary, he wanted Stewart to take over command of the Railroad Front to show the Russians that the Allies were one army. This offer, wrote Ironside,

> took him completely by surprise, for he did not answer me
> for some minutes. He then refused, saying that he would be
> exceeding his instructions if he left Archangel and though
> I pressed him hard he would not change his mind.[3]

A forty-six-year-old native of New South Wales, Australia, Stewart had enlisted in the United States Army in 1898 as a private. He won a commission in 1899 and in 1906 received the Congressional Medal of Honor for heroism in the Philippines. From the moment he arrived in Archangel, however, he was a supernumerary. He was humiliated by Poole, who stripped away two of his battalions and sent them to fronts far in the interior without so much as a murmur from the American ambassador. Poole never gave Stewart orders to convey to his regiment. Instead Poole gave orders to British colonels who transmitted them to American units.

The men of the 339th rarely saw Colonel Stewart, their commanding officer, and when they did he was preoccupied and distracted. Stewart attended the funeral of the first American casualties on the Railroad Front, but he was on his way back to Archangel before the three coffins were lowered into the ground. On another occasion he visited the Dvina, where he lost a mitten. Though he searched everywhere he couldn't find it and in anger accused one of the junior officers of having stolen it. Stewart was finally replaced on the Railroad Front by Colonel Lucas of the French 21st Colonial Battalion.

Having established command reforms in the Allied force, Ironside tried next to recruit Russian detachments without which, he was sure, the expedition would fail.

The British commander paid a call on Chaikovsky to discuss the proposition of putting several Russian regiments in the field. Chaikovsky wanted to discuss why the October Revolution had occurred. He told Ironside he personally regretted the intrusion of Lenin and Trotsky, but he was confident the Bolsheviks would soon disappear. In the meantime, Chaikovsky said Ironside could take the problem of raising a Russian force to Colonel Boris Durov, the War Minister of the Northern Provisional Government, and to Major General T. Samarin, the commander-in-chief. Ironside saw sadly that old Chaikovsky did not realize he would need force to beat the Bolsheviks. Chaikovsky "was living quietly in the past," wrote Ironside, "and was the same old plotter he had always been. Now that the chance had come to him, he had no vigorous plans to put it in effect."[4]

Samarin and Durov were not much more effective than Chaikovsky. Neither had distinguished himself in the old Imperial Army and consequently neither enjoyed prestige with the ex-Czarist officers populating Archangel. The two explained to Ironside that volunteering was alien to the Russian soul and that conscription was illegal.

Ironside snapped harshly that Russians could not mount parades in Archangel while the Allies did the fighting. If indeed the Bolsheviks were to be defeated, it was the White Russians who would have to do it. Therefore, ordered Ironside, Durov and Samarin would restore discipline at once. Anyone wearing a uniform would present himself for duty or discard the uniform. Within the week, Ironside wanted Samarin and Durov to present a model company from the Slavo-British Legion.

When Durov and Samarin published this order, the Slavo-British Legion mutinied. On October 29, the men refused to leave their barracks and parade for Ironside's inspection. When they informed their officers of this decision, the officers democratically left since they were in the minority. Colonel Durov betook himself to the barracks, where he harangued the mutineers for two hours, then asked questions. The men wanted more meat, jam and cigarettes, better living conditions, better working hours, and equal rations with the British and American troops. To the cries of "Tovarish," Durov left to confer with the Allied ambassadors. High Commissioner Lindley put a damper on Durov's solution. No power on this earth could alter the rations prescribed by the British War Office. "Characteristic but unwise," noted Ambassador Francis.

Ironside, however, immediately recalled two White Russian colonels from the Dvina who had proved steadfast under fire. With these two officers Ironside went to the mutinous barracks. In stern Russian, Ironside explained to the Slavo-British Legion that they were about to receive orders. To assure the men that any disobedience would bring upon them his own vengeance, Ironside held up his hands, which were as big and hard as canned hams, and said they were perfectly capable of tearing a man's ears from his head. The Russian colonels stepped forward and ordered the men to the parade ground. The men fell in.

The shame of the episode forced Chaikovsky to remove Samarin and Durov. Durov left for England on the last transport able to break through the gathering ice. Samarin enlisted as a private in the Archangel detachment of the French Foreign Legion. Chaikovsky thought the whole affair would have blown over if only Ironside had left the men alone.

In early November, the 21st Colonial Battalion also mutinied. The poilus, hearing the rumors of an armistice on the Western Front, refused to go forward at Verst 445 to relieve the Americans. "The war is over," they chanted when their officers tried to coerce them. Colonel Lucas hurriedly summoned some Yanks. The Yanks persuaded the poilus that they needed them at the front. The French liked the doughboys, and the 21st Colonial responded by calling off their mutiny and going forward.

The approaching armistice comforted the Allied ambassadors, who tacitly assumed it meant as well a cease-fire in North Russia. Ironside tried to convince them that indeed the campaign in North Russia was another war, but the ambassadors had a "detached attitude about military operations. In many ways," wrote Ironside, "they regarded themselves as neutrals, though their position was so close to the front line."[5]

Only two Yanks were added to the American Expeditionary Force in North Russia before the Armistice. The first was Admiral Newton A. McCulley. McCulley reported to Ambassador Francis on October 24 as the flag-ranked officer approved by the State Department to command American naval forces in North Russian waters. McCulley had served as a naval observer on the Russian side during the Russo-Japanese War and later as an aide to the American consul in St. Petersburg. He was knowledgeable about Russia and fluent in its language. In his first report to Admiral William Sims, McCulley saw clearly that Chaikovsky's government was too top-heavy and complicated for the average Russian, that it dealt only vaguely with questions important to the peasant and workingman.[6]

The other Yank was Colonel J. A. Ruggles, who was the head of the American Military Mission in Murmansk. Ruggles transferred his staff to Archangel because that was where the fighting was. Ruggles felt morale must steadily decline among the Americans because their officers could not explain the reasons for achieving certain objectives nor the overall reason for the war. Friction between the different Allied troops was also bound to take its toll. It would have made more sense, Ruggles concluded, to have put all the Yanks on the Railroad Front, all the British on the Dvina, all the French in Onega.[7]

Only one American left Archangel before the armistice. He was Ambassador David R. Francis, who boarded the *Olympia* November 8 on a stretcher carried by sailors. In ill health for some time, confined to his apartment during much of his stay in Archangel, Francis was bound for London and a healing prostate operation. Francis was the first of the Allied ambassadors to leave North Russia, and with him went the last powerful friend of Chaikovsky's government. Noulens, who succeeded Francis as the dean of the diplomatic corps, was neither as favorably disposed toward Chaikovsky nor as inclined to challenge the British military command. Francis was replaced by DeWitte Clinton Poole, who moved over from Finland as *chargé d'affairs*. But DeWitte Clinton Poole could not exert the influence of an ambassador and did not. When the *Olympia* with Francis aboard began to grind through the ice, it bore away the American presence in Russia for the next fifteen years.

When the armistice came, Archangel celebrated with great solemn masses and *Te Deums* and small but spirited parades. The remaining Allied ambassadors made extemporaneous speeches. The Armistice Day was another hallmark date in the history of the intervention. It marked the beginning of the Russian counteroffensives that were to continue throughout the winter.

Ironside had expected the attack since he took over command. He had just three weeks to prepare for it. It started on November 4 when the Bolos hit the Railroad Front. The Yanks and the poilus weathered the attack. But an Allied plane accidentally bombed the American position, taking the life of Floyd Sickle, M Company's barber, and wounding several others.

On the 5th, the Bolos flanked Kodish. Heavy artillery supported their assault. "Iron Mike" Donohue and K Company held on until November 8, when a Bolo regiment drove Yank machine gunners from their outposts and at midnight Donohue ordered his troops out. They crossed the Emtsa hearing the wild shouts of the Bolos behind them.

But the real thrust of the Bolo offensive was along the Dvina.

Four Bolo gunboats appeared off Toulgas on the east bank of the river on November 7 and began shelling the well-fortified position. Captain Thomas Boyd commanding three hundred doughboys of Company B and three hundred Royal Scots with two batteries of the Canadian Field Artillery simply ordered his command to hold on. It was obvious to the Allied command that if the Bolos took Toulgas they could lay siege to Bereznik, thus trapping the Shenkhurst force.

At dawn on November 11, a Bolshevik company that had circled through the supposedly impassable forest fell suddenly on Toulgas from the north, Boyd's rear. Bolo riflemen swept through the rude collection of huts known as Lower Toulgas and opened fire on the backs of surprised Tommies and Yanks. To the south, which was Boyd's front, one thousand Bolo infantrymen rose and began shouting as they broke into a running charge. The double assault front and rear achieved surprise that should have given the Bolos victory.

But the Bolos sweeping through Lower Toulgas in the rear stopped to search for food, to relieve themselves, or to kick in doors to flush defenders. This small respite gave the Canadian gunners in Toulgas time to wheel their cannons a full 180 degrees. Loading with shrapnel fuse 5, the Canadians began firing at point-blank range. Dismembered bodies flew into the air. Blood and brains began to soak the ground. The Bolsheviks stormed toward the batteries. But now the batteries were supported by a Yank seven-man Lewis machine-gun section that had also reversed its position. It opened a withering fire. The Canadians threw a hurricane of death. The Bolsheviks stopped and pulled back out of range. The Canadians wheeled their artillery 180 degrees again and opened the same galling fire on the Bolos attacking the front. The Canadians slowed them. The Bolsheviks dived for cover.

This pause in the attack gave Lieutenant Harry M. Dennis time to pull his thirteen-man squad from the point, a village called Upper Toulgas. Quickly Dennis led his men over a single narrow bridge that crossed a deep and treacherous stream into Toulgas. One group of riflemen took cover behind a house that belonged to a priest and another group set up across the road behind the village

Bolos Fail at Toulgas

church. Their rifle fire beat the Bolsheviks back. Yank machine guns in the blockhouses started up. Keeping the Bolos from crossing the bridge was the crux of the battle.

Captain Thomas Boyd judged that he was cut off from downriver support. Only his river flank was safe from Bolo attack. But for the moment, his command had beaten off the Reds. Boyd counted over one hundred Bolsheviks dead or writhing with wounds. Some were crawling off from the perimeter. Boyd ordered Dennis to take his men back over the bridge and clear Upper Toulgas of snipers. Dennis and his squad did a thorough job. Boyd also ordered the Canadian gunners to level Lower Toulgas to deprive the Bolsheviks in the rear of cover. They did a thorough job, bringing down everything save the one long building used as a hospital.

The Allied soldiers within the hospital had to count themselves doubly blessed. They had been awakened that morning when the Red leader, named Melochofski, broke into the aid station and ordered his two men to shoot every patient. This order was immediately countermanded by a beautiful woman wearing Bolo battle gear and carrying a weapon. She said she would kill the first Communist who raised a rifle. She was, the Yanks later learned, Melochofski's mistress. Melochofski shrugged and went out in time to catch the first burst of the Canadians' shrapnel. The Yanks were then privy to a tender love scene as he crawled back to die in her arms.

Nor was Melochofski the only Bolo commander to meet death on Armistice Day. After the battle, the Yanks found the body of a Bolshevik commander named Foukes who died with his last dispatch in his hands:

> We are in the lowest village—one steamer coming up river —perhaps reinforcements. Attack vigorously— Melochofski and Murafski are killed. If you do not attack, I cannot hold on and retreat is impossible.

Though they had saved Toulgas from surprise devastation on November 11, the Allied garrison was still endangered. On the morning of November 12, the Bolshevik gunboats put ashore two field howitzers to the south which began shelling the position with a savagery the Yanks had not experienced before. The Red gun-boats also brought their six-inchers to bear. The main target of the Bolo artillery was the blockhouse which commanded the field of fire on the narrow bridge. Inside the blockhouse was a machine-gun crew and six Yank riflemen, Sergeant Floyd Wallace their noncom. Twice Wallace left the protection of the blockhouse to clear the loopholes of debris piled against it by exploding shells. The second time he took a serious wound but got back to safety and stayed at his post.

At noon on the 12th, this blockhouse took a direct hit. The shell killed three of the Yanks within, although Wallace and two more wounded crawled out. Another wounded Yank, Private Charles Bell, stayed with the machine gun and when the Bolos rushed the bridge brought fire to bear. Another machine-gun section dashed from the priest's house to a ditch alongside the road, and the crossfire from the two caught the Bolsheviks and drove them back.

The shelling continued through the next day. The Bolsheviks made rushes for the bridge. Each time they were repulsed. In the late afternoon of the 13th, the Bolos increased their barrage, hoping to take the Toulgas stronghold by concentrated artillery fire. Though several hits decimated the Royal Scots, the bombardment did not weaken the Yanks. But the garrison was rapidly approaching defeat through hunger and fatigue. Boyd saw that the Bolo gunboats precluded Allied help from the flotilla.

Boyd and the British officers planned a counterattack to relieve the pressure. Before dawn on November 14, Lieutenant John Cudahy leading Company B and one platoon of Company D under Lieutenant John W. Derham crawled south toward the forest, where they circled around to attack the Bolo flank at daybreak. The small force overran two Bolo observation points and plunged to attack a now deserted log hut which they found was the Bolo ammunition dump. Whooping and shouting, they set it afire, and when the bullets and shells began exploding from the heat, they made their way back.

The Bolsheviks in Upper Toulgas thought this violent commotion behind them signaled Allied reinforcements and they abandoned their posts. The Yanks were able to cross the vital bridge and take up positions again in Upper Toulgas. Above the sound of battle, Boyd had heard the giant groans and thumps of the river as ice newly frozen began to lock it all into place. The Bolsheviks heard it, too, and the Bolo commander had to order his gunboats upstream before the ice trapped them. The whole of his force soon withdrew.

That afternoon the Yanks burned the little settlement of Upper Toulgas, whose presence menaced their security because it provided cover. Captain Boyd gave the inhabitants three hours to evacuate their homes, although these Russians were as dazed and bewildered by the fight as the soldiers. "It was a pitiful sight to see them turned out of their dwellings," wrote Captain Joel Moore, "where most of them had spent their whole simple, not unhappy lives, their meagre possessions scattered awry on the ground."

Soon the houses were roaring flames. The first snow floated down as old women gave themselves to paroxysms of weeping, children shrieked at the terror and the moujik men looked on in silence. The engagement had cost seven Americans their lives and another twenty-three were wounded. The Royal Scots had more than sixty casualties. The Russian church and the priest's home had been smashed by the Red artillery, and in going over these ruins Lieutenant John Cudahy found the bearded priest dead, the top of his head neatly severed by an artillery splinter. His two children, a boy and a girl, who had gone to sleep "trusting in a Providence who surely would not desert them through this malignant turmoil that had descended," were dead beside him.

When Boyd reopened communication with General Finlayson at Bereznik that evening, he was able to tell the men of Toulgas that the Great War in Europe had ended in a forest in Compiègne four days before. However, no orders came down for the 339th to quit the fight. The only message the soldiers heard came from the south, where Commissar Leon Trotsky promised to come back and drive the Allies under the ice at Archangel.

Long before Woodrow Wilson issued his *aide-mémoire*, the young American vice-consul at Archangel, Felix Cole, warned the

State Department of the consequences of a North Russia intervention. It will begin, said Cole, on a small scale and it will grow in its demands for ships, men, money, and materiel; it will come to an area not wholeheartedly pro-Ally; the intervening forces will have to feed a population numbering anywhere from 500,000 to 1,500,000; the intervention cannot depend upon active Russian support—the Russians who urge intervention, the Mensheviks, the Socialists, and the democrats lead only when they advocate peace; the intervening force must really contend against the Bolsheviks, who do indeed lead Russia and who oppose intervention. Cole concluded:

> Every foreign invasion that has penetrated Russia has been swallowed up and unless we are to invade the whole of Russia, we shall not have affected that part of Russia where the population is massed, namely the center and the south where the industrial, mining and agricultural strength of Russia lies.[8]

Everything Cole predicted had come to pass in the weeks preceding the armistice. Yet the messages that went out to the Allied troops did not promise withdrawal. They were simply the congratulatory telegrams signed by Clemenceau, King George V, and Woodrow Wilson.

The Allied world had three reasons for remaining in Archangel. The first of these was the most compelling. By Armistice Day the expedition was frozen in place. With Archangel icebound, there was no way to evacuate nearly ten thousand troops.

Winston Churchill, soon to become British Secretary of State for War, gave a second reason when he told the House of Commons that it was easy to say, " 'Clear out, evacuate and come away' here in London but quite another thing to say it on the spot face to face with the people among whom you have been living, with troops by the side of whom you have been fighting in defense of the small government created by your insistence."[9]

A third reason that kept the Allies from pulling out was that shortly the victorious nations would sit down at a peace conference to restructure the world. That restructuring needed a proper settlement of the Russian frontiers. The Allies could not draw these frontiers with the Bolsheviks in power. Perhaps the military forces intervening in Russia would depose the Bolsheviks before the impending peace conference. It was a long shot that the North Russian Expedition would succeed, but within days of the armistice a new White government appeared in Siberia. The Allies wanted to bet that somehow this government would bring down the Red regime.

NOTES

1. Strakhovsky, *op. cit.*, p. 89.
2. "Report on the Expedition to the Murman Coast." Colonel George Evans Stewart Papers. Special Collections, USMA Library, West Point, New York.
3. Field Marshall William Edmund Ironside, *Archangel: 1918–1920.* London: Constable, 1953, pp. 31–32.
4. *Ibid.,* p. 112.
5. *Ibid.,* p. 27.
6. Charles Weeks and Joseph A. Baylen, "Admiral Newton A. McCulley's Mission to Russia, 1904–1921." *Russian Review,* Vol. 33, January 1974.
7. "Report on AEF." Historical Files of the American Expeditionary Force, North Russia, 1918–1919, 32-11:4. National Archives, Washington, D.C.
8. Quoted in Kennan, *op. cit.,* pp. 363–64.
9. George Stewart, *The White Armies of Russia. A Chronicle of Counter-Revolution and Allied Intervention.* New York: Macmillan, 1933, p. 245.

CHAPTER 12

OMSK:

NOVEMBER 18, 1918

Throughout the fall there had been two governments in Siberia, both of them contending for Allied support, each, however, at odds with the other. One of these governments was at Samara, the so-called Komuch. The other was at Omsk and was known as the Siberian Provisional Government.

The Komuch was a Socialist regime. It promised to redistribute the land. It requisitioned grain, cattle, and draft animals from the prosperous peasants. It promulgated laws which made men and women equal.

The Siberian Provisional Government was conservative. It held that private property was a venerable institution. It commanded the loyalty of thousands of Czarist officers and the multitudes of the old Imperial Bureaucracy. It made divorce a crime.

Neither of these governments was able to get soldiers in the line to help the Czechs. Consequently, the military task masters from Britain and France were not particularly impressed with either. The Allied representatives wanted to see a stable government in Siberia with an army ready to fight Bolsheviks before dispensing largess. The Allied task masters forcibly made their point.

The Komuch met with representatives from the Siberian Provisional Government at Ufa, a railroad station midway between

Samara and Omsk. The conference produced an amalgam: the All-Russian Provisional Government. The government was administered by a board of commissioners from Samara and Omsk who called themselves "the Directory."* Still it was riven by Socialists and conservatives, men, as Winston Churchill later characterized them, "hampering in council, feeble to help but powerful to embarrass."

The Directory of the All-Russian Government, for example, conscripted an army of 200,000, only half of whom it could arm, and it armed those in the rear rather than those at the front. The Directory did not convince the peasant to bring his produce to the market because it could not control or even pretend to control the inflation that threatened Siberia. Nor could the Directory get factories into production because it could not coordinate the distribution of raw materials and workers.

There were many Whites who believed the quickest and surest way to establish a stable and fighting Siberian government was by military dictatorship.

On the night of November 17, Ataman Krasilnikov, a Cossack opposed to the Socialist proclamations of the Directory, moved through the streets of Omsk at the head of a mounted squadron. Outside the official government building, which had once been a technical school, he and his men dismounted and, flailing with knouts at the guards, walked into the council room of the Directory and arrested two Socialist Revolutionaries, Arkentov and Astrov. Krasilnikov bound the two men and marched them through the streets to the Cossack encampment. No one interfered with the arrest because Colonel Ward's Middlesex Regiment, which had come to Omsk a few days before, commanded the fields of fire down the main streets with machine-gun emplacements.

What the Cossacks had done was to remove those ministers of the Directory more concerned with short-term liberties than with the final defeat of the Bolsheviks. The Cossacks did not sug-

* One minister served in absentia. He was Chaikovsky, the Premier of the government at Archangel.

gest new policy. They did not have to. The Cossacks for this night at least had the support of the Middlesex Regiment.

The remaining members of the Directory, General V. B. Boldyrev and the Premier of the Siberian Provisional Government, P. V. Vologodsky, saw what was needed immediately. Summoning a council meeting, they urged the ministers to offer the civil and military powers of the All-Russian Government to Admiral Alexander Kolchak. Kolchak demurred momentarily, then accepted the appointment as Supreme Ruler.

Alexander Kolchak was forty-five years old in 1918, a veteran of the Russo-Japanese War, later a noted Arctic explorer and more recently the commander of the Black Sea fleet. When his sailors mutinied in 1917, Kolchak hurled his sword overboard rather than surrender it to the mutineers. Kerensky's Provisional Government sent him to the United States on a technical mission in July 1917, and he had reached Tokyo on his return when he learned of the October Revolution. Promptly he offered his services to the British, volunteering to fight in the trenches. "I considered it my duty as one of the representatives of the former government to fulfill my obligations to the Allies," Kolchak explained later. "Russia's obligations were my obligations. I wanted to serve as a private soldier because I knew the British would have no important naval command for me."

The Englishman to whom Kolchak addressed himself was General Alfred Knox, who saw in the admiral shining prospects. Admiral Kolchak realized Siberia needed development and was of the opinion that the British were the best developers. This as well as the fact that Kolchak was obviously a man without political passions and without a political past appealed to Knox.

At first, Knox sent Kolchak to Harbin to take charge of Dmitri Horvat's army. Kolchak, an honorable man, could not bear the cowardice and corruption of Horvat's pseudo-regime. He resigned his post in Horvat's government and was about to entrain for Mesopotamia when General Boldyrev, at Knox's insistence, asked Kolchak to come to Omsk as the War Minister of the Directory. Kolchak was recognizably England's man in the

All-Russian Provisional Government, and for that reason the French and the Czechs and the White Russians subscribed to the view that the British staged the coup in Omsk. Perhaps they did. Certainly, the British displayed a notable penchant for coups in Russia. Colonel Ward was to claim his regiment only "stabilized" conditions, but to stabilize conditions after a *coup d'état* is in effect to certify it. General Knox was in Omsk two days before the coup but was wisely out of the city on the night itself.

There is, however, a larger and more meaningful explanation for the ascension of Admiral Kolchak as dictator. Siberia had taken on a life of its own. It had become a hemisphere where hunger was beginning to swell the bodies of children, where typhus felled hundreds in the streets, where murder had become commonplace, a hemisphere in which neutrality, moderation, and wisdom had been extinguished. Such conditions have always bred dictatorships, the trust that cruel power can remedy cruel conditions. But Kolchak's dictatorship failed to ameliorate Siberia's agony.

The Kolchak dictatorship, which tried to direct the Russian civil war, was in the end remote and disoriented from the Siberia whose destiny it tried to control. Kolchak assumed command of an army whose military objective was the occupation of Moscow. But the Siberians who fought, fought for independence and autonomy. They fought for their homes and their fields, not for the streets and factories of a European city. The army would defend Siberia, but it would rarely move forward.

Though Kolchak promised to repay Imperial Russia's debts to the Allies, his All-Russian Government could not collect taxes from its people. Surely taxation is the one constant contract which must exist between a government and the governed. Kolchak's police and soldiers, his White Russian administrators, extorted money, stole it, seized upon it where they found it, but Omsk never established the systematic levy without which no government can succeed. People pay taxes only to governments they trust are perpetual.

Not from Russians came the arms and armaments, the food and medical supplies which supported the White armies—but from the Allies. Kolchak possessed neither the authority of the Imperial

autocracy nor of the Revolution—again Winston Churchill's succinct judgment. Sensing too well he had neither the love of the
people nor their respect, Kolchak often resorted to harsh measures.
The knout and the gun were the emblems of his rule. White atroc-
ity augmented Red barbarity. Suspected Bolsheviks were seized in
their homes at midnight and marched naked to the banks of a
nearby river where soldiers doused the victims with buckets of
water until frozen in a mound. In Ekaterinburg Kolchak's deputies
allowed Cossacks to massacre two thousand Jews. Wrote the
American ambassador to Japan, Rowland Morris:

> All over Siberia there is an orgy of arrest without charges;
> of execution without even the pretense of a trial; and of
> confiscation without the color of authority. Fear—panic
> fear—has seized everyone. Men suspect each other and live
> in constant terror that some spy or enemy will cry "Bolshe-
> vik" and condemn them to instant death.[1]

The more the civil war spread, the less could Kolchak make
use of his command. Socialists opposed him. Communists condemned him. His staff and supply were not only disorganized and
inefficient but criminal and corrupt. Where the German High
Command could make do with roughly one thousand staff officers
for a two-front war and the American General Staff sent only
forty-two officers with Pershing to France, Kolchak maintained
four thousand staff officers. There were Kolchak quartermaster
generals of whom the most junior had 179 subordinates. All drew
pay and allowances. Kolchak's chief-of-staff, a young colonel
named Lebedev, was duplicitous, inefficient, and sadistic. General Knox asked the Supreme Ruler why he kept him. Kolchak
replied, "I am sure he will not stab me in the back." Wrote Knox,
"Kolchak forgets the post requires more positive qualities."[2]

The Supreme Ruler could act with vigor and intelligence and
he looked the part. His military bearing had presence. There was
an immense difference between him and other ex-Czarist officers.
And there is no question that Kolchak wanted to regenerate
Russia, to make it great again. He was determined and stubborn.
Knox said that Kolchak possessed two characteristics uncommon

in a Russian—a quick temper which inspired useful awe among subordinates and a disinclination to talk for talk's sake. Rudolph Gaida said the admiral lived with a fever of 101 degrees. That quick temper neurotically disabled Kolchak in perilous moments.

When the Czech Legion, for example, deplored his assumption of dictatorial power, Kolchak ordered them from the front, a glorious gesture but in essence suicidal. "I was struck," wrote one of Knox's subordinates, "by the harsh and ungrateful manner in which Kolchak spoke of the Czechoslovaks. He said they were no good and the sooner they cleared out the better." Knox himself was astute. He weighed the alternatives: pressure Kolchak to retain the Czechs or let the Supreme Ruler have his way. In the long run, thought Knox, if Kolchak were a real wolf, then the English would have to let him bare his fangs on this occasion. Kolchak's unreasoning antipathy toward the Czechs was one of the first of his serious mistakes and, in the end, the most fateful.

NOTES

1. Quoted by White, *op. cit.,* p. 119.
2. Quoted by Fleming, *op. cit.,* p. 95.

CHAPTER 13

SIBERIA:

NOVEMBER 21–DECEMBER 25, 1918

On November 21, the Czech National Council in Vladivostok described Kolchak as a reactionary and censured his coup. General Syrovy remarked, "This change of government has killed our soldiers. They say for four years they have been fighting for democracy and now that a dictatorship rules at Omsk they are no longer fighting for democracy."[1]

Indeed the Czechs had a lot to say about the causes for which they were now asked to risk their lives. They were no longer stateless men. The Austro-Hungarian Empire had collapsed. A Czechoslovak government ruled in Prague. The legionnaires had won the great prize for which they fought for so long. Now they were worried about their homes and families. They longed for safety. They were homesick, weary of battle. The legion had seances at which legionnaires asked the old warrior Zizka, "How much longer?" Their morale was low because they realized the Allies had been simply "swinging" them with the promises of relief. "Swinging," explained Gustav Becvar, "was the catch phrase of the legion. It meant pulling the leg of an innocent victim. We even published a monthly magazine titled *Swings*."

They said they would not fight for Kolchak.

"I shall have to disarm the Czech forcibly," threatened the neurasthenic Kolchak when he learned of the council's censure and the legionnaires' criticism. "I shall place myself at the head of the troops and blood shall flow." Cooler heads persuaded the Supreme Ruler that there were other ways to deal with criticism and contumacy.

Czech aspirations rose when Milan R. Stefanik arrived in Siberia at the end of November. Stefanik, who had enlisted in the French Army as a poilu in 1914, had risen from the ranks to become the commanding general of the Czech National Council. Now he was the Minister of War in Masaryk's first cabinet. Supposedly he had come to Russia to expedite the Czech evacuation.

"Brothers," said Stefanik to the legion, "the date of your return depends upon our unity and faith. We must finish with dignity our task as unselfish Slavs and honest Allies. We will abandon the Volga Front. But the moral front we cannot forsake. The Allies need us."[2]

They were not going home after all. Governments make policies, not armies. There can be no quarrel with Stefanik's decision. Would the British Government allow an army corps in India to disregard the wishes of London? he asked Syrovy's staff. The Czech Legion was going to stay on. The legionnaires cursed Stefanik. They said they didn't like his blue French uniform. They didn't like what he was doing to the legion. In the fighting since Chelyabinsk, the legion had transformed itself into a band of brothers. It had evolved its own discipline, which was administered at the company level; devised its own commendations and medals; and written its own military code. But Stefanik disbanded the legion's soldiers' congresses and its soldiers' committees. He ordered that troops no longer elect their own officers. He abolished field promotions. And he organized a war cabinet of his own appointees to sit in Omsk. The one order the legionnaires found tolerable was that they withdraw from the fighting front and mount guard on the Trans-Siberian Railway from Chelyabinsk and Ekaterinburg to Irkutsk. Then Stefanik went home.

It took the legion four months to transfer their 250 troop trains from the Urals to their designated stations, a movement hampered and made difficult by heavy snows and subzero temperatures. The legionnaires had to watch each other's ears and noses for frostbite. To repair locomotives or rails, they had to work with flashlights under heavy tarpaulins, relieving each other every thirty minutes. To protect their vans from the cold, the legionnaires built a second interior wall and filled the space between the two walls with ashes shoveled from their saucepan stoves.

Keeping the line running across the steppes was far from police duty. Soon enough the Czechs found themselves in the fight again. Partisan detachments attacked the railway. The Bolsheviks in central Siberia had become dangerous and daring guerrilla fighters who raided key points along the line, wiping out lonely outposts, terrorizing White communities. No sooner did the Czechs disperse a band in one place than partisans banded together in another. To keep the railway open, the Czechs had to mount expeditions north and south, sometimes deep into the *taiga*. Now they waged the never-ending tedious fighting not because of inspirational promises from the Allies nor to secure a lever for independence but because their government ordered them to. Ironically, their efficient antipartisan operations helped secure the Kolchak regime.

The discipline of the legion, the devotion of the legionnaires to one another, their skilled industrial background produced a military unit of superior organization quite unlike the regiments and divisions of the European war.

Each echelon, for example, carried along an official artist. The sides of the Czech van were decorated with bucolic or religious themes and the handiwork was preserved by official photographers. Each echelon had its own post office, its own doctor (though he may not have attended medical school), and its own historian, who contributed to the Historical Branch of the Czech General Staff.

The legion also published a newspaper, *Ceskolovensky Denik,* edited by Rudolph Medek, assisted by Pavel Halecek, both of whom roamed east and west along the tracks, digging out the news. Months before the legionnaires had onloaded the typesetting machine. Publication was continuous enough to wear out the original die casts. Still the Czechs got hold of another rack of type. A Czech-language daily in Pittsburgh donated old molds to the legion. The type went across the United States, the Pacific, to Tokyo, where legionnaires moved the racks to Vladivostok. A special train brought the type to Medek's mobile city room.

The type had priority in shipment because the Czechs were Kolchak's minters, printing money on rice paper imported from Japan. The Bolsheviks flooded Siberia with counterfeit money. Only the exquisite work of the Czech mint kept the real recognizable from the queer.

The Czechs also established a bank, a flourishing affair, founded and managed by Captain Josef Sip, an actuary from Prague. Though the legionnaires were so meagerly paid that Gaida complained they could not purchase a pack of cigarettes after a month of fighting, they were still paid in hard currency.* Money for the legion's payroll came from France, deposited in francs in Tokyo to be converted into roubles. It was Sip's idea, unanimously approved by the congress, to use the francs to purchase copper, rubber, cotton, and other valuable commodities that could be sold dearly in Czechoslovakia once the legion was evacuated. The anti-Czech Russian general Sakharov insisted the legionnaires confiscated over twenty thousand freight cars for their holdings, which was one for every two legionnaires.

The specter of starvation had come to Siberia, accompanied by the specters of lawlessness and anarchy. Only where the Czechs held the line was there pity and help and order. The commanding officer of every Czech echelon tried to adjudicate the disputes that distract people no matter what their time and condition. A bearded Jew came to Lieutenant P. Spala with the complaint that a Magyar prisoner of war had seduced his wife. Spala explained that he couldn't shoot a Hungarian prisoner of war because a married woman loved him. The best he could do was transfer the Magyar

---

* A soldiers' committee reasoned that democracy "permitted a pay scale of four to one" in the rates for officers and enlisted men. Lieutenants, therefore, made four times as much as privates and generals made four times as much as lieutenants.

to a prison camp at Samara, which he did. But the woman followed him.

The echelons took on refugees. Nuns, priests, young students, and nursing mothers found shelter in the vans. The legionnaires stretched a blanket across the rear of the interior behind which the women slept and bathed and in their turn cooked and sewed for the legionnaires. The soldiers' committees had voted to prohibit marriages because there was no room. But men make room for this. There were Czech children born during the Anabasis. One thousand Czechs, in fact, did marry Russian women.

There was only one priest among the legionnaires, Father Chaidin, and he would often solemnize a dozen marriages at once. He always warned the Czech Romeos that the kitchen ovens in Russia and back home were radically different and that Russian girls might never learn to cook in Bohemia to a man's eternal satisfaction.

When the legion withdrew from the Urals in November 1918, General Milo Dietrichs and Colonel Bruno Voitsekhovskii joined Kolchak's White Russian Army. Though both were of Czech descent, they were native-born Russians and, as anti-Bolsheviks, felt strongly they belonged in the forces of the All-Russian Government.

Rudolph Gaida joined them by obtaining a leave of absence from Stefanik. Gaida's enlistment, though not common, was neither anomalous nor atypical. Many other legionnaires, both enlisted men and officers, volunteered to fight in Kolchak's northern army. At the end of his novel *Anabase,* Rudolph Medek's protagonist, Jiri Skala, dives from the ship which would bear him home to swim back to Vladivostok and fight on with the tattered remnants of the anti-Bolshevik forces.

Kolchak put together three small armies which held a front roughly five hundred miles long which extended from the Volga south of Samara to the Urals north of Ekaterinburg. The army in the south was commanded by Ataman A. I. Dutov. It was to proceed in a western offensive south of Samara. It was to cross the

Volga and invade Transcaspia and eventually hook up with the armies commanded by White generals Denikin and Wrangle which were fighting along the Don.

Kolchak's central army, commanded by General M. V. Khanzin, was to retake Samara and Simbirsk, then move in a straight line toward Moscow.

Kolchak's northern army, commanded now by Gaida, was to move from Ekaterinburg to Perm, then from Perm to Viatka, where it would join the Archangel force fighting its way up the Dvina.

The capture of Perm was Kolchak's most significant victory. Gaida, who planned the campaign, took the city on Christmas Day, 1918. He took 31,000 prisoners and a vast quantity of armaments and field guns. Two days after Christmas, Gaida moved out toward Viatka. He knew the chance to gain a great victory was now, in the intense cold, when the enemy did not expect fighting. But he failed. He quickly discovered commanding Russians was far different than commanding Czechs. A thoroughly inefficient supply system and a totally disorganized rear warned him to pull up short. Gaida stopped at Glazov.

He was supposed to command an army of 120,000 men. He knew that he had at best only 60,000. These 60,000 were drawing supplies from Omsk for 270,000. Gaida knew his staff was implicated in disastrous fraud. He tore the epaulets off Czarist officers. He punched corrupt colonels. He threw one Kolchak general down the stairs. He documented charges for Kolchak. Kolchak ignored these depositions.

Gaida came to Omsk to argue with Kolchak that the three armies were hopelessly overextended. He begged Kolchak to desist, to break off the offensive, which could not succeed, and concentrate instead on a defensive line behind which the Whites could ward off the Red counterattacks in the spring. There was, Gaida pointed out, no coordination between the three Kolchak armies let alone coordination between them and the armies they were to join. But Kolchak repeated the conviction that to gain recognition from the Allies he needed a great victory against the Reds. The Czar had persevered in his folly by insisting the war had to go on. Kolchak persevered in his folly by insisting that only by the capture of Moscow could he defeat Bolshevism.

Gaida said there wasn't a chance they could take Viatka. Kolchak ordered him back. Gaida knew he could not drive demoralized men to victories.

NOTES

1. Stewart, *op. cit.,* p. 245.
2. Quoted by Baerlein, *op. cit.,* p. 198.

CHAPTER 14

ARCHANGEL:

DECEMBER 29, 1918–JANUARY 27, 1919

As president of the Provisional Government of the Northern Region, Chaikovsky had every reason to dispute the assumption that Kolchak ruled all of Russia. He could point out that certainly Kolchak did not rule North Russia. Nor industrial Russia. Nor South Russia. Moreover, Chaikovsky had been a member in absentia of the Directory at Omsk. He had not given his assent to Kolchak's ascension. But in *pourparlers* with High Commissioner Lindley and Ambassador Noulens, Chaikovsky was blackmailed into recognizing Kolchak. The ambassadors told him if he did not extend recognition to Kolchak, the Allies would refuse to go on with some much needed financing.

Chaikovsky had only recently succeeded in arranging a loan through a complicated arrangement with the Bank of England. For collateral, he had to put up the timber resources of his province. The English had then issued new rouble notes which had been printed in London and were countersigned by Mr. Thomas Harvey of the British Treasury. Unfortunately, when the money reached Archangel, Chaikovsky discovered the notes bore the imperial crown, which made them unacceptable. The crowns had to be blocked out and, as Ambassador Noulens wryly remarked, the effigy of Mrs. Harvey substituted for the Empress Catherine.

In addition, the governments of the United States, Britain,

and France had underwritten $15 million to supply the popula-
tion of Archangel and Murmansk with food. These governments
were about to extend the same help to Kolchak and would not tolerate two White factions opposed to each other. Chaikovsky
grasped the truth that Kolchak's regime diminished the *diplomatic*
importance of Archangel. But he made the best of a bad bargain
and in mid-December recognized the hegemony of the Kolchak
regime in Omsk.

For the Allies, this represented a tidying up of political loose
ends. But in actuality, considering the vast distances between
Omsk and Archangel, the differing conditions under which Russians in each struggled to survive, the decision to make one the
authority for the other and all others was as perilous and imprac-
ticable as trying to make Zaire the authority for all Africa, from
Algiers to Capetown.

As the British were tidying up political loose ends, so they
expected a tidying up of military loose ends. The War Office told
Ironside to expect a wing of the Czech Legion under Gaida coming through Perm to Viatka to Kotlas to Archangel. This was
almost a terrifying prospect to Ironside. He was aware that he
could not feed and house another army along with his own unless
he extended his positions. He drew up the plans for a campaign,
hoping against hope he would not have to implement the plans,
but as Gaida closed on Perm, Ironside issued his orders.

No matter what the attack in North Russia, it had to be of
short duration and have shelter as one of its ultimate objectives.
Ironside saw that the way to consolidate, strengthen, and widen his
perimeter in North Russia was to deprive the Bolsheviks of the
shelter they now had, to drive them from it, make them fall back
long distances, and use their abandoned positions for additional
Allied troops.

To achieve this, Ironside planned a number of limited offensives. The first of these was staged in the northwest, along the
Pinega River, which guarded Archangel's rear. If the Bolsheviks
intended to ambush the Czechs, this was where they would stage

their attack. Ironside sent a small American force with a larger detachment of White Russians along the Pinega River to take Karpogora. Karpogora had once been the principal seaport of North Russia when trading vessels did not exceed the size of a ketch. It still had good port facilities, which could serve an organized Red force.

Captain William Conway had a full complement of G Company of the 339th at the village of Pinega and 350 White volunteers. More correctly, he had 350 White volunteers when he organized them in October; he was soon to discover that every time he sent out a reconnaissance patrol under the command of a junior officer or noncom only the American officer or noncom came back. However, Conway detailed 1st Lieutenant William Higgins and thirty-five Yanks of three machine-gun sections to accompany 210 Russians along the Pinega, take Karpogora, garrison it with Whites, and return. Higgins set off on November 15 and four days later, thirty miles away, led his detachment safely into Kurga. But from Kurga onward, misadventure plagued him.

Near Karpogora, the doughboys beat off a feeble Bolshevik attack and on December 5 Higgins came into the port minus several dozen of his Russians, who had deserted, and five of the Yanks, who had been wounded. He told the villagers of Karpogora that the Provisional Government of the North and the Allies had come to protect them. After establishing the Whites in secure positions, Higgins started back. He had not gone ten miles when the White volunteers, having deserted Karpogora, caught up with him. In his report, Higgins wrote:

> These people are fighting for their own homes, families and their lives and really everything they have, and I never saw a bigger bunch of cowards. They won't turn over a hand to help themselves. They expect us to do it all. After we have done it and when the volunteers do get to their own homes, they leave us and are perfectly satisfied. A great many of them are only boys from 15 to 16 years old.[1]

By December 27, the Yanks were skirmishing with the Bolos outside Pinega.

The second of Ironside's limited offensives was aimed at the occupation of Emtsa, a large village midway between Verst 445 on the Railroad Front and Plesetskaya. With Emtsa and Shenkhurst in Allied hands, Ironside could shelter a heavy concentration of men.

To take Emtsa, Ironside planned a three-pronged attack. He would bring a force down the Onega River to attack the Bolshevik western flank; from the east he would bring over another force to retake Kodish and move through Avda and Kochmas to attack Emtsa on the eastern flank; and he would push straight ahead on the Railroad Front.

Ironside thought he had a good chance of success in this offensive. The Bolsheviks were exhausted and fought out. He also had the element of surprise. The Allied troops were ready and capable and Ironside reinforced them by bringing down the King's Liverpool Regiment, which had been garrisoned on Ekonomie Island in the White Sea. He would have numerical superiority.

Each of these assumptions was mistaken. Ironside was attempting an offensive which Poole had attempted. It had failed then and had failed because of problems of terrain and timing which the Allied force had far from overcome. It had also failed because the Bolos proved flexible in containing it. It would fail again because the Bolsheviks were neither exhausted nor were their soldiers in short supply.

Not even the Allied unit commanders knew their orders until December 29 when Ironside ordered them to bring up their reserves in absolute stealth. The offensive got under way when Lieutenant Edmund Collins and three platoons of G Company along with a detachment of Russian volunteers moved up the Onega River. Collins' force made it past Chekuevo and as far as Turchasova, where it was to turn east and come upon Emtsa. Here, however, Collins encountered no lonely outpost but a garrison defended in depth. On December 30 and 31, Collins led his men against Turchasova. The Bolos repulsed each attack. His force had taken serious casualties and the survivors were so fatigued that Collins knew even if somehow his men took Turchasova they would be unable to continue. Late on December 31, Collins got orders to withdraw. It was obvious that the Bolsheviks were along the Onega in force and that force was far from fought out.

Similar misadventures befell the Allies on the Railroad Front. The key here was a flanking attack to be launched on the Bolo rear at Emtsa at the moment the Yanks jumped the logs at Verst 445. The flanking column, known as the "Snowshoe Detachment," was made up of Russians who had enlisted in the French Foreign Legion. They were under the command of Captain Henri Barbeteau, an experienced woodsman from Canada who had led many commercial and scientific expeditions in the American Northwest. Barbeteau had purchased seven thousand pairs of snowshoes for the expedition, among them several hundred of his own design which would enable men to track through light and fluffy snow, precisely the snow that made the going so hard in the Archangel province.

Gliding through the forests on these new shoes, this Russian detachment was to infiltrate the rear of the Bolo position like a dirk between the ribs. Their devastation would signal the main attack on the railway. Unfortunately, when the men of the Snowshoe Detachment drew their issue, they discovered the specially designed Barbeteau shoe had been sent to Murmansk. They would have to rely on the ordnance issue, which was made for tracking through wet or frozen snow.

The men of the Snowshoe Detachment found soon enough that the ordnance hoop went through the fluffy snow to the ground, which made movement fatiguing after one mile of tracking and torturous after two. In addition to their weapons, they were man-hauling sleds with supplies and sleeping bags. When the detachment reached its turning point five miles west of Verst 445, Barbeteau sent back the message that he could not continue. He needed an additional forty-eight hours to reach his destination and attack.

Learning of the delay, Colonel Lucas postponed his attack. He pulled back the six companies of Yanks on December 30 and told them the jump-off time was December 31.

The Bolsheviks promptly canceled whatever additional preparation Lucas wanted to make by opening up an accurate artillery barrage at noon on the 30th. The Bolshevik cannon destroyed the station house and moved north to cut all communications between the forward post at Verst 445 and the staging area at Verst 455. The barrage also cut the rail line at four different points. In twelve hours of bombarding, the Bolsheviks poured in 1,500 shells, which persuaded Lucas to cancel the attack. He recalled the Snowshoe Detachment.

Despite Ironside's precautions, the Bolos were forewarned. Before every battle, a small number of White Russians always defected and hurried over to the Red lines with the latest information on Allied operations. Any delay at all in an Allied operation provided the Reds with the time to blunt Allied attacks.

Hearing of the cancellation, Ironside rushed to the Railroad Front. He was dismayed to discover that Colonel Lucas had no coordinated plans with the force of Yanks moving on Kodish, a direct violation of orders.

The attack on Kodish was spearheaded by Companies K and E of the 339th accompanied by a machine-gun platoon. These Yanks crossed the frozen Emtsa on December 30 and with Canadian artillery in support attacked Kodish on its eastern perimeter. Captain Mike Donohue directed the fighting.

In weather twenty degrees below, Lieutenant John Baker led three platoons to the outskirts of Kodish and signaled for the mortars to lay in shells. Seven Stokes mortars hurled 1,000 shells in fifteen minutes. The Canadian cannons began their barrage. The Yanks moved forward from tree to tree, falling prone to fire, then up to dash for advance cover. Lieutenant Baker, however, took a Bolo bullet. The infantry charge halted. Some began dropping back. First Lieutenant Emil Tessin, directing the fire of the mortars fifty yards to the rear, saw the confusion. Ordering a sergeant to assume command, Tessin ran to the skirmish line, moved up and down its length, encouraging the men, promising them that extra ammunition was coming up.

It was hard going. Kodish was defended by two thousand Bolsheviks. But the infantry cleared Bolo machine guns from the outermost defenses. The 339th kept pushing. As dark morning edged toward gray noon, it became obvious to Donohue that the flank support he expected was not forthcoming. It was also obvious to him that the Bolsheviks were giving him the town, although they made the Yanks pay for every step.

By late afternoon, Donohue's men were in Kodish. Three platoons started down the Avda-Kochmas Road. The Bolos had given the Yanks the town so that they could prepare their eastern defenses of Avda. Well-emplaced Bolo machine guns halted the advance and drove the Yanks under the snow or into the dense woods for cover. Bolo artillery began shelling Kodish. Donohue painfully and agonizingly realized there were to be no diversionary attacks on the Bolshevik rear.

These attacks were to have come from the north and south. The Archangel Regiment composed of White Russians was to stay north of the Emtsa River until it was past Kodish, then cross over and take up positions to harry the Bolo retreat. But when a guerrilla force attacked the regiment on the morning of the 30th, the Russians informed their commander they did not want to fight and without orders began a retreat.

To the south, a machine-gun company of the King's Liverpool Regiment was also to bypass Kodish and help secure the Kochmas-Avda Road to cut off Red reinforcements. But this company withdrew when their colonel failed to show up to command the operation.

American intelligence later reported that agitators within the Archangel Regiment kept it in a tumult. As for the British force, as Ironside grimly put it, "The colonel in question had succumbed to the festivities of the season."

The double failure north and south had created a salient into which the Yanks in the center rushed. The Bolsheviks had the opportunity of directing fire on Donohue from three sides. Apprised of this at the Railroad Front, Ironside ordered Donohue to pull back into Kodish. Ironside himself began speeding from the Railroad Front to Kodish by pony sleigh accompanied only by his batman, a Canadian of Russian extraction named Piskoff.

It took Ironside several hours to make the trip. The sleigh drivers had to halt every half hour to break off the long icicles that formed on the ponies' noses. Then they would get going again with the soft "Per-rrooo, per-rrooo," which is the Russian

"Giddyap." At every halt, Ironside thought he saw stalking Bolos and he swiveled left and right, his pistol cocked. But the sounds which startled him, he realized, came from birds leaving white-laden trees which cascaded snow.

At Kodish, Ironside relieved the drunken colonel. He turned over command of the Liverpool Regiment to its executive officer, a lieutenant colonel by brevet, in actuality a subaltern. He settled down in a blockhouse with Donohue to spend New Year's Eve. There was a sudden Bolshevik challenge, he wrote,

> and looking out of the embrasure in the blockhouse I saw some faint figures moving in front of us as if they were float- ing in air above the snow. Several of our machine guns opened fire and a Stokes mortar left off half a dozen rounds. After five minutes there was complete silence. The captain decided he would go out and see what happened, and when he left with his orderly I followed with Piskoff at my heels. Some hundred yards beyond the wire we came across six bodies lying in the snow. They were dressed in long white smocks and were on short skis, which were bound with rough skins to keep them from slipping. All were quite dead and frozen stiff in the intense cold. Two had been wounded in the legs and had died of exhaustion and loss of blood. They must have died within minutes of being hit.[2]

Ironside left Kodish for the Dvina Front the next day. He ordered Donohue to hold the position, but on that afternoon of January 2, the Bolo artillery heated to a point where holding Kodish was impossible and the two companies of the 339th moved three versts north to the banks of the river. They held on, as Lieu- tenant John Commons put it, because they were proud that they were once "a sidekicker and a buddy to some of those fine fellows of the various units who unselfishly and gladly gave the last that a man has to give for any cause at all."[3]

Donohue's grip near Kodish was tenuous at best. Even Iron Mike realized that to try to hold the town was to perish. Geo- graphically, Kodish was a catch basin. It was hedged south, west, and east by hills on which the Bolos had brought artillery. The gunners simply had to drop shells into the basin without worrying about coordinates. Bolo artillery outdistanced the Canadians. Donohue told the Yanks they had to let go. He burned what was left of Kodish and after this no one would ever have to fight for it again.

In late December, Chaikovsky received a telegram from Prince Georgi Lvov in Paris urging him to leave Archangel to take a seat at the coming peace conference. Chaikovsky would be able to represent himself not only as a delegate of Kerensky's old Provisional Government but also as a delegate representing Russia's millions of anti-Bolsheviks. Chaikovsky accepted. He was tired of his role as a figurehead. His northern government had been superseded by Kolchak's Siberian dictatorship and his political programs in Archangel made little headway against the British High Command. To succeed himself, Chaikovsky appointed Lieutenant General Eugene Miller as Governor-General and Minister of Foreign Affairs.

Eugene Miller, whose family was of Baltic extraction, had served in the Imperial Army for thirty years. During the war, he was chief-of-staff of the 5th Army and later commander of the 26th Army Corps. In 1917, Miller had been posted to Italy as head of the Russian Military Mission. He was fifty-one years old when Chaikovsky recalled him, a convinced monarchist and a brave and resourceful fighting man. In effect, Chaikovsky was investing a chancellor for the Provisional Government of the Northern Region, making Miller in Archangel what Kolchak was in Siberia.

Miller arrived from Stockholm via Murmansk on January 13. Twelve days later, after a solemn service in the cathedral, Chaikovsky left Archangel aboard an ice-breaker. The old Socialist was never to take a seat at the Paris Peace Conference. Nor was he ever to see Russia again.

After the failure of the December–January campaign, Ironside's consuming concern was how to hold on to what he had. He knew he was overextended in Shenkhurst. He decided to see for himself how vulnerable the position was. He left Archangel with his batman Piskoff and arrived by sled at Bereznik on January 14.

He went over the situation with the commanding officer of the Dvina and Vaga Fronts, Colonel C. Sharman of the Canadian Artillery (who had relieved Finlayson). If the Reds came on against Shenkhurst, Sharman was to do everything in his power to extricate the troops along the river. But he was on no account to relieve a besieged Shenkhurst.

Ironside proceeded on to Shenkhurst. Its commander, Colonel C. A. L. Graham, thought his defenses strong enough to beat off any limited offensives the Reds mounted. Ironside was not sure the Reds were about to launch *limited* offensives. The Bolos might feel they were strong enough to annihilate the Allies.

The trip deepened his concern because he and Piskoff found the Russian villagers along the way remote and cautious. As he started back for Archangel, Ironside turned in the darkness to watch the flashes of the big guns. They seemed to increase in their intensity and to become more menacing.

Three outposts to the south protected Shenkhurst. The nearest to Shenkhurst was Visorka Gora, then Ust Padenga and the farthest Nijni Gora. They were like three eggs rolled from a basket, each coming to a stop a little beyond the other, all on the west bank of the Vaga.

Company A under Captain Odjard was deployed in Visorka Gora. A company of Cossacks with two pieces of field artillery were in Ust Padenga. Twenty-three riflemen from A Company along with twenty engineers from the 310th were in Nijni Gora. Twenty-two more infantrymen under Lieutenant Harry Mead held the knoll just outside the village. Mead was therefore the first to know of the great Bolo offensive.

On the morning of January 19, Mead was awakened by heavy shelling. Over the crust of snow thirty inches deep, Mead saw a long skirmish line of gray-coated Bolsheviks emerge from the forest two thousand yards away. The Bolos were advancing with fixed bayonets. Mead rang Captain Odjard and told him the Bolos meant business. Odjard told him to delay the attackers as long as he could before pulling out.

Mead got his small unit in a line and waited for the Bolos to draw closer for more telling fire. From immediately below the

Yanks, suddenly materializing like ghosts on Walpurgis night, white-clad Bolshevik infantrymen leaped from hiding places in the snow to charge upon Mead's startled platoon.

One of the Yank machine guns raked the attackers and drove them back into the ravine. But the Bolos took a toll. Many of them bypassed the point itself and charged into Nijni Gora, where they killed unsuspecting Yanks who were rousing themselves from sleep.

Mead signaled his men to get out. They dashed down the slope, darting to the right of the main street, which they discovered was covered by a Bolo machine gun. Yanks struggled through the back streets, hard movement because the snow reached their waists. Dashing from one peasant hut to another, they paused to gasp for breath in the rarefied air. They kept on until they came to the open space between Nijni Gora and Ust Padenga. Here there was no cover and no path, nor was there helping fire, for the Cossacks had deserted at the first sound of battle. The temperature was forty-five degrees below. When a man was wounded his blood froze before he hit the ground. Of the forty-five men Mead had in Nijni Gora that morning, he counted only seven when the last of them made it to Ust Padenga. They ran through the streets of the now deserted village, keeping near the river, heading toward Visorka Gora.

Behind them, the Reds momentarily halted. The Bolo commander counted the price he paid for Nijni Gora. Crumpled gray blotted the snow, and the wind whipped the white smocks of the dead snow troopers. During this respite, Lieutenant Hugh McPhail in Visorka Gora asked for volunteers. With two sleds he and six men went out to rescue the wounded. They brought back nineteen. From their vantage point on the brow of Visorka Gora's lone hill, Odjard and Mead saw the Bolos grouping for an assault on Ust Padenga, not realizing it was abandoned.

Odjard got two cannons of the Canadian artillery down from Shenkhurst. That afternoon, the Bolsheviks made one of their serious mistakes: They charged Ust Padenga, offering their flank to Allied cannon and rifle. The Reds lost forty men to seize deserted realty.

Visorka Gora was a more defensible position than either Nijni Gora or Ust Padenga. It had five blockhouses, each with a machine gun. Odjard had seven Stokes mortars. He also had three hundred determined men. Visorka Gora withstood the shelling, which commenced on January 20. When the Reds charged, Lieutenant Douglas Winslow of the Canadian Artillery ran his guns into the open and fired muzzle burst after muzzle burst of shrapnel. The Red commander called off the attacks.

Bolo artillery, however, outdistanced the Canadians and it began raining shells on the outpost. The Reds, with one thousand men, were in better shape to wage a war of attrition. One Bolo shell smashed through the walls of the makeshift hospital and flared in the operating room. It killed four medics outright, sheared off the leg of a patient, and fatally wounded the detachment's medical officer, Lieutenant Ralph C. Powers.

The British command at Shenkhurst realized now that the Reds had launched an enveloping attack. They were hitting the outposts in the south and, at the same time, Bolos, gliding through the woods on skis, were moving on Shenkhurst itself. An enveloping attack can be compared to the difficulty a man has in putting a burlap sack over a small wildcat: He must move fast to seal the end lest the cat badly scratch him and turn around and get away. The British command in Shenkhurst ordered its cat in Visorka Gora to get away.

As A Company and the Canadians left Visorka Gora, an incendiary shell hit one of the warehouses. The flash of burning supplies and exploding ammunition lit a lunarscape over which tired, stooped soldiers shuffled. Odjard and his men made it to the small village of Shalosha, where they rested during the day of January 23. Odjard was aware that the Bolsheviks had cut his A Company force from the Shenkhurst garrison by occupying the small villages on both banks of the Vaga. To get by them, Odjard resolved to follow the frozen river bed itself rather than trails on either bank. Because it was dark night and because there was movement on both sides of the river, the Bolos on the west bank of the Vaga confused the American line with Bolos on the east bank. So on January 24, Odjard led his men into Spasskoe, about six versts south of Shenkhurst. Here they were met by Captain O. A. Mowat, a Canadian commanding an 18-pounder (Winslow, having preceded the retreat, reached Shenkhurst with his two guns the day before).

Mowat had orders that Odjard was to make a stand at Spasskoe. The enemy was coming on Shenkhurst from four sides, having earlier in the day attacked garrisons well to the rear. Odjard and Mowat could see hundreds of Reds moving slowly but inexorably toward them. Shells began to land in Spasskoe, and the two officers could hear even larger shells crashing into Shenkhurst.

They made their stand. Later in the day, a Bolo shell landing directly on the Canadian field piece, killed its gunners, and wounded Mowat. Shrapnel also felled Odjard. Doughboys loaded the two men on a sleigh that had drawn the cannon and sent it to Shenkhurst. Odjard made it; Mowat did not. Lieutenants Mead, Saari, and McPhail saw that without artillery they could not possibly hold. It was only a matter of time before the Bolo shelling cut their telephone communication with Shenkhurst. Mead simply shouted over the phone that A Company was on its way. The men staggered into Shenkhurst at 4:00 P.M. on the 24th, some of them so utterly exhausted they did not have the strength to strip off their field packs before they fell into a stuporous sleep.

The British command at Bereznik saw that the Vaga force had only two choices: run or be annihilated. Colonel Sharman's last message to Graham was to get out if he could. Graham didn't need the advice. By the afternoon of the 24th, Shenkhurst was completely pocked with shell craters. The big guns the Bolsheviks had moved up were pulverizing the town and the soldiers in it. Graham ordered the evacuation to start at midnight, January 24–25.

The position was surrounded. The one chance of slipping past the Bolos was by a little-used logging path that plunged straight north through the forest, sheering away from the roads and paths along the river. Reconnaissance told Graham that in bypassing Shenkhurst the Bolos had neglected the path. If the men followed it, they could get to Shegovari for a rest before crossing the Vaga to the east and plunging again through the woods for

Kitsa, which had prepared defenses. It was twenty miles to Shego-vari, ten more to Kitsa.

To get out of Shenkhurst, Graham had to withdraw stealth-ily, leaving behind large stores of clothes, ammunition, and food. To burn them would alert the Bolos. It would not be hard for Red troops to catch this cumbersome, near-defeated column. Graham had to march before dawn because even now the Bolshevik snow troops were wriggling forward to mount a morning assault. He told the men to leave everything behind, including the hospital wounded and the big guns. The Canadians would not hear of abandoning their field pieces. The Yanks would not leave the wounded. Graham patiently explained to the Yanks and Cana-dians that the chief value Shenkhurst now had for the Bolos was to trap within it a military force capable of stemming an attack on Bereznik. Neither Yanks nor Canadians would listen.

The wounded left in a caravan of hastily requisitioned sleighs on January 25, two men strapped to a sleigh, wrapped in blankets, fortified with medicine and blessed with "good luck" and "God speed" from their buddies. After the wounded came the Cana-dians, driving exhausted ponies hauling the guns. Two companies of mounted Russians, recruited in Shenkhurst, followed, ordered to deploy along a parallel path as decoys. Once out of Shenkhurst, the Russians decided it was every man for himself and his horse, and that was the last ever seen of the "Shenkhurst Battalion." Leaving last were the infantry, the Yanks, the Tommies, and the loyal Russians, all of them ordered to defend themselves with the bayonet and to fire only as a last resort. They carried rations for three days. Some foolishly tried to carry more—prizes of war, extra cans of tinned salmon, Bibles, packets of love letters. Behind everyone came the sleighs of the Russians turned refugees. Com-panies A and B held the perimeter fortifications until Graham's column, nearly a mile in length, was fairly under way. Then, as Russians who stayed behind began to loot the warehouses, the two companies, led by Lieutenant Colonel Corbley, who had come over from the Dvina, got going.

It was, remembered Mead, an incredibly quiet line of march. But the sleighs and the cannons had chewed the forest path to ruts.

The infantry was climbing the Matterhorn. The luckiest soldiers were those of McPhail's platoon who had followed the lieutenant's advice and cut away their long coats over the knee. After an hour, the doughboys and the Tommies began shedding their excess. They threw away their packets of love letters, their extra tins of salmon, their Bibles, and their booty. They were stumbling every five or six paces. Soon they shed their overcoats, which dragged them down like heavy weights. Their footing was unsure in the Shackleton boot. Men fell asleep on their feet, roused only by the strenuous efforts of the officers and the noncoms. When the barely perceptible dawn overtook them, they heard the thunder of Bolshevik artillery falling on empty Shenkhurst.

At Yemska Gora, a tiny forest settlement, the soldiers drank hot tea poured from samovars along the street. Some chewed on chunks of black bread. Mead even gulped the pasty concoction of herring baked in slippery dough whose coarse smell had heretofore sickened him. At 5:00 P.M. on January 25, the column reached Shegovari, where it met two platoons of C Company. Pursuing Bolshevik units were catching up. Though the Canadians had finally been forced to leave behind four of their six guns, they wheeled the remaining two into action front and with open-sight marksmanship brought these Bolos to a halt. C Company took up the defensive perimeter to give the others time for sleep.

Three thousand Bolsheviks were in the area. They could not concert their grouping fast enough to pin the column in Shegovari. At dawn on January 26, the Allied column crossed the Vaga and proceeded through an unblazed forest with neither settlement nor crossing. Behind them, wrote Lieutenant John Cudahy, ". . . Shegovari was added to the sum of Russian villages fed to the fires of the Allied cause and became another charred ruin on the Vaga."[4]

By the night of the 26th, the column reached Vistavka, six versts in advance of Kitsa. The town was plentifully supplied with food and ammunition. It was one in a line of several small villages from which Graham thought at last his troops could beat back attacking Reds. The soldiers dug snow trenches and strung barbed wire.

The Bolsheviks brought up artillery on January 27 but did not press the attack. The cat had escaped the bag.

Mulling it over in Archangel, Ironside surmised that the Bolsheviks had for their objective the retreat of the force on the Vaga. They had mounted the offensive when they learned Gaida had captured Perm. They left off when they had severely limited Ironside's opportunities to bring Archangel and Siberian forces in close communication. Now the Bolos turned east and south where more dangerous foes threatened. Nevertheless, Ironside realized, the Allies had paid for too blindly extending their line when extension was tempting and not strategic. By driving the Allies from Shenkhurst, the Reds had pulled the rim of the wheel from a spoke. They had also won something more than a tactical advantage. "The withdrawal," wrote Ironside,

> undoubtedly made our task heavier in the future, for the villagers in the northern region had seen the strength of the Bolsheviks, and it made them all the more unwilling to oppose them.[5]

Colonel George Stewart heard Lieutenant Mead's report. Mead was now A Company's senior officer. When Mead described how the medical detachment had brought back all the wounded save one, the colonel asked him to repeat how the caravan was outfitted at Shenkhurst. Mead repeated. Stewart laughed and said, "You must have made quite a sight."

Mead never forgave his senior officer for the laugh.

NOTES

1. "Report." North Russian Historical Files. 23-33:2.
2. Ironside, *op. cit.*, p. 91.
3. Moore, Mead, and Jahns, *op. cit.*, p. 134.
4. Cudahy, *op. cit.*, p. 186.
5. Ironside, *op. cit.*, p. 103.

CHAPTER 15

PARIS PEACE CONFERENCE:

JANUARY 12–FEBRUARY 18, 1919

When the State Department informed the military commands in Archangel and Vladivostok that the President would make no decision about ending the Russian intervention until after the peace conference, it did not mean that Woodrow Wilson was postponing a decision because more timely and pressing matters occupied him; it meant that American policy *vis-à-vis* Russia would be resolved by the peace treaty itself.

The work on this treaty began on January 12 in the French Ministry of Foreign Affairs on the Quai d'Orsay* when commissioners from twenty-seven nations plus the delegates from five British dominions (which gave Britain five extra votes) convened. The five American delegates, called Peace Commissioners, were Woodrow Wilson, Secretary of State Robert Lansing, Colonel House, General Tasker Bliss, and Henry White, a diplomat and a Republican, the only commissioner who spoke French and whose daughter had married a German baron.

* Technically, the Peace Commissioners in Paris constituted the Preliminary Conference of the Allied and Associated Powers. Because of the inordinate length of time it took them to draft a comprehensive treaty, the Preliminary Conference became the Final Conference. The document the conference produced in late May was the Treaty of Versailles, so called because it was signed by the Germans in the Hall of Mirrors in Louis XIV's Palace at Versailles, a suburb of Paris.

Russia was not represented. But according to most observers of the time, the Russian problem was *the* problem of the peace conference. On the very first day of the conference, Marshal Foch of France suggested to the commissioners that an Allied force, composed mainly of Americans, march on Moscow to crush the Bolsheviks. Woodrow Wilson rose to reply that he doubted whether Bolshevism could be checked by force; it was at any rate unwise to bring such an Allied force into being until the conference agreed on a joint objective.[1]

For the next four days, the delegates discussed Russia. Wilson wanted a world order of liberal capitalist states in which Russia was included. So did David Lloyd George, Prime Minister of England, who argued that world peace was unattainable as long as immense Russia was unregulated by a League of Nations. But Georges Clemenceau, Premier of France, wanted a watertight bulkhead between Russia and the West, a *cordon sanitaire* that would economically and physically starve the Bolsheviks by preventing them access to the Ukraine, Poland, the Caucasus, and western Siberia. The *cordon sanitaire* would starve some decent Russians as well as Bolsheviks, a sacrifice Clemenceau was prepared to make for France.

On January 16, Lloyd George attempted a compromise. He suggested that the peace conference call upon the warring elements in Russia to agree to a truce. During the truce, all Russian factions could send delegates to Paris, where the Peace Commissioners could assist them in putting aside their differences.

Clemenceau would have none of it. He said he refused to sit down with criminals and he would not let murderers and anarchists run loose in the streets of Paris.

Woodrow Wilson then proposed that the conference invite the Russian factions to confer with the Allies at some other place. Rather than destroy the hoped-for unity of the conference, Clemenceau, who presided, acceded and deputized Wilson to issue the invitation. He said he chose Wilson because in part it was his idea and because writing peace notes seemed to be the American President's favorite hobby.

Wilson designated as a site the island of Prinkipo in the Sea of Marmora near Constantinople. Prinkipo, literally "Princes Island," was named in honor of the sons of Czar Alexander II. Winston Churchill wrote that "Very near to Prinkipo lay another island to which the Young Turks before the war had exiled all the *pariah* dogs which formerly infested the streets of Constantinople. These dogs, shipped there in the tens of thousands, were left to devour one another and ultimately to starve. I saw them with my own eyes, gathered in troops upon the rocky shores, when I visited Turkey in 1909 in a friend's yacht. The bones of these dogs still whitened the inhospitable island, and their memory noisomely pervaded the neighborhood. To Bolshevik sympathizers the place seemed oddly chosen for a conference. To their opponents it seemed not altogether unsuitable."[2]

On January 22, Wilson sent off invitations to the interested parties. Prince Lvov, chairman of the White Political Conference, turned the invitation down in one paragraph. In Archangel, General Eugene Miller said the same thing in a lengthier note. In Siberia, Kolchak complained that the invitation undermined the prestige of the White cause. Along the Don, Denikin wondered why the Allies supplied him with arms to beat the Bolsheviks if they really wanted him to sit down with them someplace else.

But the Bolsheviks did accept. The Bolsheviks assumed that the invitation indicated the willingness of the Allies to extend *de facto* recognition to their rule. Wilson had intended the opposite. He had hoped an armistice in Russia would undercut Bolshevik authority by giving time for orderly political expression to emerge. Now Wilson and Lloyd George were stuck with a party to which only an unpleasant guest wanted to come. So the American President and the English Prime Minister commissioned William C. Bullitt, an adviser to the American Peace Commission, to proceed to Russia for the purposes of determining the exact terms on which the Bolsheviks would agree to an armistice.

Twenty-eight years old, a newspaperman who had joined the White House staff to analyze the foreign press, Bullitt was thoroughly informed on Russian affairs. He believed moderate Bolshevism was infinitely to be preferred to extreme Bolshevism. If the Bolsheviks proposed reasonable terms for an armistice, Bullitt was instructed to indicate unofficially that the United States would recommend an immediate withdrawal of all foreign troops from Russia.

But the French remained intransigent. Clemenceau thought the Allies were wasting time. He wanted a war against the Bolsheviks. He asked the peace conference to consider such a move.

Lloyd George pointed out that when the Germans needed every man on the Western Front, they were still constrained to keep one million troops in Russia simply to secure a few provinces at a time when Bolshevism was weak and disorganized. "Is any one of the Western Allies prepared to send a million men into Russia?" Lloyd George asked. "I doubt whether a thousand would go."

Woodrow Wilson rose to say that he thought that Allied troops were doing no good in Russia, that they did not know for whom or for what they were fighting. If the Allies were asked what they were supporting in Russia, they would be compelled to reply that they did not know.

The crux of the argument had been reached. Allowed to proceed, to thrash out what they could do about Russia or what they could not do, perhaps the peace conference and its important commissioners would at least have resolved their own differences. Instead, for one reason and another, the big three had to break off their discussions. The first to break it off was Lloyd George. His government, which had been returned in the "Khaki Elections" of December 1918, faced the prospect of nationwide strikes. Lloyd George went to London. To take his place at the conference he sent Winston Churchill, the new Secretary of State for War. Churchill was the antithesis of William C. Bullitt. Churchill saw Bolshevism as a world curse and he believed the time to strangle it was now, when the baby was in its crib. He took his seat at the conference on February 14, sitting beside "Clemenceau presiding, grim, rugged, snow white, with a black skull cap; opposite him Marshal Foch, very formal, very subdued, grave, illustrious, lovable. On either hand in sumptuous chairs sat the representatives of the victorious powers. Around them Gobelin tapestries, mirrors and glittering lights."[3] This was Churchill's one contact with Woodrow Wilson, a contact of short duration. Wilson himself was leaving the next day for the United States to sign the bills of the Sixty-fifth Congress, which was drawing to a close. It was not until 7:00 P.M. that the Russian item on the agenda was opened and Churchill rose to forward the idea that the Russian "situation must be judged as part of the great quarrel with Germany and unless we are able to come to the support of the Russians there was a possibility of a great combination from Yokohama to Cologne in hostility to France, Britain and America."[4] Could the conference come to a decision on Russia? What was the policy? Peace or war?

Wilson had already risen to leave for Cherbourg, but he turned back to the table and, resting his arm on Clemenceau's chair, listened to the Churchillian rhetoric. After the peroration, the President replied that Russia was a problem to which he did not know the solution. There were grave objections to every course, yet some course must be taken. If Prinkipo came to nothing, he would do his share with the other Allies in any military measures they considered necessary and practicable.

With that, the President left and sped toward the USS *George Washington*. Four days later, the conference was incapacited not only on the Russian but on many other questions as well when an assassin shot down Clemenceau. The bullet lodged in the French premier's lung and for the next month he was hospitalized, not returning to the conference until Wilson returned in mid-March.

That Woodrow Wilson left the conference with the vague promise he would go along with the others was a thoughtless statement. Woodrow Wilson was nothing if not his own man. Aboard the *George Washington* he held an interview with Ambassador Francis, who was returning with him. The interview was not a long one, and according to Francis' memoirs, Wilson ventured nothing he had not ventured before. But the fact that he had sought out Francis indicates the President was turning over the North Russian venture in his mind. Francis outlined to the President his own plan of sending a strong Allied force to North Russia for a clear and decisive victory over the Bolsheviks.

Wilson replied that sending troops anywhere after the armistice was unpopular.

Francis disputed this, arguing that many of the two million soldiers still in France were disappointed the war had ended before they could do battle. Wilson could have 500,000 of these soldiers for the asking. They would be glad to go to Russia to save a representative of the United States Government.

"What representative?" asked Wilson.

"Why, me," said Francis, who planned to return to Archangel in the summer.

The absurdity of sending an army to protect an ambassador already safe and sound aboard the *George Washington* must have occurred to the President. He already knew from Newton Baker's summaries that the 339th had taken serious casualties at Shenkhurst and he had wired the War Department to instruct him on what consideration was being given their relief. Peyton C. March had to remind the President that the Allied Supreme War Council was responsible for reinforcements in North Russia.

If he needed any more impetus to withdraw the 339th, Wilson found it in the report of Churchill's proposals to the peace conference. In the absence of the American President and the British Prime Minister, Winston Churchill had proposed that the Allies prepare a program of military action to depose the Bolsheviks. This had provoked such acrimonious debate that the minutes were deleted lest the commissioners expose their division to the world. Churchill asked the conference to get rid of the Prinkipo plan and instead issue an ultimatum to the Bolsheviks that unless Red forces left off from the attack and retreated five miles from their front lines everywhere, the Allies would immediately begin to coordinate all military efforts in Russia.

Wilson thought this intemperate polemic could start a war. The way to prevent such a catastrophe was to call home Allied troops. On February 16, Wilson wired Newton D. Baker to call off the North Russian intervention. On February 18, Baker addressed a letter to Senator George E. Chamberlain of the Senate Military Affairs Committee in which he explained that the dispatch of 720 volunteers for railroad duty in Russia was to "assure greater safety for American forces and facilitate the prompt withdrawal of troops in North Russia at the earliest opportunity that weather conditions in the spring permit."⁵

Typically, the orders were never directly transmitted to Stewart's North Russian command. Instead the soldiers in Archangel learned about the withdrawal through their newspaper, *The American Sentinel,* which picked it up from *The New York Times.*

The Wilson Administration may have had no choice but to break off the North Russian intervention. The Senate, which was to bear so cruelly on the peace treaty, had begun to warm to its task by bearing heavily on the North Russian expedition. Senator Hiram Johnson, the progressive and isolationist leader from California, had introduced several anti-intervention resolutions, the last of which, proposed on February 7, had been barely defeated by 37–32. Senators William E. Borah and Robert La Follette, the hard-core "irreconcilables," also raised arguments against continued responsibilities overseas. "Bring home American soldiers," shouted Borah from the Senate floor. "Rescue our own democracy. Get American business into normal channels."⁶

In the House, Speaker Champ Clark of Missouri, crossing party lines, inspired the gallery to cheers when he called for an immediate return of all American troops now in Russia and Europe. Representative Ernest Lundeen of Minnesota introduced a resolution to recall the 339th. Newly elected Congressman Fiorello La Guardia read into the *Congressional Record* the angry protests of Michigan and Wisconsin families whose sons were fighting in Russia.⁷

The influential liberal press, Wilson's determined supporters, also began to come down heavily against intervention. Oswald Villard of *The Nation* condemned the Russian expedition, and the *New Republic,* while castigating the Red Terror, also castigated the Allied blockade of Russian ports and the use of Allied soldiers to win a war the Whites could not win themselves. Even Nikolai Lenin addressed the American public in a letter to the International News Bureau, forwarded by its Moscow correspondent:

It may be that it is not war but it looks very much like war.
We do not want war with any nation, because we find that

almost always it is the workers who have to take risks and that we have to kill people against whom we have no objections and who, if they could understand us, would never fight us.[8]

NOTES

1. Donald I. Buzenkai, "The Bolsheviks, the League of Nations and the Paris Peace Conference." Soviet Studies. 19(2), 1967.
2. Winston Churchill, *The Aftermath*. New York: Scribner's, 1929, p. 172.
3. *Ibid.*, pp. 173–74.
4. Ullman, *op. cit.*, Vol. II: *Britain and the Russian Civil War*. Princeton: Princeton University Press, 1968, p. 119.
5. *The New York Times,* February 19, 1919.
6. Peter G. Filene, *Americans and the Soviet Experiment, 1917–1933*. Cambridge, 1967, p. 53.
7. *Ibid.*, pp. 53–54.
8. Ivan Krasnow, "Unknown Documents on Soviet-American Relations." *New World Review,* 1971. 39(2), pp. 99–105.

General Ironside decorates an officer of the 310th Engineers.

Archangel looking north.

The doughboys go home.

Archangel's cathedral.

A Yank pulls sentry duty with temperatures at 50° below in North Russia.

Yanks at Verst 445 of the Railroad Front.

Allied diplomats at Archangel. Ambassador David R. Francis, sitting, wears pince-nez and holds a telegram; to his right is Chaikovsky with beard.

Poilus of the 21st Battalion prepare to move up to the Railroad Front.

The sled convoy that saved the wounded at Shenkhurst.

General Poole and a Russian officer.

Secretary of War Newton D. Baker and Chief-of-Staff Peyton C. March in New York to welcome home Woodrow Wilson.

The sailors of the *Olympia* who helped start the shooting war.

Funeral cortege of a Yank in Archangel.

Home-knit socks strung up to dry on the Railroad Front.

Company M sets out to take up its position on the Railroad Front.

(*Left:*)
Engineers of the 310th building one of the many blockhouses.

(*Center:*)
View from observation tower of the Railroad Front. The men lived in boxcars.

(*Bottom:*)
The Allied Command: from left to right, the first four men—Dunlap and Lucas of the French 21st Colonial Battalion; Ironside; Colonel George Evans Stewart, CO of the American 339th Battalion.

Captain Joel Moore waves a sword captured from Bolshevik at the end of the battle for Bolshie Ozerki.

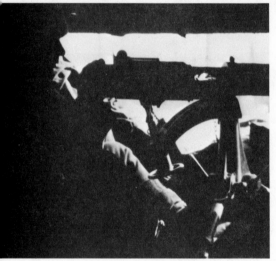

Inside the blockhouse at Toulgas.

The knoll at Nijni Gora. The church in the far background served as a Bolshevik observation post.

Machine-gun section on the Railroad Front.

CHAPTER 16

HARBIN:

FEBRUARY 10, 1919

The principal success of the American intervention was in keeping the Trans-Siberian Railway Russian. Indeed, Woodrow Wilson eventually conceived this as the true objective of the Siberian venture. He did not want the Japanese to gain control of the Trans-Siberian lest American economic interests in Russia suffer.

In May 1917, three months after the February Revolution, Woodrow Wilson sent the Advisory Commission of Railway Experts to Russia. The duties of this commission, as the President explained them, were to advise and assist the Russians in their transportation problems.

John F. Stevens, one of the world's premier railway builders, headed the commission. Born in Maine in 1853, Stevens had worked his way up from surveyor to Chief Engineer of the Isthmian Canal Commission. Later he was vice-president of the New York, New Haven and Hartford line. Assisting him were George Gibbs, Chief Mechanical Engineer of the Pennsylvania Railroad; W. L. Darling, Chief Engineer of the Northern Pacific Railway; Henry Miller, Operating Vice-President of the Wabash Railroad; and John E. Griener, Chief Consulting Bridge Engineer of the Baltimore and Ohio.

When the Bolshevik Revolution in October 1917 forced the Advisory Commission from St. Petersburg, Stevens established headquarters in Harbin, in Manchuria, where his group concentrated on keeping the Trans-Siberian continually operating.

To help the Advisory Commission of Railway Experts, Woodrow Wilson also put together the Russian Railway Service Corps, commanded by Colonel George H. Emerson, the General Manager of the Great Northern. The corps consisted of railroad officers and skilled mechanics who, once in Russia, divided into the regular station unit of fourteen men to put into practice the reforms planned by the Stevens group. Emerson and his men joined Stevens in Harbin in March 1918, and the fourteen-man units were distributed along the length of the Chinese Eastern and the Trans-Siberian as far as Omsk.

Stevens discovered that much of the Trans-Siberian's inefficiency was due to its having always run at a loss. The Czar had subsidized it. But the Kerensky and Bolshevik regimes could not afford the subsidies and both had perforce allowed a steady deterioration of rolling stock and equipment. The Trans-Siberian lacked spare parts, lubricating oils, and cotton waste, which took more and more cars out of service every month. Stevens estimated that it would take three hundred ships to bring sufficient railroad supplies to Vladivostok to run the line at peak capability.

But Stevens and his commission made many recommendations that improved service. They simplified coaling supply and saw to it that new mines were opened. They introduced dispatching, consolidated repair shops, made up train sheets for operating officers, and brought out everything the line could use from the vast store of supplies at Vladivostok.

None of this was easy. Stevens had to deal with the antiquated Russian Railway Technical Board, which consisted of twenty professors none of whom had actual railroading experience. One of these men remarked to Stevens, "These things which you propose to put into effect would better the service, move our trains and result in economy, but what object is that to us? We have life positions and the national treasury always makes up deficits."

Stevens and Emerson and their units were established along the railroads when the Japanese arrived in the fall of 1918. The

Japanese wanted to seize the roadbeds and operate the railways, but their military men could not displace the railroad units who managed the Herculean task of moving freight and soldiers in a chaotic and dangerous time; nor could the Japanese High Command diminish Stevens' influence with the various White directorates and governments which controlled the lines.

The civil war wreaked incalculable damage. Eight hundred and twenty-six bridges were blown up by one side or the other. At least twenty stations and fourteen water supply depots were leveled. Thousands of miles of track were blasted to pieces or bent out of shape. Monies held in reserve were soon exhausted and no revenues came in. Carl Ackerman reported that not only did he never buy a ticket for his many trips back and forth across the continent, but no train conductor ever asked him for one. Although the Advisory Commission assessed low rates for the movement of military forces, many countries, notably France and Britain, refused to pay anything. Yet the Trans-Siberian continued to operate because it was subsidized by the United States, which contributed 5,000,000 gold dollars; Japan, which contributed 8,000,000 gold yen; and China, which contributed 500,000 gold dollars.[1]

Realizing they could not wrest the roadbeds or the stock from Stevens' and Emerson's guardianship, the Japanese became more tractable in helping operate the road and more concerned about the inequities of financing it. When Stevens proposed that an Inter-Allied Railway Committee, whose board would be made up of representatives from different countries, run the Siberian lines, the Japanese approved the plan. The proposal, which would help finance the roads, would also give the Japanese some say in running the lines.

The Inter-Allied Railway Committee was in actuality a gang of special agencies created by Stevens to carry on the management of the railway. On February 10, 1919, the United States Government formally accepted the plans forwarded by Stevens and approved by the Japanese, Chinese, British, and French. The Inter-Allied Railway Committee made one crucially important decision: It assigned its members different sections of the road for whose guard each was responsible. China guarded the Chinese Eastern from Nikol'sk in the east to Manchouli in the west. The Japanese took up guard duty between Nikol'sk and Spasskoe and between Kharbarovsk and Karymskaya on the Amur as well as along the stretch between Manchouli and Verkne-Udinsk. The United States posted guards between Vladivostok and Nikol'sk and along the branch line which ran to the Sucgan coal mines. Farther west, Yanks guarded the section between Verkne-Udinsk and Baikal. The Czechs, of course, were posted along the line from Irkutsk to Ekaterinburg.

On learning of the agreement, General William S. Graves issued a proclamation to the Russian people. He advised them that the sole purpose of the United States was to protect the railroad and its property and insure the passage of freight and people without obstruction or interruption. But Graves saw quickly enough that the agreement did not provide for ridding the railroad of Cossack raiders who still terrified at will. Nor did the agreement end corruption and bribery. Kolchak partisans used the Trans-Siberian to further White ends and often cleared the tracks for boxcars of black-market valuables, letting grain rot in eastern sidings while Russians in the west starved.

Whatever the imperfections of the railway agreement, without it the chaos that eventually engulfed Siberia would have swallowed whole the Czech Legion—for whose rescue, it will be remembered, the American expedition was sent in the first place. When it came time to pull out the Czechs, John F. Stevens was able to raise some $400,000 worth of gold roubles and sixty cars of wheat for Russian railway men who refused to work until they were paid and their families fed.

The 285 Americans of the Russian Railway Service Corps stayed on their posts through perilous times. They finally came home in 1920 and were promptly disowned by the United States Army. All of them held commissions signed by the Adjutant General and issued by the Corps of Engineers. But upon their discharge the Army said they were civilians employed by the Kerensky Government and offered them only certificates of service, not honorable discharges, which meant they were not legally veterans. For the next fifty years these men persevered in redressing this injustice by carrying their case through the courts. On March 28, 1971, the Supreme Court ruled for the twenty-two surviving petitioners that it was not reasonable to consider that they had been paid by a nonexistent, bankrupted government. Since they had indeed been paid, they were paid by the United States Army, which entitled them to all benefits conferred upon veterans of the AEF-Siberia.[2]

The preservation of the Trans-Siberian Railway was the *raison d'être* the Wilson Administration offered Congress for the Siberian intervention. Frank L. Polk, Under Secretary of State, detailed before the Senate Appropriations Committee the aggressive thrust of the Japanese. By sending troops to Siberia, Polk argued, the President was keeping the lid on.

Breckenridge Long, 3rd Assistant Secretary of State, went before the House Committee on Foreign Affairs and in the same careful detail explained the events which led to the Siberian intervention, whose guiding policy remained the maintenance of the open door.

In his book *The Siberian Intervention,* John Albert White remarks that centralized nations have greater freedom of action in international affairs than democracies—which is why the United States Government, "knowing that the American people would be unlikely to support an aggressive policy, has been forced to find peaceful means of maintaining her commercial position in the Far East. Therefore, such concepts as the preservation of territorial integrity of a nation or the maintenance of the 'open door' in trade relationships have been found useful because they are intended to enlist general support. . . ."[3]

Nevertheless, Congress began to balk at the prospects of an extended intervention in Siberia. By the early spring of 1919 a tide of isolationism began to wash over the country which drowned even anti-Bolshevism. Senator Hiram Johnson presented a resolution directing the Secretary of State to inform the Senate immediately why American troops remained in Siberia. In the early summer of 1919, the Senate approved this resolution unanimously. In the House, Congressman T. Mason of Illinois charged that the Administration kept troops in Siberia simply to protect private investment. Montana's Congresswoman Jeanette Rankin, who had voted against the declaration of war in April 1917 and was to cast the lone vote against the declaration of war in December 1941, proposed that the United States Government purchase land in Siberia on which to settle the Yanks after their discharge since the length of their stay in Russia precluded their reintegration in American society.

Yet the Siberian intervention did not alarm the Congressional constituencies, principally because the 31st and 27th Infantry were Regular Army units whose personnel had served all over the world for many years. These outfits did not have a locus as the 339th had in Detroit, where the complaints of wives and mothers inspired a choric voice from elected officials.

There is a central reason why the Siberian intervention did not provoke acrimonious debate in Congress: It is that Woodrow Wilson did not give Congress a chance to debate the matter. He did not have to ask Congress for the appropriations to continue.

As the Commander-in-Chief of the United States Army during wartime, nothing the Congress did could have prevented Woodrow Wilson from sending American soldiers to a war zone. Congress could, however, have argued the wisdom of supplying Kolchak and replenishing the rolling stock, rails, and locomotives of the Trans-Siberian Railway. It could, that is, if Wilson had asked for the appropriations for these measures. He did not because he had an instrument at hand for such financing. That instrument was the Russian Embassy in Washington, D.C., accredited to the Kerensky Government, directed by Ambassador Boris Bakhmetev.

Bakhmetev, an engineer by profession, had first come to the United States as Chief of the Czar's Procurement Committee in 1915. He returned to Russia in March 1917 to become Vice-Minister for Commerce and Industry in the Provisional Government until Kerensky named him as the ambassador to the United States. Bakhmetev presented his credentials in the fall of 1917. He denounced the Bolshevik Revolution as unlawful and illegal and counseled that it would shortly fail. When the United States did not recognize the Bolshevik regime, Bakhmetev stayed on. When the Bolsheviks enlarged upon their power, Bakhmetev's mission lost diplomatic standing. But financially, Bakhmetev's mission assumed more and more importance because he controlled over $200,000,000 in assets which he could disperse on nothing more than his own authority.

In order to keep Russia in the war, the United States had extended to the Provisional Government millions upon millions in credits for armaments and military supplies. Contracts between the Russian Embassy and American firms had been let without stint. To declare the Russian Embassy without legal status would terminate these arrangements and undoubtedly put several American businessmen and bankers into bankruptcy. Consequently, when Congressmen and newspaper editors inquired why the Wilson Administration still recognized Bakhmetev as an official envoy, the State Department quickly replied that he was the "Ambassador of the Russian People," rather than the Russian ambassador, that the United States regarded the Bolshevik regime as a temporary aberration which would soon be replaced by a more responsible and enlightened government.

American businessmen and bankers were threatened with monumental losses where they expected profits and they would have implored the State Department to crown Bakhmetev king if that were the only way to help the Russian Embassy meet its obligations equitably. For its part, the Embassy canceled the contracts it could, reduced some more, and promised manufacturers to accept for resale on the open market materials already in production. Proceeds from such sales would repay the United States Government and private loans. But the Russian Embassy never canceled contracts for rifles, ammunition, machine guns, airplanes, and railroad supplies. Indeed, the Embassy accepted these and shipped them on to Vladivostok. While it did realize substantial monies from materiels sold on the open market, none of these proceeds went toward repaying the United States but instead for more small arms and locomotives. Instead of payment, the Treasury accepted Bakhmetev's IOUs and its officials asked bankers to cooperate with the Embassy by settling for interest payments—as unusual a financial arrangement as the intervention was a peace-keeping effort.

"By conserving and augmenting the Embassy's resources," writes Robert J. Maddox, "the [Wilson] Administration maintained what amounted to an independent treasury for use in Russia—a treasury which was immune to prying congressmen. . . . The Ambassador of the Russian People had now become the quartermaster for the Kolchak regime."[4]

NOTES

1. White, *op. cit.,* p. 293.
2. Walter A. Grayson Papers. The Siberian Collection, Hoover Institution. 74005-8:36. Box 1.
3. White, *op. cit.,* p. 133.
4. Robert J. Maddox, "President Wilson and the Russians." *American History Illustrated,* 1962. 2(1), pp. 40–47.

CHAPTER 17

ARCHANGEL:

MARCH 17–APRIL 5, 1919

At the end of February, Ironside could deploy an effective fighting force of 11,000 rifles, of whom 4,500 were Yanks, 5,000 British, 700 French, and 700 Polish. In addition, he had 5,000 Russians he counted as an integral part of the Allied expedition and another 12,000 raised by the Provisional Government, troops of questionable worth.

Against Ironside was the Bolshevik Sixth Army commanded by General Boris Kuzmin. Sixteen thousand and eight hundred troops of this army were pressing against the Allies from Chekuevo to the Dvina. Thirty-two hundred more Bolsheviks of the Sixth Army were in the north on the Pinega River. There were Red reserves of eight thousand in Kotlas and nine thousand in Vologda. These Red forces had 66 field guns and 150 machine guns.[1]

As the leaden winter passed, Ironside suspected the Bolsheviks were marshaling the regiments which would throw him back into Archangel. Though the Americans were going home when the ice broke, the British were not. Ironside doubted the Bolsheviks would wait.

Besides the mounting Bolshevik superiority, another menace threatened the Allied expedition: mutiny. Mutiny did not occur in one spot but in several and not during one period but in consecutive episodes.

The first serious mutiny transpired within the Yorkshire Battalion, which Ironside brought down from Murmansk in February to relieve the Yanks on the Onega.* When Colonel Lavie, a well-regarded professional who had spent four years in the trenches, ordered the Yorkshire to take up its position, a regimental adjutant reported that the troops refused to muster. This simply astonished Lavie.

Lavie commanded the men to fall in without arms. He asked them to repeat what they had told the adjutant. Two sergeants stepped forward, stiff as boards, eyes to the front, and bellowed that the battalion would do no more fighting. Lavie ordered a lance corporal to arm twelve men. The corporal obeyed. The colonel ordered the twelve to take the two sergeants into close arrest.

Ironside was there within hours. He hopped out of an airplane, went straight to the guard room to promise the sergeants a court-martial as soon as he could convene officers for the trial.

Lavie and Ironside turned out the battalion again and Ironside told them they were to replace the Americans. The men moved out. Ironside did indeed court-martial the two sergeants, who were sentenced to be shot, a sentence commuted to life imprisonment on secret instructions from the King that there were to be no more executions after the armistice.

The Yorkshire mutiny spread to the French. A company of the 21st Colonial Battalion refused to leave their Archangel barracks to return to the Railroad Front. An English colonel on the Emtsa refused to talk to his French counterpart because a poilu had come along as an interpreter. The British officer objected to the presence of other ranks at an officers' conference and insisted the French colonel had come to spy. Even the Poles had a day of havoc. Due to return to the front, they refused until they were blessed by their priest. Colonel Sollohub explained to Ironside that he had been forced to put the priest under arrest. The priest refused to bless the men until he was free of restraint. But to release the priest, said Colonel Sollohub, was to set a bad example.

---

* Major General C. M. Maynard's force at Murmansk totaled 15,000—7,400 British, 1,000 French, 1,400 Italians, 1,200 Serbs, and 4,000 Russians and Karelian Finns.

I Company of the 339th groused when ordered back to the Railroad Front. They complained that the Yanks did all the fighting while the Russians did all the parading.

A mimeographed pamphlet circulated among the soldiers at the front. *Facts and Questions Concerning the NREF* asked, "Where is our Monroe Doctrine? The majority of people here seem to prefer Bolshevism to British intervention. . . . We are fighting neither for Russia or for Russian wealth but for our lives. . . . We are removed 200 miles from our base, with an open country intervening, with no force except in a few villages to guard our lines. . . . There is no military reason why we should be more than 20 miles from our base." Colonel Stewart knew that Lieutenant Joel Moore had written the protest. He warned the lieutenant that such a pamphlet was treasonous and made its author liable for a court-martial.[2]

"Tempers everywhere," wrote General Ironside in a masterpiece of understatement, "were getting very frayed by this time." Taken together, these incidents indicate that Ironside was pushing the men hard and pushing them for longer and longer periods. He had no choice, since he had no army with which to relieve them.

There were mutinous acts with far more serious consequences. Archangel was a beehive of subversion, a subversion not only inspired by but also directed by the Bolsheviks. The workingmen in Solombola and Bakaritza waged strikes, planned work stoppages, and forced delays. They sabotaged and pilfered. More and more they were turning against the Provisional Government of the Northern Region, calling it reactionary and incompetent.

On the anniversary of the February Revolution, the leaders of the Archangel Council of Professional Unions staged a large rally. When the excitement of the workers was whipped up, three of the union officials declared to tumultuous cheers that the natural protector of the workingman was the soviet system and that the municipal and provisional governments had compromised themselves and Russia by relying on the force of arms wielded by foreigners.

General Eugene Miller arrested these officials. In the customary search of the union's headquarters, Miller's police came across a large cache of arms as well as secret documents which revealed a working agreement between the union hierarchy and the Bolshevik underground. The documents provided the police with the evidence which led to the subsequent arrest of the council and the discovery of several Bolshevik apparats in the White Army. Along with seventeen spies the police also arrested a key Bolshevik operator, the telegrapher on one of the trawlers who had been monitoring Ironside's reports and orders as well as passing on directives from Moscow. Firing squads executed over thirty men in late March and early April. The Archangel authorities, by Vice-Consul Felix Cole's testimony, were making more Bolsheviks with these executions than they could ever shoot.[3]

Ironside expected the Bolos to direct a dislodging move against the Allied position in North Russia. As long as ice locked the expedition in, the advantage was with the Reds. On March 3, the Bolos attacked Vistavka. After the artillery barrage lifted, the Yanks and Tommies could hear the commissars urging the men forward. The Bolos kept the pressure on for six days, and on March 9 the Yanks retreated from Vistavka to set up a new line three versts in advance of Kitsa.

But the Bolsheviks did not try to advance. There was sporadic shelling. Nevertheless the attack had ceased. A Yank patrol, hauling a sled of gasoline, crept back to Vistavka, soaked the village, and set it aflame to hamper Red occupation.

Ironside guessed correctly that the attack against Vistavka was a diversionary move. Somewhere around the bumpy and now jagged edge of the rim that was the Allied front, Ironside waited for the offensive which would attempt to make him draw the entire force into Archangel, there to be smashed to pieces against the ice. He did not have long to wait.

The Bolsheviks came out of Plesetskaya, moving north between the Onega River and the railroad, aiming at the crossroad town of Bolshie Ozerki. An enemy force of 1,200 men, hundreds of them gliding swiftly and silently on skis, surprised this outpost on March 17. Bolshie Ozerki was sixteen miles due west of Obozerskaya. It sat athwart one road running east and west between Chekuevo and Obozerskaya and on another road running north and south.

The Bolos easily wiped out the small French garrison and by moving in force into Bolshie Ozerki cleanly divided Ironside's detachment on the Onega River from the detachment on the Railroad Front. Once Kuzmin took Bolshie Ozerki, he could move his Sixth Army east, fall on Obozerskaya, and attack the Railroad Front from the rear.

On the day Kuzmin hit Bolshie Ozerki, he also separated Colonel Lucas from his command. Lucas had passed through Bolshie Ozerki on March 16 making for Chinova, several versts farther on. On the morning of the 17th, Lucas ran into a Yank patrol from H Company which had come over to investigate what it heard was a raid on Bolshie Ozerki. When Lucas and the Yanks reached the outskirts of the town, machine guns on its western approaches convinced them it was held in force. The patrol had to crawl through the snow to save itself. Once out of range, the Yanks discovered they had lost Colonel Lucas. Rather than waste time—and perhaps lives—searching for him, they hurried back to their outfit with the bad news that a sizable Red offensive was under way. Another patrol found the near-frozen Lucas twelve hours later, by which time Ironside had taken over personal command of the Railroad Front.

Ironside had a glimmering of what was coming from the reports of refugees who, getting out of the way of the Bolsheviks, began pouring into Obozerskaya on the night of the 16th. They came with reports that the snow-packed roads were littered with dead and dying horses, collapsed from the terrible exertion of hauling cannon. A priest from Bolshie Ozerki had taken the time to count the men in the Bolo advance column. The Reds were mounting their largest attack in the North Russian campaign.

Ironside scoured Archangel for healthy Yanks and Tommies, whom he impressed on the spot. He picked up mail clerks, bakers, medics, soldiers on leave, walking wounded, and men coming from the red-light districts. With a hastily composed force of five hundred Ironside left for Obozerskaya, where he found that the ever-reliable 310th Engineers had already begun to clear defensive positions twelve miles to the west with log barricades and blockhouses. Ironside designated this position Verst 18. It was halfway between Bolshie Ozerki and Obozerskaya.

Ironside ordered the Chekuevo garrison to move upon the Bolsheviks from the west. Company H with three companies of the Yorkshires attacked the Bolos on March 23, one Yorkshire company to the north, the Yanks in the center, a second Yorkshire to the south, and a third in reserve. They found the Bolo positions well guarded by machine guns. Snow impeded the advance. By nightfall, this force was running out of ammunition, and British Major Basil Monday, commanding at Onega, recalled it.

Though the Allied attack did not retake Bolshie Ozerki or even dent its western position, it still accomplished a tactical objective: It convinced Kuzmin that he was under serious pressure on two fronts. It made him hesitate in attacking to the east. Though he had superior numbers, the Red commander brought up still more men from the south before he began his advance along the road he would have to take in order to bring his artillery to bear on Obozerskaya. Kuzmin waited for the 2nd Moscow, the 96th Saratov, and the 2nd Kazan regiments.

This delay gave Ironside time to perfect his defenses at Verst 18. The five hundred men he had brought with him had hauled out to this position five big guns. Pushing these guns through the snow was a Sisyphean task, but Ironside got them to Verst 18, set them in place with their crews, and they established his front when they began shelling Bolshie Ozerki. On this front, Ironside placed D and M companies of the 339th and two platoons of E Company. He had fought the Bolsheviks long enough to gamble on Kuzmin's assault tactics: a simultaneous frontal and rear attack. Ironside consequently stripped his flanks of men and put them with the best he had—M Company—farthest east, their entrenchments facing Obozerskaya.

On March 31, the Bolos moved out of Bolshie Ozerki. Ironside's five big guns took a cruel toll. Three Bolo battalions did indeed come upon the rear where Company M behind impervious defenses drove them back.

Kuzmin's frontal assault was delayed not only by the artillery but also the weather. The daylight came earlier. Temperatures rose, the snow was wet and slushy, making forward movement tough going. Nights were still bitterly cold. Having crammed three additional regiments as well as their support units into the area, Kuzmin had to keep his troops in the snow for long periods. These rigors weakened and discouraged the Bolos. Like Czarist generals before him, the Red commissar was victimized by the delusion that a prodigal waste of men would make the mass prevail. On April 1 and 2, Kuzmin came up against Ironside's front and lost two thousand men. Many of the wounded crawled to the Allied lines in darkness to save themselves from freezing.

On April 2, the Onega force, Company H, and the three Yorkshires, roughly six hundred men, came again on Bolshie Ozerki. Again they failed to dislodge the Bolos. Captain Ballensinger of Company H found the going so tough that he had to summon the reserve Yorks to extricate his men. But the attack kept occupied a large Bolshevik contingent which might have made the difference for Kuzmin in the push against Ironside at Verst 18.

The weather stayed warm. Longer hours of daylight turned the roads into swamps from which Kuzmin would never retrieve his cannon and sleds if he did not retrieve them now. His men were exhausted and disheartened. The Yanks had captured the commissar of the Moscow Regiment when he was trapped under his horse. The commissar of the Saratov Regiment was among the dead: He had mistaken a lull in the firing for proof that his men had overrun a Yank position and, unsuspecting, rode directly up to the American barricade, where the doughboys unceremoniously shot him.

On April 5, Kuzmin broke off the engagement and began withdrawing south to Shelaxa, a staging depot a little north of Plesetskaya. The men at Verst 18 promptly moved west to Bolshie Ozerki, where they joined with the Onega Detachment. Spring had come. The weather, for the only time in history, had worked against Russia's advantage.

NOTES

1. "Strength of the Bolsheviks." North Russian Historical Files. 23-37:1.
2. Stewart Papers.
3. Strakhovsky, *op. cit.,* pp. 154–59.

CHAPTER 18

PARIS PEACE CONFERENCE:

APRIL 3–MAY 27, 1919

Neither in secret talks nor by open threats could the Allies persuade the White factions to meet with the Bolsheviks. By the time Wilson, Lloyd George, and Clemenceau returned to the conference table in mid-March, the Prinkipo bubble had burst. The American Commission to Negotiate Peace decided after a long wait that Professor George D. Herron and Mr. William Allen White, who had been selected to represent the United States at the Prinkipo Conference, should step down from their duties.

The first business anent Russia to come before Wilson and Lloyd George privately was William C. Bullitt's report. Accompanied by Walter Pettit, R. E. Lynch, and Lincoln Steffens, he had reached Russia in early March, seen that the Red Army was disciplined and numerous, that the Bolshevik Government was firmly in control and had the support of the people despite starvation but that Red leaders would discuss peace. If the Allies withdrew from Russia, Lenin promised to declare an armistice during which the Bolsheviks would discuss the settlement of issues with any White *de facto* government. Both White and Red factions would assume their share in repaying the debts of the old empire. Lenin said he was prepared to let the Whites keep what they had if the Allies would let the Reds keep what they had, subject eventually to the voluntary self-determination of the populations involved.

Certainly this was a better deal than the Allies could get by continued intervention. But Bullitt's report was suppressed. Suppression was easy since his mission had been covert. Though neither Wilson nor Lloyd George discussed the reasons for their suppression, still there are reasons that are not hard to guess. Many thought Kolchak's advance into Siberia in the early spring doomed peace. It may also have seemed to Wilson and Lloyd George that urging a *modus vivendi* with the Bolsheviks was a dangerous political ploy. Lastly, there is the truth that Lenin offered no guarantees that he could or would keep to the letter of his proposals.

Bullitt himself felt Lenin's proposals failed in the main because Woodrow Wilson chose to ignore them. Bullitt was to say later that Woodrow Wilson's refusal to burden his one-track mind with Russia may well have turned out to have been the single most important decision made in Paris.

What Bullitt didn't know, however, was that on April 3 Wilson suffered a cerebral vascular occlusion of the brain—a "little" stroke as differentiated from a "big" stroke, which is accompanied by gross paralysis and aphasia.* Though impaired, Wilson kept on working, his illness disguised as influenza by the White House physician, Dr. Cary Grayson. The President shifted much of his work load onto Colonel House. House was not nearly as prepared to consider and urge adoption of Bullitt's report as Wilson himself. And where Wilson would not venture, Lloyd George would not go. Thus neither House nor Lloyd George commented on Bullitt's report, nor did they show it to the peace conference.

Bullitt resigned. He wrote an angry letter to Woodrow Wilson: "I am sorry you did not fight our fight to the finish and that you had so little faith in the millions of men like myself, in every nation, who had faith in you."[1] In 1933, Bullitt became the first American ambassador to the U.S.S.R., a post he resigned after three years because he was sickened by Josef Stalin's tyranny.

When Wilson recovered from his influenza, he assented to

---

* *Cf.* Edwin A. Weinstein, "Woodrow Wilson's Neurological Illiness," *Causes and Consequences of World War I*, ed. by John Milton Cooper, Jr. New York: Quadrangle Books, 1972, pp. 315–46.

Lloyd George's request to keep American troops in Vladivostok until the Kolchak regime was secure. In that first April after the war, Kolchak had promised the Allies to convene the Constituent Assembly, to hold free elections, to abolish permanently the old class system of privileges, to recognize the independence of Finland and Poland, and to permit the League of Nations to draw up the subsequent frontiers of Russia. In return the Allies promised to provide him with munitions, supplies, and food as well as *de facto* recognition. This was as good a deal as the Allies could hope for, much better than Lenin's. What made it false coin was that Kolchak's White Army was not capable of beating the Reds. By the time Woodrow Wilson left the conference for good on May 27th, the Bolsheviks had turned the tide in Siberia. The White armies were in flight, in disarray, rushing pell-mell toward a winter which would impose defeat, starvation, and death. Eventually the Reds would rule.

NOTES

1. John Silverlight, *The Victor's Dilemma.* New York: Weybright and Talley, 1972, p. 189.

CHAPTER 19

ARCHANGEL:

APRIL 14–JUNE 23, 1919

The spring thaw made Ironside vulnerable on the Dvina at Toulgas and on the Vaga at Kitsa. The ice would break up in the south first and jam the northern narrows at Archangel. This would give Bolo gunboats three weeks of unopposed navigation, time to blow up the defenses for which the blood of so many men had reddened the snow.

Ironside hurried barbed wire in coil to these points. Doughboys wound it in double aprons through forests and across tundras. The Yanks stored food and ammunition in their blockhouses, enough of both to last sixty days. In the woods, the Yanks began laying booby traps. Concealed wires attached to sticks and branches detonated grenades. Dummy machine guns fired at regular intervals by an ingenious arrangement of water buckets: A higher bucket with a small hole leaked water into another below. When the water reached a certain level, the bucket tipped, pulling a string attached to a trigger.

The ice began to break up with a grinding, crunching roar. Slowly at first, gaining speed quickly, the ice floes moved, bobbing like gigantic seals as they sped down the river to smash into a jam at Archangel. Giant slabs jutted from the water. Floes pyramided against natural obstacles and the shore.

Doughboys from the 310th Engineers began drilling holes in

the jam in which to explode dynamite. They blew it in mid-April. With an incessant roar that one witness compared to the dumping of rocks by a million trucks over a precipice, the great bergs began hurtling through the estuary, spinning like tops. Old huts and tumbling boats and drowned animals spun toward the White Sea.

Sooner than the Bolsheviks expected, therefore, the Allied gunboats moved upriver to support the infantry. In a surprise attack, the Yanks, accompanied by the gunboat *Glow Worm*, retook Kitsa.

After this battle, Ironside began withdrawing the Yanks from the Dvina and replacing them with Russians. General Eugene Miller had spent the winter mustering and training a White Army. From Paris, Chaikovsky advised Miller that the Allies were putting their money on Kolchak and that it was politic for the Northern Region formally to accept the authority of the government at Omsk. Accordingly, in April 1919, to present the Allies with the fact of White Russian unity, the Provisional Government of the Northern Region unanimously voted itself out of existence. Kolchak's ministers accepted this submission and appointed General Miller governor-general and commander-in-chief of Russian land and sea forces operating against the Bolsheviks in Archangel Province. Miller was anxious to commit his army, to test it against the Reds, and Ironside was equally anxious to put Russians in the field. Consequently, Ironside gave Miller the task of defending Toulgas, and by late April Miller had relieved the Yank garrison with the 3rd North Russian Rifle Regiment.

Whatever hopes Ironside and the British still nourished for a link-up with Kolchak in the south were soon dismayed. On April 25, in a mass defection at Toulgas, the troops of the 3rd North Russian Rifle Regiment murdered their officers, joined the Bolsheviks, and drove out the few loyal Whites. Toulgas was in Red hands, and Ironside knew he had to drive them out as a matter of self-preservation. Tommies in Archangel disassembled two sixty-pound cannons and prepared to transport them overland to Kurgomen on the west bank of the Dvina below Bereznik. Here these guns could pound Toulgas. Captain Edwin Stuart, a Canadian, supervised the crash construction of big sleighs in the naval workshops. He mounted each gun on a ten-horse sleigh, each trail and carriage on another, each wheel on still others, and each buffer on six-horse sleighs. Fifty one-horse sleighs pulled the ammunition. Stuart needed 118 ponies in all. Once these big guns opened up on Toulgas, the Bolos retreated, and British infantry retook the port town in May.

Where Ironside had tragic consequences on the Dvina when he relieved the Yanks, he had comic consequences on the Pinega in the northeast. There Ironside had posted a White regiment under the command of Lieutenant Colonel Dilatorski, a Cossack from the south who had heretofore proved resourceful. Several British officers came north with Dilatorski to help launch hit-and-run attacks against the gathering Bolsheviks. Guerrilla tactics did not suit Dilatorski, who sent off an expedition to capture Karpogora once again, a movement doughboy Captain Conway had warned was wasteful. Wasteful it was. The Bolsheviks cut down the British officers and scattered the White Russians before they were fairly under way. Dilatorski compounded this ineptitude by sending out his reserves to rescue the already dispersed advance. The Bolos decimated the reserves as well.

Ruefully, Ironside confessed to himself that he should have known better. Russians were incompetent in command because they were unable to assess the military situation seriously. Ironside included as proof one of Dilatorski's orders to his troops:

> Talking to me today, Captain Akutin mentioned that Lt. Yadivin had told him that Yemetskoe and Seletskoe had been taken by the Bolsheviks. On being asked by Captain Akutin where he had heard this, Yadivin said that I was supposed to have said this to some young lady. I am not acquainted with any young ladies in Pinega, and have not been sent here to flirt but to fight. The taking of Seletskoe and Temetskoe are Bolshevik falsehoods. I demand from all officers and men, who during their free time flirt with women, not to discuss with them military matters, but to entertain their ladies with subjects more interesting for them, such as love, the moon, etc. It is scandalous for men, especially officers, to spread such panicky rumors.[1]

Brigadier Wilds P. Richardson arrived in Archangel on April 17 to take command of the 339th and provide for its evacuation. A West Pointer, class of 1884, Richardson had served for many years in Alaska, where he not only supervised the construction of roads, including the "Richardson Highway," but had also built camps, hospitals, and shelter facilities for the prospectors who failed to find gold during the Yukon rush. Richardson had received his command in March but was stranded in London without transport until the Navy, learning of his dilemma, assigned the USS *Chester* to take him, thirty-five replacement officers, and 265 enlisted men of a railroad company to Archangel to arrange the transport home of the 339th.

The first Americans sailed for Brest before Memorial Day. Another portion of the command embarked at Ekonomie on June 3, another on June 16, and the last on June 27. Headquarters left on August 5 and Richardson himself on August 23.

As these transports steamed down the Dvina a pervasive melancholy settled on many of the men. It is always sad saying goodbye to anything for the last time. It is certainly sad saying goodbye to a countryside where good friends have lost their lives. Much of Russia itself is a sad place, a brooding, mysterious plain where in most seasons the noon sky is the color of dirty snow.

One hundred and nine Americans were killed in battle; thirty-five died of wounds received in action; 100 died in drownings or accidental deaths or disease; 305 were wounded; and many were hospitalized with influenza.[2] The 339th and its support units had disproportionately fewer casualties than the Yanks on the Western Front, where 83,000 were killed in action and 250,000 hospitalized. The disproportion is significant when one realizes that the 339th fought for a longer and more continuous time than any American division in France. Yet it suffered only one suicide and only a few self-inflicted wounds (not included among the casualties).

It was not that the Bolsheviks were inept. If they had won at Toulgas in November or taken Bereznik in January or Bolshie Ozerki in April they would have inflicted far heavier casualties. Considering what the Red Army accomplished between 1918 and

1920 the Bolsheviks made pretty good soldiers. The 339th suffered less because its morale, about which the command constantly worried, never deteriorated to the point where men ambush themselves. The weather and the terrain of North Russia made combat a terrible hardship. The mystifying cause for which the Yanks fought robbed them of devotion. They were men who fought without a Crispin's Day. These factors made them unhappy and bewildered but for several reasons did not demoralize them. The men fought in small, disparate units, and soldiers will always stick longer for the love of their buddies than for the glory of the regiment or the honor of the country. The Yanks also fought from defensive positions so that they were giving more than they took; their rifle power and automatic weapons were always adequate for the killing task; they were not, like the White Russians, fighting for the protection of home and dear ones, which noticeably weakens the resolve of soldiers when the enemy savages the civilian rear or promises eternal retribution.

The 339th had one last depressing discovery to make about their British allies when they reached Brest. They had been paid in pound sterling pegged by an arbitrage board in London at a rate applicable only for North Russia. When they cashed in their pounds, the men of the 339th received fewer dollars than their fellow soldiers in France who had been paid in American currency or French francs.

NOTES

1. Ironside, *op. cit.*, p. 118.
2. March, *op. cit.*, p. 150.

CHAPTER 20

LORD OF THE EAST:

MAY 22–AUGUST 7, 1919

Soldiers, the regulars used to remark, should never drown, get kicked to death by a mule, or give in to pneumonia—soldiers should bleed. The regulars in Vladivostok and Siberia bled from unprovoked Cossack terror which claimed a dozen lives here and there. In the small railroad depot of Polsolskaya, for example, a Cossack machine gunner inadvertently or maliciously let off several rounds which killed three sleeping Yanks. There were similar incidents elsewhere. Once the doughboys leveled their rifles, however, the Cossacks always backed down. The serious incursions into Yank security came from Bolshevik guerrillas.

Armed guerrillas were nothing new to the men of the 27th and 31st regiments. They had contended against Moros and dissident Tagalogs in the Philippines for almost two decades. What was new were the strategy and the tactics of the guerrillas. These have been clearly defined by Mao Tse-tung, who himself came upon their definition by a close study of the Russian Civil War. The guerrilla's strategy in the twentieth century, wrote Mao, is that of one against a thousand; his tactics are that of a thousand against one. The guerrilla does not claim the lives of enemy soldiers, for the enemy can bury an unlimited number of soldiers; the guerrilla disrupts the economy, for there is a limit to the number of bridges the enemy can repair and blasted factories he can recommission. It was this kind of war that the Bolshevik guerrillas waged in eastern Siberia. In the beginning, the Bolsheviks concentrated on bushwhacking the Japanese.

These Red partisans did not war against the Americans or the Czechs. The Czechs were perpetually alert. The Americans were few in number and disposed to be humane. When an American company under the command of Lieutenant Fairfax Channing occupied the village of Uspenskaya, it simply confiscated firearms without making an arrest, burning a building or hanging a Russian. Pragmatic young Yank lieutenants conferred unofficially with guerrilla leaders. They argued that each of them had a duty to perform, the Yanks to guard the railroad, the partisans to free their country. The lieutenants proposed an accommodation: Stay away from the railway and no one will oppose you elsewhere. In the beginning, for the Bolsheviks at least, it was a good bargain.[1]

As the guerrillas, however, grew more adept, they began to take more desperate and damaging measures. Bold leaders emerged, ambitious and dangerous men who cared nothing for caution. Among these was Yakov Ivanovitch Triapitsyn, once a metalworker, later a sergeant in the Imperial Army, finally a fanatic partisan leader able to wring from his followers enormous sacrifices.

By mid-1919, the Bolshevik apparat in eastern Siberia had undertaken a campaign first to disrupt, then retake the Ussuri Valley, which runs from Kharbarovsk to Vladivostok. Triapitsyn, who was to gain international notoriety as the executioner of the entire Japanese garrison at Nikol'sk in 1920, began the campaign with recurring attacks on freight and passenger trains. But he saw quickly that the way to cripple the valley was to close down the Suchan mines, which supplied the coal for the entire area. This would immobilize all rail movement from Vladivostok. It would punish Kolchak. The Bolsheviks started with certain advantages. The coal miners were proletarians and, if not pro-Bolshevik, certainly anti-Kolchak. The Reds infiltrated the working force and helped stage a series of miners' strikes which lowered production.

The White commander at Vladivostok wanted to march into Suchan, seize the strike leaders, execute them, and drive the rest of the workers back to the pits. General Graves, whose responsibility it was to keep the mines in operation, forbade this, knowing that such a police action would close down the mines forever. The White press accused Graves of Red sympathies. Graves replied that American soldiers had strict orders to support the police in arresting those charged with criminal activity. A strike was hardly criminal activity.

When this explanation brought forth even more vituperation, Graves proposed to withdraw the Yanks and let the Russians run the mines themselves.

The partisans boldly occupied some of the surrounding towns. Little coal came out of Suchan, and fewer supplies, foodstuffs, and money went in. A Kolchak general named Smirnof had to mount an expedition of three hundred men to drive guerrillas out of Novitskaya, another mining village. The miners, through their unions and their *zemstovs,* passed resolutions that denied Kolchak's authority. They refused to report for army duty. A White detachment came to Suchan and at the Brovnitchi and Gordyevka mines executed nine men. The strike went on. Miners began joining the partisan bands. Even the local police fell under Bolshevik influence and many of them quit their posts. On May 22, 1919, the Suchan miners declared a general workingman's strike throughout the Maritime Province. From his headquarters on May 23, Triapitsyn demanded the withdrawal of all Allied troops from the Suchan Valley. He threatened to use force to drive out Allied detachments, the first open declaration against the Americans by the partisans.

The fourteen mines of the Suchan fields lay in the center of a fertile valley forty miles northeast of Amerika Bay. Dotted with small villages, the valley was five miles wide, running north and south. Through its center flowed the Suchan River, navigable for boats of three-foot draft as far north as Vladimiro-Alexandrovskaya.

Army intelligence estimated there were two thousand Bolshevik partisans in the area, divided into companies of 150 men each. These men were harbored in the small villages that sur-

rounded the Suchan fields. The elite among these troops were at
Kazanka. They were armed with high-powered rifles and 150
rounds apiece. Among them surprisingly were a large number of
Koreans.[2]

On June 22, the attenuating edginess between the Yanks and
the Bolsheviks flared like a Martin-and-Coy feud. At 11:00 A.M.
Corporal Harlan S. Daley and Privates Harold Bullard and Forest
Moore were kidnapped by Bolsheviks as they fished in the Suchan
River. Later in the day, two other fishermen, Lieutenant Custer
Fribley and Corporal Eastland Reed, were also marched off by
Red partisans.

Lieutenant Gilpin Rumans went out with a mounted patrol
to determine what had happened to the five men reported absent.
A Korean peasant told him they were in the hands of the Reds.
Rumans tracked them upriver to the ford, where he found three
fishing poles. He tried to communicate with the partisans across
the river, but though Rumans was sure they were there, he got no
answer.

With 110 men of Company M, 31st Infantry, Rumans came
back, crossed the Suchan, and started to ride into the little village
of Novitskaya. The troops proceeded toward the main street as
dusk was gathering. A church bell tolled twice. Bolsheviks behind
bushes, in high windows and in trenches to his front opened fire
on Rumans. Rumans spurred his men forward, gained the intersection with a wall for cover, and a Yank machine gun began
raking every available target. Dismounted Yanks dashed from
house to house flushing snipers. When the fight ended, five Americans lay dead in the street. Many Bolsheviks had perished. But the
surviving Bolsheviks had taken the five fishermen to another location, a small mining village called Frolovka.

The funeral of the dead Americans took place the next day
attended by the regiment and a platoon of Japanese troops. At
Suchan Mine No. 1 Colonel G. H. Williams considered the next
move.

No one tried to figure out why Bolsheviks would kidnap five
Yanks. The Bolsheviks were under no misapprehension that this
mischief would frighten away a disciplined occupying force. They

were, in fact, probably sure that the kidnapping would bring out a determined rescue party and when that party was fired upon, another thousand would rush to the event. In retrospect, it is probable that the partisans were in the process of making a move which the five men, innocently fishing, stumbled upon. What that move was became apparent two days later.

On the night of June 24, Lieutenant Lawrence Butler arrived in Romanovka to take over command of the third platoon of Company A. Romanovka was to the west of Suchan on the important spur which connected the mines to the Vladivostok-bound tracks five miles to the southwest. Butler inspected the camp, noting that the men had pitched it at the foot of a hill. Butler thought he would move the camp to the crest in the morning where it would be more defensible. But he never got the chance.

The single trooper on outer guard quit his post as usual at daybreak and returned to camp. When he left, several hundred partisans crept forward on their bellies through the tall grass. They opened fire from the rim of the hill into the camp below. Caught by surprise on the dangerous low ground, the platoon lost twenty-six men in the first few minutes of the fusillade. But Lieutenant Butler, despite having the lower part of his jaw shot away, got the rest into a firing line and began to fight back. Giving orders with his hands, Butler kept a sharp watch on the rapidly diminishing supply of ammunition. Butler held the platoon together. While some partisans kept up the firing into the American camp, others began destroying the railroad.[3]

Corporal Valeryan Brodnicki volunteered to try to make it north to Novo-Nezhino, where the other two platoons of Company A were on duty. Though wounded once in the arm and more seriously in the ankle, Brodnicki, who would win the Distinguished Service Cross for his heroism, got past the ring of Red fire and headed up the railroad tracks. As he stumbled along, weakening from the loss of blood, he came upon the supply train moving south. Firing his rifle to bring it to a halt, Brodnicki ordered the engineer to back it up to Novo-Nezhino. While the company medic cut away the shoe and bandaged the pulpy, discoloring ankle, Brodnicki flashed the story. Lieutenant James Lorimer, who was in command of A Company's two remaining platoons, armed the second with machine guns and BARs and decided he would take it by train to Butler's relief. He ordered Sergeant James Gardner to have the first platoon start laying railroad ties for a barricade and to entrench as soon as possible.

Brodnicki's limping dash had beaten the Bolos to the punch. When the guerrilla force came upon Novo-Nezhino later in the morning, the defensively secure Yanks beat them off, suffering only two wounded while killing more than twenty of the enemy.

In the meantime, Lorimer's force moved four miles south by train before it ran into torn-up track. Double-timing, the platoon took fire at Sitsa, three miles to the south. They suffered two wounded but kept rushing on to Romanovka. Lorimer came upon the enemy's flank. It was the guerrilla's turn to be surprised. Yank machine guns and BARs opened up with such ferocity that the tracer bullets soon set the fields on fire. The partisans withdrew to the south. Lorimer and his platoon went down to the camp, where the ground was strewn with webbing, discarded canteens, expended cartridge shells, and blood-soaked bodies. Yanks moaned from the pain of splintered bones. Dead men, kneeling like Muslims, stared with sightless eyes into the ground. Lieutenant Butler had passed out by the ammo boxes, where he was prying them open with a borrowed bayonet.

Despite the shooting war that was about to rage around Suchan, Triapitsyn offered to trade the five captured Yank fishermen for several captured partisans and a deserter named Vasily Shedko. Along with this communiqué was a letter from imprisoned Lieutenant Custer Fribley, who assured his CO that the partisans did indeed hold five Yanks, that they meant business, and was there any way the command could send on some smokes? The American command effected the transfer although Colonel Williams refused to include Shedko.

General Graves ordered Williams "to proceed with force and vigor" to clear the partisans from the Suchan area, a harder job than was immediately apparent. The partisans had cut all communications and rail lines between Suchan and the surrounding towns. The trains from Vladivostok were immobilized. Colonel Williams had no immediate source of supply for the American units which were proceeding to Mine No. 1. So the colonel turned to the sea.

By the beginning of July, the cruiser USS *Albany,* a British and two Russian merchantmen were in Amerika Bay, their crews offloading supplies on a quickly constructed wharf. Along with food and ammunition came several dozen pack mules, horses, and some 37-mm cannons, which traveled overland to Suchan. They were used to outfit Company C and auxiliary troops, which moved out under the command of Major Sidney C. Graves (the general's son) on July 2 in a crescent swinging west-northeast. Another column consisting of Company M and a Japanese infantry detachment under the command of Williams left on July 4 to swing east-northwest. Three more companies under the command of Lieutenant Colonel Robert Eichelberger left on July 5, proceeding due north from Suchan. The three columns were to clear out every Bolshevik and every guerrilla in every town.

It was tough campaigning. Lieutenant F. M. Kindsay in Eichelberger's column described the action in his "Report of Activities":

> The column left Shkotova for Maihe. To make an ideal day for battle there should be rain. So it rained. Maihe lies six versts inland on the banks of the Maihe River, a low-banked sluggish stream. The fields and roads quickly became a bottomless sea of mud. Through this the troops, wagons, guns and mules plowed to Maihe. A short skirmish gave us the town. The return to Shkotova was made after several hours of road repairing, digging out of mules and hoists on wheels.[4]

And again:

> An enveloping movement was executed on the town of Novitskaya. One 37 mm gun and two machine guns accompanied the right flank. An early start was effected and the town occupied by 7:00 A.M. Patrols and numerous

snipers in the hills caused some casualties. A platoon commanded by Lt. Fred Shepard was sent out to clean up the
hills. The 37 mm and the machine guns assisted with heavy
fire. The enemy evacuated the nearby hills.[5]

So it went, town by town, through Gordyevka, Novorosia,
Olga, and Tethune: two Yanks dying here, three wounded there,
but on the whole the three columns conducted a successful antiguerrilla campaign. They outgunned the enemy and their determination matched his.

The mud which turned the fields into a morass, the blazing
sun which made water rationing an agony, the mules who kicked
their shoes, the guns whose breeches jammed were not to be compared with the poison gas, the barbed wire, and the suicidal assaults of the Western Front. Still these soldiers in Siberia were
moving in a country where the terrain harbored ever-present danger and they were moving against an enemy who would never commit the numbers to a battle that would yield a decisive result.

Sailors and Marines from the *Albany* and the USS *New Orleans* garrisoned the captured villages. On August 7, Captain
B. H. Rhoads with a combat patrol of forty men dealt an annihilating blow to a group of thirty partisans. This convinced Triapitsyn
to withdraw from the area.

One day the Suchan Valley was charged with danger and
hidden foes and the next it was placid and empty. But before they
left, the partisans had rendered the rail lines to the Suchan fields
inoperable for several months. The guerrillas had also damaged
the paternalistic and neutral image of the Americans and drawn
them closer to the vortex. Colonel Williams noted in his final
report that "The ever-present anti-American feeling and propaganda among the governmental class of the Maritime Province
became acute."[6]

Overall, the Siberian Expedition took the lives of 170 soldiers
and another fifty-two were wounded. Fifty deserted.[7] Intelligence
estimated that the Suchan campaign killed some five hundred Bolshevik guerrillas. The casualties led Tasker Bliss to surmise in a
letter to Newton D. Baker:

Bolshevism exists everywhere; and it will exist after we have killed the last Bolshevik. The trouble is that we are trying to kill Bolsheviks and not Bolshevism. The latter can be killed but not by force of arms. After most thinking men have come to the conclusion that a way must and can be found to combat Bolshevism otherwise than by armies, I am sorry to see statements in the American press that our government has decided to lend aid to the Kolchak Government.[8]

NOTES

1. White, *op. cit.,* pp. 272–73.
2. "Report of Operations in the Suchan Valley, Siberia: June 22 to July 5." Also "Headquarters Mine Guard: Report in Compliance With Memorandum no. 36." *Historical Files of the AEF in Siberia.* 21:33-6.
3. Virginia Westall Cooper, "The Prelude and Aftermath of the Romanovka Massacre as Told by Russell C. Swihart." Joseph Longueven Papers. *The Siberian Collection.* 74064-10v.
4. "September 14, 1919." Longueven Papers, *op. cit.*
5. *Ibid.*
6. "Report in Compliance." Longueven Papers, *op. cit.*
7. March, *op. cit.,* p. 132.
8. Quoted in Unterbarger, *op. cit.,* p. 164.

CHAPTER 21

ARCHANGEL:

JULY 1–SEPTEMBER 26, 1919

The British War Cabinet knew there were compelling political reasons for evacuating North Russia. The British people no longer approved of the intervention, and the British contribution to Russia had caused a serious drain on the nation's resources. By the summer, the War Cabinet realized that there were equally compelling military reasons for evacuating North Russia. Sir Henry Wilson, Chief of the Imperial General Staff, noted that while the Mesopotamian campaign started with the dispatch of two brigades, it ultimately absorbed 900,000 men. It behooved England, Sir Henry went on, to apply what resources were still available in the most profitable direction. North Russia offered no prospects of a decisive result.[1]

The Imperial General Staff also realized that the army needed troops for Ireland, wracked by civil war, and for India, agitating for independence. Even that ardent champion of thoroughgoing intervention, Winston Churchill, saw the necessity for a withdrawal in the North. He told the House of Commons in May, "There is reasonable hope that the whole of this North Russian situation may be placed on a purely Russian basis before the end of summer without anything in the nature of a disaster to our troops or the desertion of friends."[2]

But the crucial determination for a British withdrawal came

from Ironside. Three more closely related mutinies convinced him that the cause of rallying the Whites was hopeless.

The effect of these mutinies on Ironside was traumatic. He advised London to implement plans for an early evacuation. He said without qualification that the Whites could not nor did they want to defend themselves. London believed him. London was relieved.

In speculating later why the Whites failed—why, despite their anti-Bolshevism, they could not infuse fighting spirit in their troops—Ironside thought one important reason was the failure of a national hero or heroes to emerge after the February Revolution. Such heroes had emerged in America after the Revolution of 1776 and in France after the Revolution of 1789. Ironside believed a second reason the Whites failed was that there was too great a gap between officers and men. White officers were elite egotists, too proud, too vainglorious, and too fond of drinking to become competent let alone resolute battlefield leaders.*

Ironside's realization that the war could not go on was a hard disappointment. It came on the heels of British reinforcements newly arrived—eight thousand of them, volunteers all, regulars who had survived the Western Front, led by officers with names out of Burke's Peerage. Commanded by Brigadiers G. W. St. George Grogan and L. W. deV. Sadlier-Jackson, the brigades came at the behest of Winston Churchill, who had asked for volunteers to rescue the troops at Archangel, romantically transforming the north of Russia into a snowy Mafeking. Churchill wanted resplendent and efficient brigades in case Lloyd George and the cabinet changed its collective mind about the intervention. With the British had also come a contingent of four hundred Russian officers, recruited from German prisoner-of-war camps, from a special Russian brigade in France, and from the many Russian war

---

* Ironside knew whereof he speculated. For unfathomable reasons, a cargo of Scotch whiskey had been offloaded at Archangel. The whiskey had severe and troublesome effects on many British officers. But Ironside got rid of the drunks on the instant. White Russians did not. For perhaps equally unfathomable reasons there was little drunkenness among the American contingent of officers and enlisted men.

agencies in London. Churchill hoped they would become the nerve centers and backbone of General Miller's army.

The docks and piers of Archangel, the streets and municipal buildings were as festooned and gaily decorated as they were when Poole had come ashore ten months before. But the new units had come to rescue the old, not to spearhead an advance. Knowing that the announcement of British evacuation would paralyze Miller's forces, Ironside cheerfully and hypocritically announced on the day the reinforcements arrived that "I shall move up river and take Kotlas."

Ironside had to bring out of Archangel roughly twelve thousand British troops and roughly as many Whites, who simply could not be abandoned. The British Expedition had to have a necessary respite from Bolshevik offensive moves for the evacuation. To gain this respite, Ironside resolved to use the new brigades to strike a swift, disengaging blow up the Dvina. He would stagger the Bolos, drive them back, then disengage his forces for the pull-out. It is paradoxical that the war in North Russia, which opened with the first combined air-sea-land operation, was to close with a last Napoleonic maneuver.

General Sadlier-Jackson commanded when the British struck at dawn on August 10. Behind a rolling barrage, with an observation balloon to point the way, the air controlled by an RAF squadron, the British leaped upon the surprised Bolsheviks. The surprise was made more devastating by the first use in war of "nerve" gas dropped on the Red rear. The new gas temporarily incapacitated and demoralized the Bolos.[3] The British took two thousand prisoners, eighteen field guns, and large quantities of arms and ammunition. The attack gained all of its objectives ahead of schedule. It was now obvious that the Bolsheviks could not seriously interfere with the withdrawal.

On August 11, General Henry Lord Rawlinson arrived from Britain to supervise the evacuation. Lloyd George sent him in part because he was a trusted and efficient commander—his troops had broken the Hindenburg Line—and in part because the dispatch of such a hero helped quiet growing public concern over the North Russian Expedition. Rawlinson was also something of a diplomat, having served on the Supreme War Council from time to time. He was also *pukka sahib*. "He received us," remarked a Russian officer, "like a viceroy receiving a delegation of niggers."[4]

If Ironside thought the arrival of Rawlinson diminished his own authority, he was too professional a soldier to reveal it. In no time, Ironside was calling Rawlinson "Rawly" and Rawlinson was calling Ironside "Tiny." The relationship became for Ironside a "precious friendship."*

On the night of August 11, Rawlinson and Ironside told General Miller and his staff that Britain was evacuating Archangel no later than the end of September. The British would take Russian units with them and key members of the old Provisional Government. Perhaps overly elated at the victory the day before, Miller and his entourage clicked their heels, bowed, and said they would stay on to free Russia from Bolshevism. Ironside said that such a decision condemned officers of the White Army to certain slaughter or execution and was against Russia's true interests. Miller said nonsense. Despite its perils, he would defend his post. "He chose a man's part," sighed Ironside. "All honor to him."

When he announced the British withdrawal to the Russian populace, Miller also announced a new tax for the defense of Archangel. He also forbade any Russian to apply for a British visa. Miller collected the tax, for businessmen and survivors of the Czarist regime realized that all that stood between them and the Bolsheviks was the White Army. But six thousand Russians nevertheless sailed with the British, who issued a visa to anyone who applied.

On September 10, British troops began boarding the transports. The next day Ironside and Rawlinson oversaw the destruction of British military equipment. Despite Miller's despair at what he considered wanton and purposeless deprivation, Rawlinson and

---

* Indeed it was. Rawlinson promoted Ironside to the permanent rank of major general, which kept him on active duty in a rapidly demobilizing British Army. Without Rawlinson's good offices, Ironside might have spent years tending roses beside a thatched roof cottage on half pay instead of becoming a viceroy of India and in 1940 Chief of the Imperial General Staff.

Ironside were sure that if they did not destroy this materiel, sooner rather than later it would add to the strength of the Red Army. Miller begged to keep five tanks. Rawlinson refused, saying he had strict orders to take them back.

At the end of the venture, British casualties numbered 196 officers and 877 other ranks of whom 41 officers and 266 other ranks perished in battle or of wounds received in battle. The cost to the Treasury was 18,000,000 pounds sterling or 105,000,000 dollars.[5]

The last ship carrying British troops and Russian civilians cleared Archangel on September 26, though one ship remained at the dock—a yacht that was to bear away Ironside and his staff (Rawlinson having departed for Murmansk to supervise the evacuation there). At dawn on the 27th, General Miller and his aide were piped aboard to exchange the final courtesies with Ironside. Ironside wished the Russians good luck. Miller bowed. Then Miller and his aide left, walking slowly down the gangplank. Ironside stood watching from the rail as Miller moved toward the city, hoping that Miller would turn and wave, but the Russian never looked back.

NOTES

1. Stewart, *op. cit.*, p. 198.
2. Strakhovsky, *op. cit.*, p. 193.
3. Ullman, *op. cit.*, pp. 181–82.
4. David Footman, *Murmansk and Archangel*. Oxford: Oxford University Press, 1957, p. 43.
5. Stewart, *op. cit.*, p. 204.

CHAPTER 22

OMSK:

JULY 3–NOVEMBER 14, 1919

The elite of Kolchak's armies were British-trained and equipped Ukrainians who wore the emblem of the death's-head as insignia and called themselves "The Immortals." When the Bolsheviks hit them, the Ukrainians massacred their officers, ripped off their skulls and bones in panic, and began running to the rear. It was common knowledge that the Reds inflicted particularly cruel reprisals on elite units. The mass desertion gave the Reds the rail depot of Ufa in the center of Kolchak's line. The Reds regrouped and moved north to attack Gaida's army. Gaida saw he would have to retreat lest the Reds sever his communications. His retreat also became a disorderly scramble. The Reds took Perm on July 3, and now there was no army between them and Ekaterinburg.

Kolchak fired Gaida.

The young Czech general had demanded that atrocities come to an end.

Kolchak explained he had no control over continuing White terror. White terror would end when Red terror ended.

Gaida had requisitioned private freight trains at railway stations. He had cashiered corrupt White officers. He had exposed and punished bribery and corruption, whereas Kolchak wanted Gaida to use the chain of command to insure efficiency.

The nub of their disagreement was Gaida's demand that he

pull his northern army back across Siberia as far as Omsk, that here he prepare for a defensive stand. Gaida said that until the Supreme Ruler could put Siberia in order with an acceptable land policy, with civil and criminal courts, and with some kind of representative government, offensive war against the Bolsheviks was futile. Western Siberia was convinced that the Bolsheviks were preferable to the Whites.

In a stormy interview during which Kolchak threw an inkwell at a map and broke several pens, Gaida stood unblinking and contemptuous.

"What can I expect of you?" asked Kolchak. "You have no military education."

"And you," said Gaida, "you commanded three ships in the Black Sea. Does that qualify you to govern an empire?"[1] Wrote General Janin, the representative of the French General Staff, a figurehead commander:

> That evening Gaida came to ask my signature for a Czecho-
> slovak passport as well as for an encouraging word. He had
> had a violent quarrel with the Russians who wanted to
> break up his train and he intimated he would offer armed
> resistance. . . . That's shabby treatment after all he's done
> for Siberia and for the Admiral himself. . . . The Admiral
> threw up the fact to him that he had democratic tendencies,
> that he favored Socialist Revolutionaries, and that he
> counted in his armies and General Staff officers of progres-
> sive views. Gaida replied that the reactionary orientation
> was a dangerous thing; that the promises made to Siberia
> had not been kept; hence the trouble and this was becom-
> ing dangerous. . . . To the threat of court martial Gaida
> replied he was a Czech and therefore not Kolchak's sub-
> ordinate. He asks for my protection and for eventual sup-
> port of Czechoslovak troops; he seems to fear they will
> arrest him.[2]

Janin put the French imprimatur on Gaida's passport and guaranteed him safe passage through Siberia to Vladivostok. However, Kolchak demanded that Gaida give up his train and proceed

only with his Czech escort. Gaida didn't argue. He detached the armored vans, but he stripped them of machine guns, which he mounted atop of and inside his own coach. Kolchak watched the operation and asked sarcastically, "What else do you want?"

"Only that the truth shall be spoken about me," said Gaida.

The Allies felt Gaida's dismissal was bad politics since it followed so soon after Kolchak had commissioned him commander-in-chief of Siberia and the Western Armies. Gaida's capture of Perm was the only really important Kolchak victory. The peasants among the civilian population had hailed Gaida as a hero. Soldiers trusted his leadership and judgment.

Gaida left Omsk on July 12. It was a hazardous trip. Both Bolsheviks and Whites wanted him dead. At the Onon River, he and his consort found the Bolsheviks had destroyed the steel suspension bridge. When Russian engineers surmised it would take two years to erect another span, Gaida disgustedly turned from them and brought on some Czechs from a nearby echelon. With Gaida supervising, the men promptly built a causeway by filling boxes with stones and sinking them evenly for pilings. Then the Czechs threw tracks across the river and Gaida's train passed on, two weeks after it had halted.

Red partisans tried to ambush the train at Ossa-Ochansk and were beaten off handily. Gaida arrived in Vladivostok on August 8 and declared to newspapermen:

> The Kolchak Government cannot possibly stand and if the Allies support him they will make the greatest mistake in history. The Government is divided into two distinct parts, one issues proclamations and propaganda for foreign consumption stating that the Government favors and works for a Constituent Assembly, the other part secretly plans and plots for a restoration of the monarchy.[3]

Kolchak had more on his mind now than Gaida's barbs. He had tried to flank the Reds at Ekaterinburg in a maneuver that required the skills of a Julius Caesar. He failed. He tried to make a stand at Tobol, where the Reds took fifteen thousand Whites as prisoners and left twenty thousand dead on the field. Not only did these battles devastate the White Army but used up the strategic reserve. The All-Russian Provisional Government had lost the important industrial and agricultural regions of the Urals. More importantly, it had not only lost its will but its ability to fight.

Kolchak replaced Gaida with General Dietrichs. For a dictator who despised the Czechs, he relied often enough on their leaders. Dietrichs was a deeply religious man who covered the walls of his railway coach with icons and who was often found by members of his staff in solemn, solitary prayer. Nevertheless, he was an astute military man who saw that at Ufa, Perm, Ekaterinburg, and Tobol the Bolsheviks had dealt the White Army a lethal blow. Militarily, the White cause was done for. The All-Russian Government could not prevail. So Dietrichs suggested to the Supreme Ruler that he would have to couch the war against the Bolsheviks as a Holy War. Only thus could Kolchak hope to rally men to his banner. Dietrichs planned to organize orders of the "Holy Cross" among the refugee soldiers to equip them morally for battle. He did, in fact, put together a detachment of priests who went into the line with crosses and yellow banners on high and who made a tremendous if unfortunately short-lived impression.

Dietrichs also saw that Kolchak would have to abandon Omsk, which was on the west bank of the Irtysh, and prepare his heavy fortifications on the east bank. A heavily defended line here might persuade the Bolsheviks to draw up short: Their spearheads were overextended and their armies were dependent upon rail communication. They probably would consolidate their gains to the west before crossing the river eastward. This would give Kolchak time, another winter certainly, to prop up his government and perhaps coax the Allies past Lake Baikal.

Kolchak refused to listen to either of Dietrichs' suggestions. There may well have been no merit in the concept of a holy war, but there was merit in pointing out that the line could only hold where natural barriers helped. Omsk, however, had symbolic value for Kolchak. The Supreme Ruler promised that he would, if necessary, die fighting in the streets of Omsk. He thought his promises of an election for a Constituent Assembly would finally lure the Allies out of eastern into western Siberia. The Constituent Assembly would sit in Omsk.

But this was hardly a practical hope. The Allies were having second thoughts about extending recognition. The American ambassador to Japan, Rowland Morris, thought that American recognition of the Omsk regime would put America in a pre-eminent position to assist and lead in the reconstruction of Russia, but he also advised his superiors that Kolchak was losing and the odds were that he would continue to lose. The passionate pro-White analysts of the State Department began to gauge the risks involved in recognizing and aiding Kolchak. It meant the bearable loss of money, the less bearable loss of prestige, and the loss of public support, which an Administration cannot bear at all.

Woodrow Wilson, in a direct response to Clemenceau, said the United States could furnish no more troops to Siberia, not even to relieve the Czechs. Two weeks later, at the end of August, the State Department informed Ambassador Morris that Wilson's Administration would not formally recognize the Omsk Government because the United States could not give it the support necessary to insure its survival.[4]

If this decision disappointed Kolchak, the deliberations of the British must have maddened him. The British Cabinet decided to do its best for Kolchak though it saw no reason to accept Kolchak's view of what was the best. The British view of what was best was to couple the efforts of Denikin and Kolchak. Denikin was fighting in a semicircle that extended from Odessa on the Black Sea in the west to Kiev to Veronezh to Tsaritsyn (later Stalingrad) to Astrakhan on the Caspian Sea. To have regarded Denikin's effort as one with Kolchak's is a geographic anomaly. But what the British Cabinet meant was that it would continue aid to Kolchak as long as Denikin kept winning. In October, however, Denikin's forces began retreating. The British Cabinet decided that recognition of the Kolchak regime was a matter to be decided by the Allied governments acting in concert and that His Majesty's

Government was precluded from taking any separate action in the matter.[5]

Italy changed governments in June 1919, and Francesco Nitti became Premier. His predecessors had prepared an expedition of several divisions to fight in Russia. Nitti, who knew the precarious state of Italian monetary reserves, canceled the plans.

Kolchak had to go it alone. The real trouble with going it alone was that the Bolsheviks knew it too. Once they took Chelyabinsk, where they refitted their Fifth Army, particularly the 27th Division, they were unstoppable because they knew that the only armies that could halt them were foreign armies, foreign armies that would not fight.

Physically courageous, Kolchak toured the front to show the men he would brave death with them. But physical courage can no more turn back the invincible force than the will to live can halt the growth of cancer. White troops were in such bad shape that on one occasion the honor guard Kolchak inspected came to attention with feet wrapped in rags. Yet the aides and adjutants of Kolchak's retinue wore well-tailored British uniforms and stamped across the parade grounds in shiny British boots. It was inevitable that his own men would associate Kolchak with foreigners who had lost stomach for saving Russia. "For us," said a Cossack at the time, "an admiral is a kind of civilian."

When Kolchak refused to abandon Omsk, Dietrichs resigned. Kolchak appointed General Konstantin Sakharov, who promised to make Omsk into a Gibraltar. But then the Bolsheviks came, stretching across the horizon, falling away from sight with the curvature of the earth. Now Kolchak decided to run. Too late. In November of 1919, the temperature in Siberia rose instead of fell and the Irtysh did not freeze. The Whites could escape only over the railway bridge, which would not support the transport of heavy artillery and horses.

On November 14, the Bolsheviks were in the city. There was no street fighting. The snipers quickly surrendered and were just as quickly shot. The Red Army took ten thousand prisoners, forty locomotives and over one thousand trucks, made in the U.S.A., laden with food and ammunition. That night the river froze and

Bolshevik patrols made their way across it. They encountered no secondary defenses. Kolchak was no longer retreating. He was in flight. The multitudes of Siberia were fleeing with him.

NOTES

1. The exchange is quoted in Baerlein, *op. cit.*, p. 231, and in Stewart, *op. cit.*, p. 289.
2. Stewart, *op. cit.*, p. 289.
3. *Ibid.*, p. 291.
4. Unterbarger, *op. cit.*, pp. 160–61.
5. Ullman, *op. cit.*, Vol. II, p. 250.

CHAPTER 23

LORD OF THE EAST:

NOVEMBER 17–21, 1919

As the Bolsheviks closed in on Omsk, Vladivostok became as important to the Whites as Formosa became important to the Nationalist Chinese forty years later. In 1919 the Lord of the East was the last possible capital.

In the fall of 1919, however, it was ripe for revolution. It had a revolutionary cadre of dissident anti-Kolchak and anti-Bolshevik politicians and a garrison of eight thousand Czechs who were bitterly opposed to the Omsk regime.

But Kolchak realized how inflammable the situation was even before the revolutionaries. Kolchak replaced Dmitri Horvat, who had the figurehead title of Governor-General of the Far East, with General S. N. Rozanov. Rozanov was a Cossack who had commanded one of Kolchak's armies. He was a former colonel of the Imperial Staff. He was tough, barbaric, and he knew that his job was to keep Vladivostok for Kolchak.

Rozanov's first orders to Kolchak troops in the Maritime Province were to shoot one out of every ten people in villages that failed to turn over partisan leaders; to levy heavy fines on villages that failed to point out the location of the enemy; and to burn the town after executing the male population in villages that resisted Kolchak incursions.

"Rozanov proved to be the third worst character known to

me in Siberia," wrote Graves, "although he could never reach the plane occupied by Kalmykov and Semenov."[1]

Rozanov also moved four thousand of Kalmykov's Cossacks into the outskirts of Vladivostok. Allied military representatives protested. The Allies had concluded an agreement with Kolchak that they would keep peace in the city if he would keep the predatory Cossacks out. Czech, American, British, and French representatives served Rozanov with an ultimatum: Remove these troops or else. But it was a bluff. The British Foreign Office wired General Alfred Knox that he was to do nothing to weaken Kolchak. Knox told his colleagues British troops would not be used to enforce the ultimatum. Their ranks broken, the council of military representatives withdrew their demand.

The four thousand Cossacks were soldiers of indifferent quality, hardly the men Rozanov wanted in a crunch. The best-equipped and best-regarded soldiers in the Maritime Province were the officer candidates the British were training on Russian Island. There were over one thousand of these recruits, and Rozanov asked Knox for the right to use them in the event of a revolution. Knox said yes.

For there was indeed a revolution brewing. Rozanov knew it. Rozanov requisitioned every automobile in Vladivostok and every empty room. He used the cars for Cossack patrols and he billeted as many of his Cossacks in the empty rooms as he could. The Russian censor began deleting important news from the correspondents' dispatches, hoping to prevent ominous information from reaching the Allied capitals.

The man who was making the revolution was Rudolph Gaida. No doubt he was an opportunist; he was still a man of some conscience and humanity. Once he reached Vladivostok, Gaida had plunged into intrigue, contacting the men he had used so well fifteen months before—the still democratic but now embittered and proscribed Socialist Revolutionaries, Mensheviks, deposed members of the Siberian duma, and the remnants of Peter Derber's government. These men worried that Kolchak would restore the monarchy, they feared the terror of the Cossacks, they despised the Bolsheviks.

They welcomed Gaida to their secret Committee for the Convocation of a Parliament. Gaida was the man they needed to summon the Czechs to the fight, the man to muster a revolutionary army if they were to throw off Kolchak's authority. Gaida knew this was no child's play. Rozanov was capable not only of killing revolutionaries but the children and grandchildren of revolutionaries. Gaida made plans in a railway van not three hundred yards from Rozanov's headquarters. He and his co-conspirators formed the Siberian National Directorate with Pavel Yakushev as President and Colonels Morovsky and Krakovetsky as Vice-Presidents, Gaida as military commander.[2]

Yakushev described the purpose of the Directorate: to discontinue the civil war. Gaida planned for a popular uprising waged by workingmen. Once the workingmen pressed Rozanov, they could count on the support of the Czechs. The Allies, Gaida was sure, would remain neutral.

Gaida decided to launch his attack when Vladivostok learned Kolchak had abandoned Omsk. With news of such discouraging moment, Gaida hoped the defenses of Vladivostok would sag. On the night of November 17, Gaida moved. One hundred men of his command came ashore on one of the piers and captured the telegraph offices. They wired the news of their revolt to western cities, where movements similar to theirs were under way. From the telegraph office, these one hundred men moved through the city hoping to capture Rozanov in the Great Customs House, his headquarters. They failed in this purpose. While there were no barricades to halt them, no one joined them in their march. Cossacks pinned them down at a mid-city intersection.

Gaida had launched a simultaneous attack from the railroad yards. As he, too, moved toward the center city, only a few dozen Russians ran to die with him in the streets. Cossacks drove Gaida's three-hundred-man cohort back into the yards. Still these revolutionaries kept the issue in doubt. They decimated the first charge the Cossacks mounted. They might have withstood a siege for days. But Rozanov asked the British for transport for the cadets on Russian Island. The British not only provided the cadets and the transport but some artillery as well.

At 3:00 P.M. on the afternoon of the 17th, the council of
Allied military representatives met in extraordinary conference.
Generals Syrovy and Cecek insisted that this was not the Czech
Legion's fight. The legion was neutral. They agreed with the Allies
that the need was to separate the combat zone around the railroad
yards from the city. This decision, of course, doomed the one hundred insurgents who were trying to make their way through the
city to the Great Customs House. But their courage never deserted
them. Wrote General Graves:

> During this fight I witnessed a remarkable exhibition of
> courage by some Russian soldiers. The Russians had placed
> a machine gun at an intersection of two streets without any
> protection whatever. The enemy evidently had the range
> and very soon after a man would take his place to operate
> the gun, he was killed. Without any effort to remove the
> gun or protect it, man after man was killed in the same
> place. I could see this from my bedroom window and, as
> far as I could see, the men without any excitement, will-
> ingly went to what was almost certain death.[3]

Elsewhere in the city, five trucks bearing the three platoons
of Company M of the 31st Infantry careened into a bullet-pocked
square near the railroad yards. The trucks braked to a halt under
the cover of a spattered building at whose base lay a crumpled and
bloody corpse. The Yanks leaped out and began clearing the area,
moving everyone at bayonet point south and west from the railroad yards toward the bay.

Within minutes, another convoy pulled into the area. Japan-
ese troops leaped out and they began fanning north. Immediately
the shelling stopped. Now the revolution was contained in concen-
tric circles: Gaida and his men at the core, Rozanov and the
British-trained cadets around an inner circle, the Yanks and the
Japanese defining the perimeter. That night, searchlights from the
Japanese warships and torpedo boats illumined the railroad yards.
Once again Rozanov's artillery opened up. The cadets charged.
Now it was over. Gaida's men began surrendering.

One of the Yanks who was caught up in the middle of the
fighting was Captain William E. Barratt:

Firing starts and we have to get up the hill and out of the railway yards as best we can. Abandoned the train with supplies, equipment and casket. Gaida has been recruiting Socialist Revolutionaries to overthrow Kolchak. Firing became steady at night. Harbor boats opened up. Over 300 of Gaida's men killed. At 7:00 A.M. all prisoners executed. Cost—1,000 lives. Major Johnson, who commanded the international military police, protected the city from looting during the night.[4]

Yanks near the railway yards saw Rozanov's soldiers march eighteen insurgents, hands over their heads, into a shed where they executed them *en masse*. Then Rozanov's cadets went from the shed to the warehouse, which was serving as a hospital, and shot all of the wounded. When Major Johnson protested these summary executions, Rozanov himself assured him that women and children would not be molested.

Gaida was captured last. He was wearing a Russian overcoat without epaulets, there were white and green ribbons on his shoulders, and he had been sorely wounded. His legs were bleeding from splinters and his chest was lacerated. Pushing him against a wall, Rozanov's soldiers beat him unmercifully until he collapsed, his eyes rolling to the top of his head as he passed out.

Cecek and Syrovy saved Gaida's life. They asked Rozanov to spare him. Rozanov replied Gaida could live if he left Siberia within twenty-four hours, never to return.

"The day before yesterday," reported one of the Kolchak newspapers a week later, "the wind drove a corpse ashore in the Bay. The organizer of the mutiny, former chairman of the Siberian Provisional Duma, Mr. Yakushev, was identified in this corpse."[5]

Rozanov charged that Americans had financed the short-lived revolution. What led to the charge was that Colonel Krakovetsky, the vice-president of the Directorate, and four of his junior officers had sought and found refuge in American headquarters.

Witnessing the murder of surrendered revolutionaries, Krakovetsky and his cohort raced from the railway station and bowled over the sentry at Yank headquarters. Inside, on their knees, they begged for sanctuary, at which point the young officer-of-the-day wisely decided to let the higher-ups decide their fate.

General Graves was aware of the distinction between an embassy and a military headquarters. The embassy was United States property. Headquarters was not. He was not legally justified in protecting these five men. But there was a practical matter he had to consider: Did he want to redden his hands with the blood of Krakovetsky and his aides by turning them out? Graves decided he did not.

Graves handed these Russians over to Colonel F. W. Bugbee until Washington clarified the problem. The general sent a cablegram describing the revolution and on November 19 received "Secretaries of State and War agree not possible to constitute your headquarters American territory."[6]

Graves spent little time mulling this over. He promptly informed Washington that Rozanov was still shooting all prisoners, that he would shoot these five as soon as they were released, and that as a United States Army officer he himself would rather augment American prestige by saving Krakovetsky than diminish it by sending him to his death. This, of course, is the old army game. Delay favored the revolutionaries. A few days after they had been entrusted to his care, Colonel Bugbee reported the prisoners had escaped.

It was impossible for Graves to compliment the colonel on his good sense, but the general confessed in his memoirs that he remembered no event in his whole life that removed such a load from his conscience. He decided not to report the incident to Washington since there was nothing anybody could do about it now. He was amused to receive a cable a little later in which the State Department advised that he "cause the prisoners to leave headquarters as soon as consistent with the general principles of humanity and before the question of surrender arises."

The Gaida Revolution is barely a footnote in the pages of Russian history. Yet Gaida's failure more than anything else revealed the impotence of the democratic movement in Siberia, and not only its impotence but the danger such a movement portended for the United States.

The failure of the anti-Bolsheviks and the liberals and the Socialist Revolutionaries to wrest power from Rozanov as well as the revelation that the peasant and the workingman, the soldier and the refugee had begun to look toward the Soviet Government in Moscow as the last accommodation were bitter blows to the U.S. The Russians who wanted freedom and civil rights and land reform had squandered their opportunity not only by their feuds between left and right and their inefficiency but also by a telling inability to determine the heavy cost of freedom in a country where the choice was narrowing between anarchy and totalitarianism.

Now it was too late for Siberia to close ranks. The Bolsheviks were surging past the Urals onto the steppes, into the fastness of the Sleeping Land.

NOTES

1. Graves, *op. cit.*, p. 215.
2. Clarence A. Manning, *The Siberian Fiasco*. New York: Library Publishers, 1952, p. 161.
3. Graves, *op. cit.*, pp. 281–82.
4. Barratt, *op. cit.*, The Siberian Collection. Hoover Institution.
5. "Intelligence Reports," *op. cit.*, The Siberian Collection. Hoover Institution.
6. Graves, *op. cit.*, p. 284.

CHAPTER 24

SIBERIA:

NOVEMBER 15, 1919–JANUARY 1, 1920

Siberia, a land that once groaned with the tread of convicts, now wailed with the agony of one million refugees moving eastward. After the fall of Omsk, Kolchak's soldiers, ill-organized and ill-equipped, started their retreat, moving along the Great Trakt which runs parallel to the Trans-Siberian Railway. They dragged along slowly, like fatally wounded animals. Hang-dog battalions robbed peasants. Gangs of deserters took food and draft animals from villagers. Ragged loyalists stripped corpses of boots and tunics to save themselves from the cold. As their small villages and settlements were devastated, the workingmen, the moujiks, the peasants, the women and the children, the young girls, the snow-white grandfathers began moving along with the soldiers. On the Trakt, covered with trampled snow, regiments which numbered no more than one hundred men plodded, feet near freezing, rifles dragging behind them. Artillerymen, in painful exertion, tried to keep disassembled cannons on sleds. Lunatics escaped from their asylums, orphans abandoned by their keepers, children separated from their parents and the defenseless, bewildered old kept moving into the swirling dark of a Siberian winter.

As the mass of these tortured travelers reached each city, the panic was augmented as food and shelter proved scarce and more refugees fell in line along the Trakt, a *via dolorosa,* along which typhus raced faster than the wind. There were no medical supplies, no municipal hygiene, no disinfectants. The lice, carried in clothes and on the backs of rats, spread onto the marchers and thus brought typhus into the cities. In Novonikolaevsk between November and April sixty thousand died of the disease. Typhus-laden trains were shunted off on deserted sidings or sent speeding through stations before help and succor could come aboard the pestilential coaches. Gustav Becvar of the Czech Legion described an overflowing hospital train, each and every one of its typhus victims frozen to death because not one had had the strength to stoke the potbellied stoves for warmth.

Those who secured passage on trains not typhus-infected fared little better. At each stop, hundreds tried to squeeze into coaches already filled to the point of suffocation. The strong threw off the weak. The boilers often froze, stranding trains, and the passengers were forced to lever the locomotives off the tracks, a Herculean task in the best of weather. Water tanks at the pumping stations were solid ice. Often bonfires failed to defrost them, and passengers and train crew had to fill the boiler with pails of snow. Brigands and partisans raided at will, murdering and raping when they found no loot. Thousands who had patiently waited their turn were simply left behind when baubles and jewels and gold got passage for rich from dispatchers.

The walls of every station were filled with messages: "Ivan, I have gone to Irkutsk with the children. Marya," and "Dear Masha, I have departed by echelon 15 November. I shall wait for you and the children in Dom Petrov, Vladivostok. Sergei." Sometimes the messages were pinned to the wall, sometimes carved with a penknife, sometimes scrawled with charcoal. Never did the correspondent include a last name for fear of reprisal.

At the start of the journey, there were thousands of horses along the Great Trakt pulling wagons, carts, *droshkies,* and sleds. But the intense cold forced men to halt their animals every two hundred yards to melt the ice that formed in the animals' nostrils. There was no fodder. The horses began to collapse. A British officer wrote:

They were as tame as pet dogs, but nobody had time to stroke their noses. They stood in the streets ruminating over the remarkable change that had taken place in their circumstances. They walked into cafes. They wandered wearily through the deep snow. Droves of them blackened the distant hills.[1]

A Russian survivor also commented upon the hundreds of exhausted horses that stood motionless along the roadside. Other animals, still able to move, roamed about the settlements looking for food, knocking at lighted windows with their noses. The retreat denuded Siberia of horses, and the vast number of them left to die was amazing. It was amazing because once winter gripped the land, the horse was the savior. It was the only method of transport. Yet horses died by the thousands, and the hungry stripped away what they could eat of the flesh and left the rest as carrion to putrefy the land when the thaw came.

It had been icy the winter before, noted F. A. Puchkov, a survivor of the great retreat, but in 1918 the White Army in Siberia had behind it a well-supplied rear and its operations took place in its own territory.[2] In 1919 there was no rear and the army was surrounded by a hostile population. The only transport was in the hands of the Czechs, and the authorities of the Omsk regime were scattered. There was no outside help. Even genuinely courageous men sought death in battle or took their lives during the march.

On the Great Trakt there were intolerable delays. It was impossible for the retreating soldiers to march; they could only drift along with the surging, sighing caravan. Two gigantic unbroken walls of forest oppressed all. A ravine was an inferno choked with sleighs, artillery, old furniture, and broken carts set afire by the soldiers with kerosene to force passage. The shelters were crushed with uniformed men sleeping under the tables, atop them, even balancing precariously on the rafters for rest.

Puchkov's regiment crossed the treacherous Kann Rapids because of a lightning freeze, but then it began to snow. Cliffs and forests assumed fantastic shapes. The endless line of men and carts moved in eerie silence enforced by fatigue and by the weird stillness of majestic natural surroundings.

The slow monotonous movement was lulling people to sleep; tired eyes sought in vain for some relief in the distance ahead. Behind every new turn one believed he saw the lights of a village and heard the barking of dogs. But the lights vanished, the sounds ceased.

Even for those Russians who were spared the march, who rode the railroad, the journey was torturous. It was a process of stops and starts and days elapsed when the trains never moved at all. On the Trans-Siberian there was no "up" track. Both tracks accommodated only eastbound trains. The "up" track had become the express track, but the only trains that made headway were those of the Czechs. The most difficult sector of the Trans-Siberian was the *taiga,* which extended from the Ob River to the Maritime Province. Czech echelons, collected at Tomsk, usurped the trunklines and doomed all to the west. For Russians, the Trans-Siberian and the Great Trakt had become Dante's *Guidecca,* the last ring in the Inferno where sinners were wholly imprisoned in ice.

NOTES

1. Fleming, *op. cit.,* p. 168.
2. F. A. Puchkov, "The Icy March" (translation and commentary by E. Varneck). The Siberian Collection.

CHAPTER 25

IRKUTSK-BAIKAL-VLADIVOSTOK:

JANUARY 15–FEBRUARY 20, 1920

Kolchak left Omsk accompanied by his staff in six trains *de luxe*. A seventh train, which traveled in the middle of this convoy with telephone communication front and rear, carried the gold. The bullion was the last of Kolchak's symbols. He believed the possession of this treasure would enable him to keep fighting for several years. But there is sometimes an essential sadness to great riches; there are prolonged crises when gold cannot purchase the simplest of necessities.

Though there were two locomotives attached to each one of Kolchak's trains and though he was proceeding to the east as an express on the "up" track, still he made slow time. The Czechs delayed his progress. They were no longer the masters of Siberia, but they were still the masters of the Trans-Siberian Railway. They themselves faced the alternatives of evacuate or perish. They made sure they got out first. And not only were the Czechs determined to save themselves; they were almost equally as determined to put Kolchak at a disadvantage.

The Czech National Council published an open letter in which it declared that the presence of the Czech Legion along the railway was useless since the legionnaires could not cope with deteriorating conditions. The National Council disavowed the Kolchak Government.[1]

Kolchak was infuriated. His staff said he whistled like a banshee. He said the Czechs were no better than deserters. This decision to evacuate without his express directive made them Bolsheviks. In embittered folly, Kolchak published a warning to all White Russians not to collaborate or aid the Czechs on pain of death. He also deputized Semenov as a military commander of the All-Russian Provisional Government and sent him a message instructing him to destroy the Baikal tunnels if necessary to stop the Czech withdrawal.

The Czechs intercepted it.

At Mariinsk on December 13, a lieutenant of the Czech Transportation Staff switched Kolchak's seven trains from the "up" track onto the congested "down" line where hundreds of trains waited. When Kolchak's adjutant insisted the Czech lieutenant switch the admiral back, the officer replied that he had his orders. When Kolchak threatened to have his entourage switch the trains with or without Czech permission, the lieutenant replied that the Czechs would not coal Kolchak's trains until the Supreme Ruler quietly took his place on the congested rails.

There was no mystery as to Czech motives. Switching Kolchak was not a vindictive act, though the Czechs were wreaking vengeance. Common sense dictated that a man who would destroy the Baikal tunnels and by that act cut Siberia from its one possible source of supply was no longer fit to hold command. Kolchak had literally to be shunted aside so that those who were going to get out could get out and those who were going to stay and fight could fight. The Czechs knew that the longer they delayed Kolchak the sooner they would bring down his government.

The Czechs themselves were having no easy time in putting Siberia behind them. Syrovy needed a fierce rear-guard defense. He padded the Czech rear with a Polish brigade and a Rumanian contingent, both units commanded by one Kadlac, notorious for wasting no love on Poles or Rumanians.. Both groups had been recruited from prisoner-of-war camps. They were for the most part untested. The Red 5th Army caught up with the Poles and annihilated them and a few weeks later annihilated the Rumanians.

Sacrificing these relatively innocent contingents was not manly, but from a Czech viewpoint it was militarily sound.

The legion had as protracted and torturous an exodus as any of the refugees, but the legion was better prepared to endure it. The Czechs had kept their locomotives in good repair. Their trains were typhus-free. They had rations and winter clothing. And they were disciplined. A Czech echelon proceeded from one station east to another. The transport battalion backed the vans into a siding, uncoupled the locomotive, sent it back westward to haul forward another echelon. Thus the echelons began leapfrogging to Vladivostok. Roughly, all of them were moving at the same time and all of them were moving on the express line.

The Czechs enjoyed these supreme advantages in part because they had paid the railroad workers from their own funds and were cashing in for needed favors. The hindrances that delayed other transports disappeared when a Czech echelon hit the straightaway. Kolchak had stockpiled coal but had stockpiled more of it to the east than to the west, where it was needed. Many trains failed for its lack. The Czechs maintained their own stockpiles on coupled gondolas and coal cars over which they mounted their own guards. They shared none of it.

By mid-December, Kolchak was badly in need of coal. His trains were stalled at Krasnoyarsk. The Supreme Ruler stormed up and down his coach in futile rage. His staff drank heavily. Over and over again his aides demanded that the Supreme Ruler be put in contact with General Janin, nominally in command of the legion. Janin, ignoring these urgencies, noted to General Syrovy that the Supreme Ruler was traveling with five trains more than the Czar had ever found necessary and six more than the Grand Duke. Hearing this slur, Kolchak's chief-of-staff, General Vladimir Kappel, challenged Janin and Syrovy to a duel, as though men needed pistols at thirty paces to find death in Siberia. Janin and Syrovy ignored the dare.

As Kolchak's trains inched eastward, the All-Russian Provisional Government in Irkutsk fell. A new government, calling itself the Political Center, composed of Socialist Revolutionaries,

Mensheviks, members of the League of the Toiling Peasantry, and some Bolsheviks took power by seizing Glaskov, the railway station on the west bank of the Angara that served as the Irkutsk depot. The two cities were connected by a huge pontoon bridge with a roadstead. The bridge was pulled ashore in the winter months when the river froze. The Trans-Siberian Railway, in fact, enters Irkutsk not at all but debouches from Glaskov along the southern bank of the Angara to Lake Baikal. By holding Glaskov, therefore, the Political Center had effectively cut off Irkutsk from communication with Kolchak. Irkutsk itself, however, remained under the command of Sychev, the last of Kolchak's commanders, who moved artillery up to the wharves and piers and threatened to reduce Glaskov to rubble unless the Political Center departed. Since the trains of the British, French, and Japanese High Commissioners as well as that of the American Consul-General from Omsk were in the Glaskov yards, it behooved the Allies to begin reasoning with Sychev.

Rising to the occasion, Janin declared the Glaskov station a neutral zone. After two days of frenzied debates between the Centrists and Sychev, Janin prevailed. Sychev agreed not to bombard the station if the Political Center did not attack Irkutsk. No one, not the Political Center nor the Allies nor Sychev, took Kolchak into consideration. But the admiral took counter-measures against the insurgency. He appointed Semenov the Supreme Commander of all armed forces in Siberia and the Far East and instructed the new chief to clear the Centrists from Glaskov and Irkutsk.

Semenov sped a *broneviki* from the east shore of Lake Baikal toward Irkutsk under the command of Colonel Skipetrov. Thirty miles behind Skipetrov a Japanese support battalion followed cautiously. Semenov and Skipetrov had little interest in preserving Kolchak's rule and even less in saving the life of the Supreme Ruler, but they knew his trains were escorting the fabled gold reserves.

Skipetrov reported to Sychev. They decided they could not venture west to rescue the admiral. The Czechs would never clear the express track for the *broneviki's* passage. The surest way to guarantee the safety of the admiral was to seize anti-Kolchak hostages and hold them until the Supreme Commander's convoy reached Irkutsk. Skipetrov said he would transfer these hostages to Semenov's jail in Chita the next day. Sychev notified the Political Center in Glaskov. He then removed thirty-one prisoners from the Irkutsk jail, one of them a young woman. These hostages had been clapped in jail for reasons people in such times and places are usually clapped in jail—for importuning for a friend or carrying a gun or buying on the black market or expressing a strong political conviction.

Sychev, his men, and the hostages boarded an ice-breaker bound for the east shore of Lake Baikal (the Czechs refused to let him get up steam in the *broneviki*). And that night the hostages were killed for the reasons that people in such times and places are killed—for the caprice of men who have lost their pity and their reason. For that night, aboard the ice-breaker, Skipetrov and his men, wild with drink, made each of the hostages strip, then led them one by one to the deck, where an executioner pole-axed the victim with a cleaver used for chipping ice. The body was dumped into the freezing waters below. Skipetrov made no secret of his mayhem, and terrified passengers reported what they had seen the next morning. Details of the horror passed up and down the tracks, into Irkutsk and beyond, where the news inflamed the Political Center.

These insurgents violated the truce and began crossing the frozen Angara to attack Irkutsk. Sychev's artillery could have broken the still treacherous ice, but he judged the game was up and, after raiding the state bank, absconded. The Political Center took Irkutsk and promptly convened court-martials to settle old scores with the Kolchakists who had remained. One of these court-martials charged Kolchak with the murder of the hostages, which was, of course, not accurate but was certainly a truth of sorts about his rule. The court not only charged him but found him guilty *in absentia* and judged him an enemy of the people.

The Allied High Commissioners realized that the Political

Center was as determined as a lynch mob and in a joint directive they instructed General Janin:

> If Admiral Kolchak finds himself obliged to appeal for the protection of Allied troops, it is incontestably the duty of such troops to afford him protection and to take the necessary steps to assure his conveyance to whatever place shall be designated by the Allied Governments bearing in mind the need, should it arise, of negotiating with all parties concerned.[2]

The only Allied troops who could possibly protect Kolchak if he needed protection were the Czechs, specifically the 6th Regiment at Nizhne-Udinsk. The Political Center had already informed this regimental headquarters that it wanted to imprison Kolchak, strip him of the dictatorship and the gold; and if the Czechs did not cooperate, the Political Center would sabotage the railroad and strand Czech as well as White Russian trains.

Janin instructed the 6th Regiment to transfer Kolchak to a single coach that flew the flags of the United States, Great Britain, France, and Japan. The legion was to shepherd this coach and the gold train from Nizhne-Udinsk to Irkutsk, a distance of two hundred miles.

Kolchak's enormous staff melted away with the realization that the Allies considered them expendable. Only a dozen officers and Kolchak's mistress, Madam Anna Vasilevna Timareva, accompanied Kolchak in the flag-festooned coach. On January 15, 1920, the 6th Czech Regiment with the admiral and the gold in tow rolled east on the "up" track, the last of the Czech echelons on the tracks west of Irkutsk.

Four legionnaires guarded Kolchak's coach by day and twelve by night. The officer-of-the-guard was Lieutenant Gustav Becvar. At every small station, angry citizens gathered, shaking their fists, demanding the Czechs turn Kolchak over to face punishment for his crimes. The Czechs unlocked the safeties on their rifles and let their officers do the talking. But not even the Czechs were tough enough to convoy Kolchak past Polovina. "Polovina" means "half" in Russian, and this station marked the midway point between Moscow and Vladivostok. In Polovina the Bolsheviks had taken over the direction of the Political Center. They threatened that if the Czechs did not release Kolchak to their custody, they would storm the train. The Bolsheviks were emerging from the chaos of Siberia as the one force capable of taking action. The legionnaires knew they meant what they said. Becvar compromised. He allowed the Political Center to assign soldiers to guard Kolchak's coach and the gold train along with the Czechs.

The red coloration of the Political Center, its quick alliance with the Bolsheviks were sources of concern to legion commander Syrovy. If his Czechs could not find an accommodation with these Bolsheviks, it meant his last echelons would have to fight their way out. Having sacrificed thousands of legionnaires as well as Poles and Rumanians to get this far, Syrovy was hardly disposed to waste more men in saving Kolchak and the gold, although he had recently received an order signed by Beneš and Clemenceau ordering the legion to keep the bullion, an order Syrovy saw it was impossible to obey.

Syrovy concluded that the way to save these last echelons was to do business with the Bolsheviks. In a late-afternoon rendezvous, Syrovy proposed an armistice to the leaders of the Political Center, who now called themselves the Bolshevik Revolutionary Committee. Syrovy wanted his echelons to have unimpeded passage through Trans-Baikalia. In return, he would hand over Kolchak and the gold. The four conferees who conversed in the space between two parked limousines did not even draw an agenda. The Bolsheviks said yes to the proposal and Syrovy had to take them at their word.

Back at his headquarters, Syrovy by telegraph instructed Becvar that the legion was to escort Kolchak no farther than Irkutsk. When the Czech general told Janin of the decision, the Frenchman immediately decamped for Vladivostok with the comment that he was sure Syrovy would do his best to maintain the honor of the Czech name.[3]

On the morning of January 15, when the Czech echelon and Kolchak's coach drew into Glaskov, a company of Bolsheviks awaited their arrival. Becvar's instructions were to turn over Kolchak and his Prime Minister, Victor Papelieve, to Bolshevik authorities, who would appear the next dawn. Becvar thought Kolchak was getting a raw deal. But orders are orders, a phrase that has overcome more good sense and right conscience than all the blind rage in history. In his memoir Becvar wrote:

It was nearly midnight. Miserably I tramped through the darkness, challenged several times by the guards. Kolchak was quartered in a corridor carriage. Only the door at one end of the coach was unlocked. I entered, watched suspiciously by the Russian on duty. The first two compartments were open. They were packed with Siberian staff officers. The officers looked at me inquisitively. I asked them for the Admiral. A young adjutant appeared, and I introduced myself.

"I will announce you to the Admiral."

Presently he returned. I was asked to enter a closed compartment. In the narrow, badly lit room stood Kolchak, deposed Dictator of Siberia. His face was pale, but composed. He was a dignified figure. A handsome man, he looked magnificent in his uniform.

"I bring an important message, sir," I said.

"Sit down." The Admiral pointed to a seat, but remained standing himself. "Well, what is it?"

"We have just received orders to hand over both yourself and Minister Pepelyaev to the Political Center tomorrow morning. The government representatives will arrive at dawn."

"This order came from your headquarters?" inquired the Admiral.

"Yes, sir, headquarters in the town."

The Admiral paced up and down for a minute or two. I felt the perspiration start on my forehead. Suddenly Kolchak halted, and faced me. When he spoke his voice was calm.

"I should like to speak to General Syrovy. Can that be arranged?"

"I will try, sir. But it is after midnight already."

"Please do. I particularly want to speak to him at
once."

"I will see that your message is sent to headquarters
at once, sir." I saluted and left the compartment.⁴

Of course Syrovy could not be reached. The dozen officers
who had stuck with Kolchak tore off their epaulets and leaped out
of the coach windows. Others forced the door and raced across
the tracks. The Red Guards sniped away at them and then
mounted the coach and relieved the legionnaires. An hour later,
the Czechs handed over 5,143 boxes and 1,680 bags of gold.
Only two bags had been stolen since the Czechs had come across
the train at Kazan fifteen months before.⁵

On January 15, Kolchak, Papelieve, and Madam Timareva
were placed under arrest and housed in a separate wing of the
grim Irkutsk jail. For three weeks an Extraordinary Investigation
Committee took testimony from Kolchak, holding nine all-day
sessions. On the morning of February 7, a firing squad arrived by
truck and led Kolchak, whose nerves stood him well, and
Papelieve, whose morale fled, out of prison and onto the ice to a
point where a hole had been chopped. In the glare of the truck's
headlights, the firing squad in ragged barrage executed the two
handcuffed men. Then the prison commandant kicked the two
bodies into the black Angara. The official Soviet account remarked that Kolchak died like an Englishman. Madam Timareva
was released and eventually made her way to London, where she
survived Kolchak by more than forty years.

Coincident with this execution, the Czech National Council
in Vladivostok was able to conclude another armistice with the
Bolsheviks. This agreement provided for the peaceful withdrawal
of the legion through Trans-Baikalia, along the Amur and down
the Ussuri to the Bay of the Golden Horn. Moscow ordered the
Siberian Bolsheviks to expedite this armistice. The apocryphal
remark of one of the Moscow authorities was "Russia at last sees
the back of the Czechs."

The Czechoslovak Republic and the legion itself chartered
Japanese ships, which started steaming from Vladivostok for

Trieste on February 20 and finished the evacuation in May 1920. Fifty-seven thousand, four hundred and fifty-nine legionnaires were evacuated with another twelve thousand wives, children, Russians, and Czech officials in all. Thirteen thousand Czechs died in Siberia.[6]

The last Czech contingent to leave Vladivostok, however, did not make for Trieste but for San Francisco, thence to Washington, D.C., and then New York. This contingent numbered one hundred amputees who were fitted in the United States for artificial limbs paid for by the American Red Cross. In the capital, they passed in review before Woodrow Wilson.[7]

Only one legionnaire ever returned to Communist Russia. He was Lieutenant Ludovik Svoboda, who, in poor health and diminished vigor, went to Moscow in 1968 as President of Czechoslovakia to seek the freedom of Alexander Dubcek, whom the Russians had imprisoned for declaring Czechoslovakia's independence.

Of all the Czechs who fought in Siberia, perhaps the one the world remembers best is Jaroslav Hasek, who entered world literature with his novel *The Good Soldier Schweik,* which mentions Russia and Bolshevism and heroism and freedom not at all.

NOTES

1. Stewart, *op. cit.,* p. 297.
2. Fleming, *op. cit.,* p. 187.
3. Luckett, *op. cit.,* p. 344.
4. Becvar, *op. cit.,* pp. 240–41.
5. Stewart, *op. cit.,* p. 344.
6. Matamey, *op. cit.,* pp. 296–97.
7. *The New York Times,* July 6, 1920.

CHAPTER 26

LORD OF THE EAST:

JANUARY 16–APRIL 23, 1920

After the fall of Omsk, sentiment in the State Department favored the withdrawal of American troops. Practical, on-the-spot considerations forced this change. August Heid, the American representative of the War Trade Board at Vladivostok, reported to the State Department that his work was finished. The Kolchak Government, he said, had become directionless; its armies had disintegrated. Siberia was bankrupt and railway transport was rapidly deteriorating. It was wasteful, concluded Heid, for the United States to continue expensive economic relief.

Consul Ernest Harris and Ambassador Rowland Morris confessed that they were discouraged by Kolchak's formal recognition of Atamen Semenov and Kalmykov. This meant that the United States found itself in disagreement not only with Japanese policy but with the official representatives of the Kolchak Government in eastern Siberia.

Colonel George Emerson resigned from the Russian Railway Service Corps, citing as his reason that he had been opposed in every way by the Russian military faction and the technical railroad officials. The Omsk regime was unable any longer to carry out the terms of the Inter-Allied Railway Agreement.

Military opinion, which had always opposed the Siberian expedition, now counted heavily. Major Robert Slaughter,

Graves's chief intelligence officer, was at pains to point out that Kolchak's soldiers were losing ground by the thousands of versts each week, that with each backward verst desertions increased, that morale had fallen to the point of panic.

As Kolchak's military situation worsened, Graves advised that for the safety of his troops he was forced to begin concentrating them in and around Vladivostok, necessarily abandoning areas in the American sector. "We are fast arriving at the place where we join Semenov and Kalmykov in fighting the Russians who claim that they are trying to establish a representative government in the East."[1]

Two events determined Wilson to pull out of Siberia. The first of these was the failure of the United States Senate to ratify the peace treaty, thereby dooming American participation in the League of Nations. It was no longer as important for Wilson's Administration to work in close harmony with the British and the French in Russia.

The second event was the sweeping electoral victory of liberal Naimoto Hara over General Tanaka in Japan. Tanaka had campaigned on the promise of a full-scale Japanese occupation of the Maritime Province and Trans-Baikalia. Japan was obviously having second thoughts about the intervention. When the new cabinet, in fact, asked for a clear definition of Allied policy in Siberia, Secretary of State Robert Lansing laid the request on the President's desk prefaced by the single paragraph:

> The truth of the matter is the simple fact that the Kolchak Government has utterly collapsed; the armies of the Bolsheviki have advanced into Eastern Siberia, where they are reported to be acting with moderation. The people seem to prefer them to the officers of the Kolchak regime. Further, the Bolshevik Army is approaching the region where our soldiers are, and contact with them will lead to open hostilities and to many complications. In other words, if we do not withdraw we shall have to wage war with the Bolsheviki.[2]

Wilson agreed with this. In a public statement released by the State Department on January 16, Wilson noted that the steadying efforts at self-government or self-defense on the part of the Russians impressed the United States with its political instability and grave uncertainties. [The United States] is disposed to the view that further military effort to assist the Russians in the struggle for self-government may, in the present situation, lead to complications which would have exactly the opposite effect, prolonging the period of readjustment and involving Japan and the United States in ineffective and needless sacrifices.[3]

The note engendered great bitterness among the European Allies. The United States had entered Siberia as one of several Allies ordered there by the Supreme War Council. To undertake a unilateral withdrawal meant desertion. This argument was specious in the light of the evacuation of British and French missions from Siberia. The unilateral American withdrawal punished only the Japanese, who had to shoulder the entire expense of the occupation once the Yanks left.

Graves received an "Eyes Only" directive in mid-January ordering him to begin the evacuation of American forces as soon as the last Czechs had cleared Vladivostok. Since Wilson had sent the Yanks to Siberia to insure the safety of the legion, the American expedition would remain true to its original purpose.

It was over.

The last contingent of Yanks left the Lord of the East on April 1, 1920, and General Graves and his staff departed on April 23.

Some might have liked us more, commented the *Literary Digest* in September 1920, "if we had intervened less and some might have disliked us less if we had intervened more but having concluded that we intended to intervene no more nor no less than we actually did, nobody had any use for us at all."

NOTES

1. Graves, *op. cit.*, p. 302.
2. Unterbarger, *op. cit.*, p. 177.
3. Jados, *op. cit.*, p. 45.

CHAPTER 27

JULY 12–OCTOBER 6, 1920

The only Americans left in Vladivostok in the late spring of 1920 were Red Cross workers. The Red Cross Mission to Siberia had originally numbered 314 volunteers, among whom were sixty doctors, 130 nurses, six dentists, fourteen pharmacists, garage mechanics, bookkeepers, and business executives.[1] All of these had left with Graves except for Dr. Raymond Teusler, head of the mission; Riley Allen, the Red Cross director in Vladivostok; and a small contingent of youth workers headed by Hannah B. Campbell who were running a children's colony on Russian Island. The colony numbered 805.[2] These children had been lost or separated from their parents in St. Petersburg or Moscow by the dislocations of the civil war. Now that the war was over, the International Red Cross had located their parents or close relatives, and Mrs. Campbell thought it was time to repatriate the children. After four months and a 14,622-mile sea and land hegira, she succeeded in reuniting all of the children with their families.

There were others who participated in the intervention, however, who remained permanently displaced. One of them was General William Sidney Graves, who, though he served subsequently as the commander of the 1st Division and later as the commander of the Panama Canal Zone, was constantly shadowed by the FBI as a potential subversive. When Graves learned of the presence of FBI agents at a formal banquet in the Waldorf-Astoria, where he was to speak, the tough old Texan canceled the affair on the spot. His outspoken and bitter book on the Siberian intervention did little to rehabilitate him. It was published in 1931 at a time when Americans realized that Russia and its worldwide Communist Party were troublesome. Since many Americans simplistically believe that such trouble can only be the work of domestic traitors, Graves was a likely target: He had refused to crush Bolshevism when he had the chance. He died in 1940 in Shrewsbury, New Jersey, in the very house where Ulysses S. Grant had played poker on Fridays when the eighteenth President lived in nearby Long Branch.

When the Allies withdrew from Siberia, Ataman Semenov fled to Manchuria, where he continued to work for the Japanese, in fact commanding a Japanese division in World War II. But when Russia invaded Manchuria in August 1945, Semenov wasn't fast enough and he was one of the first high-ranking Japanese officers captured. He was also one of the first war criminals to be punished when the Russians unceremoniously hanged him in September.

General Maurice Janin rescued from Ekaterinburg the remains of the Czar and his family—some shards of bone, some jewelry, and a handful of ashes. He took these back to France to turn over to the Grand Duke or to the Louvre. However, neither the Grand Duke nor the curators wanted these pitiful mementoes, and Janin finally disposed of them through the Russian diplomatic service. He published a book of his adventures, *Ma Mission en Sibérie,* of which British General Alfred Knox wrote, "Many factors brought about the final tragedy in Siberia. Perhaps one worth mentioning, but naturally omitted by the diarist, was the French Commander's failure to discipline properly the Allied contingents put under his charge."[3]

Rudolph Gaida returned to Czechoslovakia, where he became a general, organized a *putsch* against the republic that failed, was court-martialed, and dismissed from the service. He founded the Czech Fascist Party, which lived an uneasy life under the Nazi occupation.

The other legionnaires became the government, the army, and the civil administrators of the burgeoning republic. The Munich Pact of 1938 did many of them in. Gustav Becvar was a member of Parliament until the arrival of the Nazis, when he fled to England. Cecek and other legionnaires were executed by German firing squads in Poland in 1939, where they had gone to found another *Ceska Druzhina*.

Once upon a time there was a Woodrow Wilson Railroad Station in Prague. Beyond it was a Woodrow Wilson Square and a Wilson Park with a statue of Woodrow Wilson in the center. There were Wilson avenues, Wilson squares, and Wilson statues in Belgrade, Bucharest, Warsaw, and other cities of East Central Europe. They are no more. The Russian intervention was a last effort to save from displacement the world of which Woodrow Wilson and these people dreamed.

NOTES

1. *Second Semi-Annual Report of the Siberian Commission of the American Red Cross.* The Siberian Collection. Hoover Institution.
2. Hannah B. Campbell, "The Children's Ark." The Siberian Collection. Hoover Institution.
3. Alfred Knox., "General Janin's Siberian Diary." *The Slavonic Review.* Vol. 3, No. 9, 1925, p. 724.

CHAPTER 28

LAST SPECULATIONS

If nothing else, the Russian intervention is one of the classic examples of where war starts: in war rooms all over the world; warm, well-appointed rooms where men can play politics and dwell on the certainty of results rather than the magnitude of catastrophe.

In April 1919 Winston Churchill suggested that the Czech Legion leave off guarding the Trans-Siberian Railway and accompany Kolchak on his western offensive. Churchill thought the Czechs could take up the left wing in the south and smash through the Bolshevik defenses around Orenburg. From there the legion could make its way farther west to join Denikin and eventually be evacuated through the Black Sea.

Eduard Beneš pointed out the terrible logistic difficulties of equipping the Czechs first on the steppes and then along the Don. The plan was abandoned.

But it was certainly no more erratic or misguided a plan than those which evolved from the Hotel Trianon in Versailles or the second-story room in the White House or Poole's headquarters in Archangel.

The Bolsheviks had their war rooms, too. Though they were the most ruthless and determined of men, Lenin, Trotsky, and the members of the Central Executive Committee temporized with the Allies, never sure whether it was wise to invite them in or promise unequivocally to repel them. If the Bolsheviks had threatened to kill the force who came, the Allies would have come anyway.

George F. Kennan in *Russia Leaves the War* and *Decision to Intervene* suggests that the Cold War began with the American intervention. The Allied intervention was probably the animating cause that turned Communist leaders resolutely from the West, a turning inward which had far-reaching effects. One of these was the withdrawal of one-sixth of the world from the international economy of the 1920s and 1930s. The full meaning of this withdrawal was cruelly apparent in the devastating economic crisis of 1929–1932 when huge surpluses of commodities and capital piled up in Western countries for lack of outlets while want and unemployment devastated workingmen. Even in the better times of 1959, when he was Dwight D. Eisenhower's guest, Soviet Premier Nikita Khrushchev told American reporters in Los Angeles that "We remember the grim days when American soldiers went to our soil headed by their generals to help our White Guard combat the new revolution. All the capitalist countries in Europe and America marched upon our country. . . . Never have any of our soldiers been on American soil, but your soldiers were on Russian soil."

However, an equally eminent authority, the English historian David Footman, argues in *Murmansk and Archangel* that there is no conclusive evidence that the Cold War descends from the intervention. There are powerful economic and political reasons that would have brought on the Cold War if the United States had shipped diamonds to Archangel instead of troops. It is a mistake to think that nations hold grudges; nations have relented too often. Nations do not think or feel or remember. Only the members of a nation's Presidium or Parliament or Congress think, feel or remember, and these men serve in these bodies to realize their nation's best interest. Bitterness was not to Russia's interest in 1941; Lend-Lease was; nor was bitterness to its best interests in 1972; *détente* was.

Whichever it was, the Allied intervention was certainly folly in that it failed abysmally.

If the Siberian intervention did not set in motion the great rivalry between the two Pacific powers that ultimately resulted in a rain of bombs at Pearl Harbor, certainly it greased the gears. It was during the Russian intervention that the military men saw that Japanese ambitions were a threat to American security. Major Sidney C. Graves, the general's son, who served as assistant chief-of-staff in the Siberian AEF, described Japanese aggression for *The New York Times* in May 1921. Vladivostok, charged young Graves, had become a Japanese city. He argued that if Japan were allowed to pursue aggressive expropriation, to turn the wealth of other nations to her advantage, "America, in a relatively short time, will face an enemy almost as great as Germany." In his 4,000-word article Sidney C. Graves never once mentioned Bolshevism. General Robert L. Eichelberger, who directed several of the Pacific campaigns in World War II, also served as assistant chief-of-staff in the Siberian AEF. Lieutenant Colonel Eichelberger wrote in his intelligence reports of 1919 that he was more impressed with the dangerous Japanese military than with the future dangers of the Red regime. Working closely with the Japanese, witnessing the way a small and unpopular military clique influenced the Diet, Eichelberger was sure of a future war.

Could the intervention have changed the world if managed differently? World War I was the incubator of the totalitarian state. The intervention did not allay this growth in Russia, possibly because it tried to reverse it with inadequate military means. At any rate that is Winston Churchill's thesis in *The Aftermath*. Two more divisions in Archangel would have succeeded in taking Moscow, he writes, and one last massive effort would have saved Kolchak.

There were soldiers who knew far better than Churchill that two or twenty or fifty divisions would still have failed. These soldiers were the German generals. It was they who learned as Napoleon learned that it is not easy to overthrow Russia. Though the Kaiser's armies inflicted a catastrophic defeat on Russia in 1915 and moved through Poland easily into the heartland, they soon slowed down when they came across the same obstacles that had weakened Russian armies—swamps, inoperable railways, the lack of water and fodder for the horses, disease, and the tactics of the ever-present guerrillas. Even when no armies opposed the Germans in early 1917, the generals realized they could not move Russia out of the war by force; they would have to settle for a negotiated peace, which indeed they did at Brest Litovsk.

The Allies could not harmonize their national interests in the struggle against Bolshevism. Japan wanted to exploit the Maritime Province. Woodrow Wilson wanted to see a democratic Russia. France wanted her money back. The British wanted trade concessions and protection for the Empire. It was, of course, impossible to marshal patriotic Russians under such diffuse banners. But more than that, the intervention failed because the statesmen and generals who devised it in 1918 lacked a historical precedent. It was hard for the men of that time to comprehend how one great power or several could infringe on the sovereignty of still another by intervening directly in internal affairs. Men have since learned how.

The American intervention does have one special area of meaning. It is as intervention *qua* intervention. Intervention is certainly a crucial necessity for great powers, which cannot stay at peace unless they *keep* the peace, whether keeping the peace means stifling dissent, installing puppet governments, or seeing to it other nations always take you seriously. From the American viewpoint, intervention depends upon a strong-willed President disposed to intervene. William Howard Taft refused to intervene in the Mexican Revolution which began in 1910, but Woodrow Wilson did intervene in 1914 at Vera Cruz and in 1916 in Chihuahua. The difference between Taft and Wilson was not one of courage or nerve or recklessness but rather that Woodrow Wilson was the first President who clearly apprehended that America had become a great world power and would have to assume the commensurate responsibilities if it wanted to remain one.

A strong President often confuses his own moral and political certainty with what he thinks the people want him to do. Often he blurs policies to preserve moral certainty. Wilson told the American constituency he went to Russia to steady the efforts of the Russian people toward self-government. The harsh reality was that the Bolsheviks were the only steady faction in Russia. Wilson went to Russia in the hopes an intervention would transform Russia into a nation with whom other nations had congruent interests.

Harry Truman said he went into Korea to save the democratic republic of Syngman Rhee, and John Kennedy said he went into Vietnam to save a Southeast Asian democracy. But Harry Truman intervened in Korea because he wanted to insist that agreements made between the United States and Russia were agreements the rest of the world had to respect. John Kennedy committed the United States to Vietnam to help a client state withstand the shock of civil war.

Yet in these complex situations, there was a clear and discreet moment when the policy which led to intervention became obsolete and when the United States in good conscience could pull out. That moment for the Russian intervention came with the signing of the armistice when an Eastern Front was meaningless. That moment in Korea came when the North Korean Army retreated above the 38th Parallel after General Douglas MacArthur's invasion at Inchon. That moment in Vietnam came when the Vietnamese generals deposed and murdered Ngo Dinh Diem and were free to constitute a regime more likely to enlist the sympathy and call forth the sacrifices of the Vietnamese people. These were good moments in which to get out because it was obvious that the United States was not going to realize its goals quickly or easily. A successful intervention is one in which a President realizes military goals so that political ends emerge sooner than the next American election. Neither Woodrow Wilson nor Harry Truman nor John Kennedy nor Lyndon Johnson nor Richard Nixon wanted to tell the constituency they'd gotten into a war. Presidents who are harbingers of bad news do not long survive. No joke that.

BIBLIOGRAPHY

PUBLIC PAPERS
AND DOCUMENTS

Hoover Institution of War, Revolution and Peace, Stanford, California.

The Siberian Collection

William S. Barratt, "The Diary of a Russian Wolfhound." TS Russia SS6 B16.

Hannah B. Campbell, "Children's Ark."

George H. Emerson Papers.

William S. Graves Papers 600009-94.

Walter A. Grayson, "Four Military Intelligence Studies." 74005-8:36.

Intelligence Studies: AEF—Siberia.

William H. Johnson Papers.

Colonel Edwin Landon, AG, "Report on Trip Through Western Siberia and Eastern Russia." VW Russia. VSL 259.

Joseph Longuevan Papers.

Polsolskaya Incident. DK 766: P854.

F. A. Puchkov, "The Icy March."

John F. Stevens Papers.

National Archives, Washington, D.C.

Deck Log, USS *Brooklyn:* May–June, 1918. 17.3.

Historical Files of the American Expeditionary Force, North Russia, 1918–1919: 23-8.3 to 23-66.1.

Historical Files of the American Expeditionary Forces in Siberia, 1918–1920: 21-4.7 to 67.4.

Special Collections, United States Military Academy Library, West Point, New York

Benjamin Dickson Papers.

Colonel George Evans Stewart Papers.

BOOKS

Carl Ackerman, *Trailing the Bolsheviki.* New York, 1919.

Ralph Albertson, *Fighting Without a War.* New York, 1920.

Henry Baerlein, *The March of the Seventy Thousand.* London, 1926.

Thomas A. Bailey, *Woodrow Wilson and the Lost Peace.* New York, 1944.

Ray Stannard Baker, *Woodrow Wilson: Life and Letters.* Vol. 8: *Armistice.* New York, 1939.

Gustav Becvar, *The Lost Legion: A Czechoslovakian Epic.* London, 1939.

Eduard Beneš, *My War Memoirs.* London, 1928.

Henri Bergson, *Ecrits et Paroles: Textes Resemble par Tome Troisième.* R. M. Mosse. Paris, 1959.

John Bradlee, *Allied Intervention in Russia.* London, 1968.

James Bunyan, *Intervention, Civil War and Communism in Russia: April–December, 1918.* Baltimore, 1936.

Field Marshal Sir Michael Carver, *The War Lords: Military Commanders of the Twentieth Century.* Boston and Toronto, 1976.

A Chronicler (John Cudahy), *Archangel: The American War with Russia.* Chicago, 1924.

Winston Churchill, *The Aftermath.* New York, 1929.

John Milton Cooper, ed., *Causes and Consequences of World War I.* New York, 1972.

R. Ernest Dupuy, *Perish by the Sword: The Czechoslovakian Anabasis and Our Supporting Campaign in North Russia and Siberia.* Harrisburg, Pennsylvania, 1939.

Miroslav Fic, *The Origin of a Conflict Between the Bolsheviks and the Czechoslovakian Legion.* Chicago, 1958.

Peter G. Filene, *Americans and the Soviet Experiment, 1917–1933.* Cambridge, 1967.

Peter Fleming, *The Fate of Admiral Kolchak.* New York, 1963.

David Footman, *Murmansk and Archangel.* Oxford, 1957.

David R. Francis, *Russia from the American Embassy, April 1916–November 1918.* New York, 1921.

Paul Fussell, *The Great War and Modern Memory.* New York and London, 1975.

Rudolph Gaida, *Moje Pameti.* Prague, 1924.

William S. Graves, *America's Siberian Adventure, 1918–1920.* New York, 1941.

A. Whitney Griswold, *The Far Eastern Policy of the United States.* New York, 1938.

E. M. Halliday, *The Ignorant Armies.* New York, 1960.

William Edmund Lord Ironside, *Archangel, 1918–1920.* London, 1953.

Stanley S. Jados, *Documents on Russian-American Relations.* Washington, D.C., 1965.

John Keegan, *The Face of Battle.* New York, 1976.

George F. Kennan, *Soviet American Relations, 1917–1920.* Vol. 1: *Russia Leaves the War.* Vol. 2: *Decision to Intervene.* New York, 1967.

Sylvian Kindall, *American Soldiers in Siberia.* New York, 1945.

Margarete Klante, *Die Geschicte der Tschechischen Legion in Russland.* Halle-Wittenberg, 1929.

———, *Von der Volga zum Amur: Die tschechische Legion und der russische Burgerkrieg.* Berlin, 1931.

Phillip Knightley, *The First Casualty.* New York and London, 1975.

Arthur S. Link, *Wilson.* Vol. 5: *Campaigns for Progressivism and Peace.* Princeton, 1965.

David Lloyd George, *Memoirs of the Peace Conference.* New Haven, 1939.

Richard Luckett, *The White Generals.* New York, 1971.

Clarence A. Manning, *The Siberian Fiasco.* New York, 1952.

Peyton C. March, *The Nation at War.* New York, 1932.

Thomas G. Masaryk, *The Making of a State.* New York, 1927.

Victor S. Matamey, *The United States and East Central Europe, 1914–1918.* Princeton, 1957.

Arno J. Mayer, *Politics and Diplomacy of Peacemaking: Containment and Counterrevolution at Versailles, 1918–1920.* New York, 1967.

Rudolph Medek, *Anabase.* Prague, 1928.

——, *Ostrove v. Bouri.* Prague, 1928.

——, *The Czechoslovak Anabasis across Russia and Siberia.* London, 1929.

Joel R. Moore, Harry H. Mead, and Lewis Jahns, *The History of the American Expedition Fighting the Bolsheviki: Campaigning in North Russia, 1918–1919.* Detroit, 1920.

James William Morley, *The Japanese Thrust into Siberia, 1918.* New York, 1957.

G. Barnard Noble, *Policies and Opinion at Paris, 1919.* New York, 1968.

Frederick Palmer, *Bliss: Peacemaker. The Life and Letters of Tasker H. Bliss.* New York, 1934.

John J. Pershing, *My Experiences in the World War.* New York, 1931.

Konstantin W. Sakharov, *Die tschichischen Legionen in Siberien.* Berlin-Charlottenberg, 1930.

Hugh L. Scott, *Some Memories of a Soldier.* New York and London, 1928.

John Silverlight, *The Victor's Dilemma.* New York, 1972.

George Stewart, *The White Armies of Russia: A Chronicle of Counterrevolution and Allied Intervention.* New York, 1933.

Leonid I. Strakhovsky, *Intervention at Archangel.* New York, 1971.

William Strobridge, *Golden Gate to Golden Horn.* San Mateo, California, 1977.

Seth P. Tillman, *Anglo-American Relations at the Paris Peace Conference.* Princeton, 1961.

Pauline Tompkins, *American-Russian Relations in the Far East.* New York, 1949.

David F. Trask, *The United States in the Supreme War Council.* Wesleyan University Press, Middletown, Connecticut, 1961.

Harmon Tupper, *To the Great Ocean: Siberia and the Trans-Siberian Railway.* Boston, Toronto, 1965.

Richard H. Ullman, *Anglo-Soviet Relations, 1917–1921.* Vol. 1: *Intervention and the War.* Vol. 2: *Britain and the Russian Civil War.* Princeton, 1968.

Betty Miller Unterbarger, *America's Siberian Expedition: A Study of National Policy.* Durham, North Carolina, 1956.

Elena Varneck and H. H. Fisher, *The Testimony of Kolchak and Other Siberian Materials*. Stanford, California, 1935.

John Ward, *With the "Die-Hards" in Siberia*. New York, 1920.

John Albert White, *The Siberian Intervention*. Princeton, 1950.

Dorothea York with the cooperation of Sergeant Edward McCloskey *et al.*, *The Romance of Company A*. Detroit, 1923.

JOURNALS

Donald I. Buzenkai, "The Bolsheviks, the League of Nations and the Paris Peace Conference." Soviet Studies, 1967. 19(2).

Raymond Estep, "The Saga of the Far Eastern Railway." *Explorer's Journal*, March 1970.

Sidney C. Graves, "Japanese Aggression in Siberia." *The New York Times Current History*, *XIV*. May 1921.

Alfred Knox, "General Janin's Siberian Diary." *The Slavonic Review*. Vol. 3, No. 9, 1925.

Ivan Krasnow, "Unknown Documents on Soviet-American Relations." *New World Review*, 1971. 39(2).

Robert J. Maddox, "President Wilson and the Russians." *American History Illustrated*, 1962. 2(1).

Noble Rust, "The Wolfhounds Pick a Winner." *The American Legion Monthly*, September 1934.

Arthur J. Slavin, "Churchill's 'Bolshevism on the Brain': Intervention and Hypocrisy." *Bucknell Review*, 1967. 15(1).

Russell E. Snow, "The Russian Revolution of 1917–1918 in Transbaikalia." *Soviet Studies*, 1971. 23(2).

Charles Weeks and Joseph A. Baylen, "Admiral Newton A. McCulley's Mission to Russia, 1914–1921." *Russian Review*. Vol. 33, January 1974.

Virginia Cooper Westall, "AEF-Siberia—the Forgotten Army: Recollections of General Robert L. Eichelberger." *Military Review*. U.S. Army Command and General Staff College, Fort Leavenworth, Kansas. Vol. XLVIII, No. 3. March 1968.

INDEX